CAPTAIN BLIGH'S OTHER MUTINY

THE TRUE STORY OF THE MILITARY COUP THAT TURNED AUSTRALIA INTO A TWO-YEAR REBEL REPUBLIC

STEPHEN DANDO-COLLINS

RANDOM HOUSE AUSTRALIA

Random House Australia Pty Ltd
Level 3, 100 Pacific Highway, North Sydney, NSW 2060
www.randomhouse.com.au

Sydney New York Toronto
London Auckland Johannesburg

First published by Random House Australia 2007

National Library of Australia
Cataloguing-in-Publication Entry

Dando-Collins, Stephen.
Captain Bligh's other mutiny.

ISBN 978 1 74166 798 1 (pbk.).

1. Bligh, William, 1754–1817. 2. Macarthur, John, 1767–1834. 3. New South Wales – History – Rum Rebellion, 1808–1809. 4. Australia – History – 1788–1851. I. Title.

994.402

Cover image: English sword, c. 1808. Collection: Powerhouse Museum, Sydney. Photographer: Paula Bray.
Cover design by Christa Moffitt
Text designed and typeset in 13/16pt Adobe Garamond by Midland Typesetters, Australia
Printed and bound by Griffin Press, South Australia

10 9 8 7 6 5 4 3 2 1

Stephen Dando-Collins is the author of a successful series of popular histories about the legions of ancient Rome published by Wiley in the US, UK, and Australia, and which are increasingly being published in foreign translation. He is also the author of the American history *Standing Bear is a Person*, Da Capo Press, US and UK. His historical novel *The Inquest* was published in the US, Canada, Spain and Italy. Stephen lives in Tasmania.

Awake, bold Bligh! The foe is at the gate!
Awake! Awake! – Alas! It is too late!

Lord Byron, *The Island*, 1823

Contents

List of Illustrations

Acknowledgements

For his encouragement on this project I would particularly like to thank my longtime New York literary agent Richard Curtis, who was quick to see what an important chapter this was in Australia's history. My grateful thanks, too, go to Meredith Curnow, Random House Australia's astute publisher, and senior editor Roberta Ivers, for their support and advice.

My gratitude also goes to Louise Doyle, Head Curator at the Museum of Sydney in 2006–2007, and helpful staff including Annie Campbell; also to Brad Manera, Head Curator at Hyde Park Barracks; and to the efficient staff at the Mitchell Library and Reference Library, State Library of New South Wales; at State Records of New South Wales; the National Library of Australia in Canberra; the State Library of Tasmania; and the library of the Royal Society, London. And to the Hon. Malcolm Turnbull MP, who shared a slice of his family history with me.

Most especially, I extend my thanks, and my love, to my dearest wife Louise, who has put up with my mutterings about Bligh and Macarthur for almost two decades. She has been my Betsy Bligh, my Elizabeth Macarthur, my Mary Putland, my secret strength and my continual inspiration.

Author's Note

This is the true story, never before told in full, of the only military coup in Australia's history, and of the two-year rebel republic that followed it.

On 26 January 1808, the New South Wales Corps, a British army regiment, carried out a military coup, overthrowing and imprisoning the British governor of the colony of New South Wales. The coup was plotted and executed by a military junta. Australia was subsequently ruled as a republic (a term applied to the rebel regime at the time) for twenty-three months, by successive rebel dictators. The overthrown governor, William Bligh, made famous by the mutiny on the *Bounty* nigh on nineteen years before, was kept a prisoner by the rebels for a year, then escaped and was a fugitive for close to another year. I was taught none of this at school while growing up in Australia.

Throughout the nineteenth century the uprising was known as the Great Rebellion. It wasn't until the 1930s that the term Rum Rebellion came into vogue, and the unit responsible dubbed the Rum Corps, because an officer cartel based around the Corps had, in 1807, been banned by Governor Bligh, on orders from London, from trading in wine and spirits. As it happens, the coup may as well have been called the Red Wine Rebellion, because the Corps was almost certainly drinking South African wine on the day of the uprising.

The title Rum Rebellion unjustly trivialises the coup of 26 January, a day that, coincidentally and perhaps ironically, is today Australia's national day. And it trivialises the crimes of the subsequent dictatorships. As Governor Bligh attempted to escape his imprisonment and wrest back control, brave men who stood up for him found themselves being dragged from their homes. Opponents of the junta disappeared or were convicted in kangaroo courts and sent to jail or the coal mines. Men were unlawfully hanged. For twenty-three months, the junta plundered the British government and exploited the colonists. These were young Australia's darkest days.

As if to excuse it, some twentieth-century writers treated the coup as something of a jolly joke, almost a prank, an example of celebrated Australian larrikinism. Some painted the London trial that followed the coup, when a man's life hung in the balance, in equally light-hearted terms, claiming that the British public took no interest in it, that those involved were of minor importance, and even that members of the court fell asleep while the trial was in progress. None of this was true. As you will see, the coup was a mean and greedy grab for power, while the later trial involved leading men of the day, attracted a vast public audience, and was reported by the press throughout Britain.

Today, the names of inner-Sydney streets recall chief players of the 1808 coup and its aftermath: Bligh, King, Hunter, Campbell, Palmer, Riley, Harris, Jamison, Foveaux, O'Connell, Bent, Kent, George, Macquarie, Castlereagh, Liverpool, Regent. Ironically, one name is missing, that of John Macarthur, the man behind the coup, William Bligh's greatest foe.

Captain Bligh's Other Mutiny is a dramatic, authentic narrative pieced together from archived records – letters, dispatches, journals, newspapers, official records and the transcript of the landmark London trial that followed the uprising. This is what really happened, seen through the eyes and via the recorded words of numerous men and women on both sides who were present at the time, and whose lives were inexorably changed by the rebellion and its aftermath.

This book slowly came together over a period of almost twenty years, inspired by my first reading of the Johnston Court Martial transcript back in 1988. What a revelation it was! Reading the books then available about the events and the leading players of this story, I was amazed that some historians had, apparently quite deliberately, left out some facts and distorted others when describing the coup, to paint Bligh as a despot and to make Macarthur the hero. This became the accepted vision of the rebellion, a picture that lasted well into the 1980s, and the occasional writer who took an opposing view, such as Justice H.V. 'Doc' Evatt in 1937, was ridiculed.

No one before now has told the story of the coup as it happened, from the points of view of those involved. And certainly no one has pointed out that several women – Elizabeth Macarthur, Elizabeth Bligh, and Mary Putland in particular – played vital behind-the-scenes roles in the story of the coup and what followed; in doing so, they have denied these women their due credit.

In between research for my Roman histories and American histories in various parts of the world, I would always come back to the story of the Sydney coup, drawn like a bear to honey and driven by a determination to set the record straight. Gradually, I built the catalogue of facts that forms the basis of this book, setting myself the goal of publication in time for the 2008 bicentenary of the coup. It is my hope that it informs, entertains and separates the facts from the fictions of the past.

Introduction

Before we become spectators to the coup itself, it is necessary to set up the story of the New South Wales rebellion with a brief description of the events that preceded and triggered it. As in a Shakespearean play, the plot and the characters involved were complex and colourful. Here then are the stage directions for the drama that unfolded on the stage that was Sydney on 26 January 1808.

At the beginning of the nineteenth century, the British penal colony of New South Wales occupied half the continent of Australia. From north to south it extended from the top of Queensland's Cape York to the bottom-most tip of South Cape in Tasmania. From east to west it ran from the Coral Sea shores of the eastern coast to the desert wastes of the 135th degree of longitude. This vast area covered all of the present-day states of Queensland, New South Wales, Victoria and Tasmania and the Australian Capital Territory, as well as much of South Australia and the Northern Territory.

By 1806, the colony had been in existence for eighteen years. Its population consisted of around 1400 women, 4200 men and 1600 children. With its capital at Sydney Town, on Sydney harbour, the colony had smaller settlements at Parramatta; at Green Hills (later Windsor); at Coal River (Newcastle); at Hobart, Yorktown and York Cove on Port Dalrymple, and Patersonia (Launceston) in Tasmania, or Van Diemen's Land as it was then called; and on Norfolk Island, way out in the Pacific Ocean.

Some of the inhabitants were soldiers of the New South Wales Corps, a unit raised in England for service in the colony. The majority of residents, three in every four, were either convicts transported from Britain and Ireland and serving their sentences or convicts whose sentences had expired and who were now trying to make a new life for themselves in the colony. A smaller number of colonists were free settlers who had been given large grants of prime farmland and convict labour by the British government, on condition that they invest a specified amount in the colony. The supreme official in New South Wales at this time was the military governor, who was appointed by the British government to be the representative of His Majesty the King in the colony.

In August 1806, the colony's fourth governor arrived at Sydney to take up his open-ended appointment. This was Captain William Bligh, of *Bounty* fame. The *Bounty* mutiny had taken place seventeen years before. Cleared of blame for that mutiny by a court martial, Bligh, who already had a name as a master navigator, went on to win recognition for his courage and determination as master and commander of several warships in major Napoleonic sea battles, serving alongside Admiral Nelson in one bloody battle. Commended by Nelson, Bligh was awarded a medal and made a Fellow of the Royal Society.

Bligh's patron, Sir Joseph Banks, had been able to convince the Secretary of State for War and the Colonies that Bligh was the perfect man for the vacant job of Governor of New South Wales. The colony had been in disarray after leading settlers and profiteers among the officers of the New South Wales Corps had manipulated the administration to suit their own ends. By 1797 the elite members of this cartel had formed a pact; an injury to any one of them was to be considered an injury to all. Two governors previous to Bligh had been recalled after losing the battle with the officer cartel. In a four-year period when there was no governor in the colony, New South Wales was administered by the military, and the cartel flourished. Controlling imports, allocating convict labour to themselves, cartel members built their fortunes. William Bligh, who was known to be a brave, no-nonsense man, was given the job by the home government of cleaning up the corruption.

Until Bligh arrived, wine and spirits had been the chief currency in New South Wales, and the 'huxter officers'[1] – as an Irish rebel doing time in the colony called them – had cornered the liquor market, and every other market besides. A former gentleman prisoner, one of the Scottish Martyrs, would tell a House of Commons committee that the officers were illegally selling government stores. But, more profitably, he said, they were monopolising the goods that were being landed from ships from Europe and India. 'The officers purchase them, and retail them at perhaps 500 per cent profit.'[2] Men of the Corps, even humble drummers, were allocated convict servants, and using free labour, many serving soldiers set up wives and mistresses in businesses.[3]

Bligh had arrived with very specific instructions from London, and well-briefed on who his chief adversaries would be. Setting to work to destroy the power of the cartel, he regulated the importation of wine and spirits; the import was taken out of private hands and administered by the government. Bligh also required that all transactions in the colony now be carried out in pounds, shillings and pence. He was sparing with the granting of land, strictly controlled the allocation of government food stores and livestock, and put limitations on the use of convict labour by settlers. He stipulated that a person could not be arrested without a warrant, and banned the torture of suspects to obtain a confession, both of which had been permitted prior to his arrival. He urged the magistrates to issue less harsh sentences – 1000 lashes had not been uncommon prior to Bligh's arrival – and to instead attempt to rehabilitate offenders. He encouraged the endeavours of the many smaller farm owners, whom he saw as the future of the colony, and provided food from the government stores for the poor. At the same time, he looked for every opportunity to embarrass, frustrate, and incriminate cartel ringleaders. He knew he was making enemies, but he had a job to do, with the full support of the British government back home. Bligh had come to make improvements, not friends.

John Macarthur, a captain with the New South Wales Corps until 1803, had arrived in New South Wales in the Second Fleet heavily in debt. Within a decade he had become one of the colony's richest men, with several large properties, thousands of head of stock, and interests in a handful of ships. An intelligent, persuasive and combative entrepreneur, Macarthur had been a significant thorn in the side of previous governors, one of whom described him as having a 'restless ambition and litigious disposition'.[4] Macarthur had a history of taking men to court, or fighting them in duels. He'd fought one such duel on the way to New South Wales, another in the colony. Seriously wounding his commanding officer in this second duel, Macarthur had been sent back to England under arrest, but charges were later dropped and he'd returned a civilian.

Nicknamed in some quarters 'the Perturbator' and 'the Arch Fiend', Macarthur believed that the future of the colony depended on the economic success of men of the officer class, men such as himself. Expressing the view to Governor King that local regulations imposed by a governor were illegal unless sanctioned by an act of the British parliament,[5] he passionately resented any intrusion that His Majesty's governors made into his affairs. There can be no doubt that before Governor Bligh left England he had been forewarned by both the Secretary of State and friends including the Reverend Samuel Marsden that Macarthur had the influence, the ability and the determination to destroy any governor who stood in his way. So Bligh set out to destroy Macarthur before Macarthur could do to him what he had done to others.

For more than a year, the pair circled each other like fighters in the ring. Macarthur found Bligh a much tougher opponent than his predecessors, but Bligh found Macarthur as slippery as an eel. While Macarthur looked for grounds to have Bligh recalled, Bligh sought a way to nail Macarthur with a criminal charge. After initial skirmishes had failed to give either party an advantage, by late 1807, Bligh was winning the war of attrition. To Macarthur, New South Wales had become 'a perfect hell', and he wrote to a close friend in October that, while Bligh now had the officers of the Corps squabbling among themselves, he had so alienated them that the Corps was galloping into a state of warfare with the Governor.[6] This was more wishful thinking than fact. The leaders of the cartel had been so effectively thwarted by the Governor's measures that they had in fact fallen into a 'despairing lethargy'.[7]

By December 1807, all of the cartel members had given up the fight against the governor, except one – Macarthur never surrendered, to anyone. But it would take a great deal of manipulation of people and events before all the military officers could genuinely be steered into a state of warfare with the Governor. One, Captain Anthony Fenn Kemp, had by that time even resorted to secretly begging favours of the Governor. Bligh, meanwhile, had been looking for a window of opportunity, a chance to pin a serious charge on Macarthur. In December, that window opened, and Bligh ordered the arrest of Macarthur on criminal charges.

At 11.00 o'clock on the evening of 15 December 1807, Francis Oakes, Chief Constable for the Parramatta district, arrived at

Elizabeth Farm, the Parramatta residence of John Macarthur, twenty kilometres west of Sydney. When Macarthur came to the door, Chief Constable Oakes announced that he had a warrant for his arrest. An Irish convict had escaped on a ship which Macarthur part-owned, the schooner *Parramatta*, and at Tahiti the man had transferred to a ship bound for the United States, with the help of the schooner's skipper. Colonial regulations designed to prevent convicts escaping aboard ships trading out of the colony required that the *Parramatta*'s owners now forfeit a bond of £900, because this man had escaped aboard their vessel. Macarthur and his business partner and *Parramatta* co-owner Garnham Blaxcell refused to pay up. Hence, the warrant for Macarthur's arrest.

Now, on the night of 15 December, to the astonishment of Chief Constable Oakes, Macarthur refused to acknowledge the legality of the warrant. He sent Oakes packing with a note that said of the warrant: 'I consider it with scorn and contempt, as I do the persons who have directed it to be executed.'[8] Next day, as Chief Constable Oakes set off for Sydney to report to the colony's Judge Advocate, he was waylaid by Macarthur's eighteen-year-old son, Edward. The youth tried to convince Oakes to give up his father's defiant note, but Oakes refused to part with it – he would tender this to the Provost Marshal as his reason for returning to Sydney without his prisoner.

Macarthur senior followed Oakes into Sydney that same morning, and was arrested at the residence of his friend, Surveyor-General Charles Grimes, just four doors from Government House. Now, Macarthur was also charged with contempt of court as a result of his contemptuous note of the night of 15 December.

Macarthur was committed to appear for trial at the Criminal Court on 25 January 1808, and released on bail of £1000 put up by his friends Garnham Blaxcell and Nicholas Bayly. The bench of magistrates for that 25 January sitting would be made up of the colony's Judge Advocate, Richard Atkins, and six officers of the New South Wales Corps.

Now began a series of unprecedented shenanigans.

Five days after his committal, on 21 December, John Macarthur called on Judge Advocate Atkins and produced a bill of exchange for £26 drawn by Atkins fifteen years before, and demanded payment in full, plus £56 in interest. At least two years earlier, Macarthur had purchased this bill of exchange from the person who originally held it, a colonist named Bond, and had kept it in a drawer ever since. Even though it could be argued that the Statute of Limitations made the bill worthless, the Judge Advocate indicated he might pay the bill, but disputed the amount of interest. Macarthur demanded payment in full, and twice wrote to Governor Bligh asking him to intercede. The Governor's secretary, Edmund Griffin, wrote back suggesting that Mr Macarthur sue Mr Atkins in the Civil Court.

On 12 January, two weeks before his trial was due to begin, Macarthur wrote to the Governor saying he feared that Judge Advocate Atkins would treat him unfairly at the upcoming trial because of their financial dispute. He declared that he was going to write in protest to the Secretary of State for the Colonies in London. On 22 January, Macarthur again wrote to Governor Bligh, this time objecting to Atkins sitting at his trial for the novel reason that, if Macarthur won, Macarthur could sue Atkins for false arrest, and therefore Atkins could not be expected to acquit him. The Governor's reply was that, as the Judge Advocate was appointed by the authorities in London, he had no power to remove him. All this letter-writing by Macarthur was a smokescreen for what he really had in mind.

On the evening of Sunday, 24 January, the officers of the New South Wales Corps held a mess dinner at their Sydney barracks. So integrated into the community had the military officers become that this was the first time they had all eaten together at the barracks in years. The commanding officer in Sydney, Major

George Johnston, had sought Governor Bligh's permission to hold the dinner, reminding His Excellency that the occasion would give the officers the opportunity to celebrate the twentieth anniversary of the founding of the colony, which was coming up on 26 January. Bligh had given his permission.

The dinner was attended by all nine officers of the Corps then based in Sydney, plus several civilians including the two men standing bail for John Macarthur, as well as Macarthur's son Edward and nephew Hannibal. While the dinner was in progress, Macarthur himself strolled on the Parade Ground outside the officers' quarters. The officers drank heavily, and at one point the Orderly Sergeant on duty noticed Major Johnston take a bottle of wine away from the inebriated Captain Anthony Fenn Kemp, who would be the senior officer sitting at John Macarthur's trial next day, saying, 'Look here, Kemp, remember tomorrow'.[9] The officers had ended the night dancing drunkenly with each other to the music of the regimental fife band.

Next day, when Macarthur's trial began, the gallery was packed. Many of those present were soldiers of the New South Wales Corps, in full scarlet uniform and wearing their sidearms, sent there on the orders of the Corps' Adjutant. Before the indictment could be read, Macarthur rose and read a long speech in which he objected to Judge Advocate Atkins sitting in his case. He gave eight specific reasons, including the fact that he and Atkins were locked in a dispute over an unpaid bill. As a result, said Macarthur, Atkins could not be expected to be impartial. Strangely, although Macarthur had held that bill for at least two years, he had not objected to Atkins sitting in several other cases in which Macarthur had been involved over that time. Macarthur had obviously been holding the bill for a rainy day, and that day had come.

When the Judge Advocate attempted to terminate Macarthur's speech, declaring it libelous, and threatened to throw Macarthur in jail at once, magistrate Captain Anthony Fenn Kemp threatened to instead throw the Judge Advocate in prison. Incensed, Atkins stormed from the courtroom and headed for Government House to report this outrage to Governor Bligh. Realising he'd left his legal papers behind, Atkins sent a constable back for them, but Captain Kemp would not hand them over.

At 11.15 am, the six officers on the bench wrote to Governor Bligh demanding that he appoint another Judge Advocate in Atkins' place. At 12.30 pm, the Governor wrote back that he had no power to replace Atkins, reminding the officers that without the Judge Advocate, the court could not legally sit. The officers replied with a refusal to sit with Atkins. At 2.15, Bligh sent a note to the officers demanding the return of the Judge Advocate's papers. The officers refused, and at 4.00, although they had no legal power to do so in the absence of the Judge Advocate, they remanded Macarthur on his previous bail. At 5.30, after the officers had again refused to surrender Atkins' papers, Bligh sent his Orderly Sergeant to ask the Sydney commandant of the Corps, Major Johnston, to come to see him at Government House. Major Johnston was then at his property, Annandale, six kilometres outside town. Some time later, Johnston replied via the Governor's Orderly Sergeant that as a result of a fall he was unable to either travel or write.

The following day, 26 January, at 9.00 am, William Gore, the colony's Provost Marshal and Superintendent of Police, together with John Redman, Chief Constable of Sydney, and two armed constables, arrested John Macarthur at the Sydney house of Macarthur's good friend, Captain Edward Abbott, commander of the military detachment at Parramatta. The policemen led Macarthur to the County Jail, where he was locked away. At 10.00, Captain Kemp and his five colleagues reconvened the Criminal Court and wrote to Bligh demanding that he appoint an acting Judge Advocate and that Macarthur be again released on his existing bail. The Governor, deep in consultation with his civil advisers, did not reply. At 3.00 pm, the six officers again met, and announced that they would proceed against Provost Marshal Gore for arresting Macarthur after they had extended his bail.

At 3.30, Bligh wrote to Captain Kemp and the other five officers of the Criminal Court individually, requiring them to present themselves before him at Government House at 9.00 next morning. He also wrote to Major Johnston, suggesting that if he was still too unwell to meet with him, perhaps Captain Abbott should be directed to come in from Parramatta to take command in Sydney.

Both sides had reached a precipice, with neither apparently prepared to turn back. The stage was set for the coup, just as John Macarthur had planned.

1

The Overthrow

Tuesday, 26 January 1808 had been a hot day in Sydney Town. Things would become much hotter before the day was out, for a military coup was in the making. Yet in the late afternoon, there was little to suggest that hundreds of armed troops would soon be marching through the town with bayonets fixed, colours flying, and band playing, to overthrow His Majesty's Captain-General and Governor-in-Chief, William Bligh, and set up a revolutionary government on Australia's shores.

It was 4.20 pm. Sentry Private John Gray had come on duty twenty minutes earlier. The New South Wales Corps redcoat smothered a languid yawn and leaned a little more weightily on his 'Brown Bess', his flintlock musket. Standing in the sentry box on the northern side of Sydney's sloping military Parade Ground, today's Wynyard Park, Private Gray was hot and uncomfortable. Sydney's average high for 26 January is 26.2 degrees Celsius[10], and the temperature can frequently reach well into the 30s, accompanied by high humidity.

When asked later, under oath, Private Gray would state categorically that at this time there was no unusual activity around the town, no agitation or state of alarm. Here and there, groups of off-duty soldiers lingered beneath the shade of barrack verandas, talking, laughing. And in surrounding streets a few clusters of townspeople stood in earnest conversation. Nothing out of the ordinary about that. Gray had seen the dragoon Sergeant Charles Whalley, Governor Bligh's orderly sergeant, trot by on his mount and head for Government House, a two-storey building on a rise 600 metres to the east. But again, this wasn't unusual; Sergeant Whalley was always out and about delivering messages from the Governor.

Now, hearing voices he recognised, Gray quickly came to attention. Two officers of the Corps and a former officer, now a civilian, came onto the Parade from the direction of the town, bearing documents. Deep in conversation, they hurried by Private Gray, the two officers returning his salute as they passed, making for the barracks on the hill. Again the private relaxed.

Ten minutes later, at 4.30, a two-wheeled chaise drawn by a single horse bumped noisily along dusty High Street, today's George Street, from the west, then slanted along Church Street, now York Street, beside the Parade. The driver was Lieutenant William Minchin, Adjutant of the Corps. The preoccupied passenger of the little carriage was the Corps commandant in Sydney, grey-haired Major George Johnston, who, Private Gray noticed, had his right arm in a sling. Major Johnston was popular with the men of the Corps. He was amiable and fair, and there were no airs or graces about him – after all, he'd kept a beautiful convict girl as his live-in mistress for years. It was the worst-kept secret in the colony that the Major was the father of six of his 'housekeeper's' seven children.

The chaise pulled up at the military barracks complex. As Gray watched, Johnston and Minchin alighted, and the commandant went directly into his own quarters, a substantial double-storey house. Lieutenant Minchin, tall, slim, fair-haired, and sporting a neat moustache, paused to speak privately with two sergeants who seemed to have been awaiting his arrival, before sending them trotting into various parts of the town on errands. Then Minchin, an Irishman from Tipperary, raised his voice, and speaking loud enough for Gray to hear, called to off-duty soldiers nearby.

'You men, go to your quarters. Put on your accoutrements, and come quietly into the barracks through the back way.'[11]

Minchin then followed Major Johnston indoors and the troops scuttled away. Within minutes, soldiers began to return, in full uniform and with their handsome black cylindrical shako headwear and their arms, via the back way as ordered. At the same time, a handful of leading settlers hurried by sentry Gray's post to the commandant's quarters. Shortly after, Private Gray, certain that something unusual was now in the works, spied two civilians leaving the commandant's quarters and heading toward the County Jail further along High Street. Gray knew them both: Nicholas Bayly, once an officer of the Corps and now a settler, and Garnham Blaxcell, Provost Marshal during the administration of the previous governor, Philip Gidley King, and now a merchant.

The pair returned to the barracks a little later accompanied by a tall, handsome figure Gray recognised instantly as Mr John Macarthur. Nicknamed 'Jack Bodice' by the troops and convicts in the colony[12], forty-year-old Macarthur, now a prominent settler, was a former captain and paymaster with the New South Wales Corps. Of Scottish ancestry, he had been born not far from Governor Bligh's childhood home at Plymouth. Private Gray knew that Macarthur had been made a prisoner in the County Jail that morning, and that a dispute had been raging between Macarthur, the Criminal Court and the Governor. The private, like many of his comrades in the ranks of the Corps, had not paid too much attention to the affair. In New South Wales, disputing with the governor of the day had long been a sport popular with the wealthy.

After the three men disappeared into the commandant's quarters, several more civilians arrived at Major Johnston's barrack. Three of them paced back and forth outside. Several men went inside, soon came back out and spoke to the others, then went inside again. Private Gray had to wonder what could be going on behind the closed doors at the officers' quarters.

Looking down to the U-shaped Guard House in Bridge Street, outside Government House, Gray noticed that, apart from a lone soldier stationed in the sentry box to the left of the Government House gates, there was no sign of the men of the Main Guard – the Governor's Guard as they were commonly known. A Governor's Guard of twenty-six men, two sergeants and an officer usually stood duty at the Guard House. During the day, men of the Guard would lounge on the veranda overlooking the Governor's garden, which ran all the way down to the waters of Sydney Cove – Warrang as the Aborigines of the local Cadigal tribe called the little bay. There, the guardsmen would gossip, joke, and, if they could get away with it, smoke pipes. Yet Gray had seen neither hide nor hair of the Guard. He could only assume that the officer in charge of the Governor's Guard, Ensign Archibald Bell, had ordered his men to stay indoors out of the heat.

All was quiet. To Gray, the town of 4000 inhabitants seemed its usual peaceful self. The smoke of cooking fires hung on the still air as, at or shortly after 5.00, most people in Sydney, of all classes, sat down to their supper. The chained convicts of the Jail Gang marched back to the convict barracks at five o'clock after ending their ten-hour working day. Some of the convicts had been rebuilding Fort Phillip, a dilapidated six-sided fortification high on Millers Point, near the government windmill, which would eventually form the foundation of Sydney Observatory. Others had been working inside the handsome new Anglican house of worship, the New Church, later the first St Philip's Church, putting the finishing touches to its circular tower and interior. Others still had been employed elsewhere around the town with paintbrushes, adding a final coat of ochre paint to the walls of the barracks and storehouses, all of which had been recently plastered on Governor Bligh's orders. Now those buildings, which had previously been whitewashed, glowed in their earthy new colour scheme.

Gray's eyes went to the few vessels riding at anchor out in Sydney Cove. Today, skyscrapers block the view to the harbour from where Gray stood, but back then he was able to see that the colony's two major armed naval vessels HMS *Porpoise* and HMAT *Lady Nelson* were not in port – both were at sea on His Majesty's service. The only government vessel currently at Sydney was the handsome little schooner, *Estramina*. She was flying Governor Bligh's commodore's broad pennant in his capacity as commander of all ships of the Royal Navy in the South Pacific. In the still, humid air, the pennant hung from the top of the schooner's mainmast like a damp sock.

There was also an assortment of small fishing boats and several local trading craft in the cove, including the sloop, *Speedy*. An American brig was riding at anchor – the *Jenny*, of 170 tons, out of Boston; she had been trading into Sydney since 1800. Private Gray would have heard that the *Jenny* was to sail for China before the week was out. She would have to take her cargo of 5000 gallons of brandy and rum with her, for Governor Bligh had only given her captain permission to land the wine that formed part of his alcoholic cargo. Not that Private Gray and his mates of the Corps would go thirsty – in addition to the *Jenny*'s wine, a shipment of good red wine from South Africa's Cape Colony had also recently been unloaded, with the Governor's approval, from the *City of Edinburgh*.

Troops in the colony received an official alcohol ration, but additional gallons of wine had recently been promised to soldiers in Sydney at a very reasonable rate. According to Sergeant-Major Thomas Whittle, the troops had settler Mr

John Macarthur to thank for that; Macarthur had confided that he would soon have wine from the shipments sitting in the government storehouses, and was offering it to men nominated by Sergeant-Major Whittle for just five shillings a gallon. How peeved Private Gray would have been now, as he stood in his sentry box dripping perspiration and with a throat as dry as dust, knowing that all the enlisted men sitting down to supper at the barracks were just then being served half a pint of wine, to wash down their meal and embolden their hearts.[13]

Six o'clock came and went. Suddenly, there was movement at the barracks. The commandant's door opened and officers emerged in a rush. Orders were issued by Adjutant Minchin. The Corps' drummers appeared, formed a line, and beat 'To Arms'. Now this was unusual. The Corps normally paraded once a day, early in the morning. The hollow drum tattoo that echoed ominously throughout the town was now summoning every soldier of the Corps to form up on the Old Parade Ground, today's Lang Park, outside the barracks buildings, to receive orders. Only 120 single soldiers lived at the barracks. The majority of the men of the Corps lived in cottages in the town, in Soldier's Row, Pitt's Row, Barrack Row, Spring Row and Camden's Row, with their wives or mistresses and children.

As troops came running past John Gray's sentry box, coat-tails flying and holding onto their tall black felt shako caps and muskets, heading for the Old Parade, the private noticed Lieutenant Minchin give orders to the Corps' handful of artillerymen. With 559 officers and men at all stations, the New South Wales Corps was seriously undermanned. Seven years before, its establishment had been twenty-one officers and 600 men, but a number had since been invalided out, or drummed out, or had settled in the colony. A few had gone 'home' to Britain. No replacements had arrived from England. The country was, after all, at war with France and could not spare troops for its most distant colony.

The Corps had been under strength from the day it landed on Australia's shores, and, to bolster the ranks, in the early 1790s, 200 convicts then in the colony had been enlisted into the unit. By the time Governor Bligh arrived in 1806, only seventy former convicts remained in Corps ranks. Replacement officers had been even harder to come by, requiring most existing officers to perform a variety of extra duties as colleagues resigned or were forced out of the Corps via court martial. So, in addition to being the Corps' Adjutant and the Colonial Engineer, Lieutenant Minchin also had the role of Artillery Officer, for which he received an additional five shillings a day.

The gunners consulted by Minchin now ran toward Private Gray's sentry post. Led by Private John Gillard, an ex-convict, the gunners, who received an extra pair of boots each year as payment for artillery duty, came jogging to two heavy cannon located beside Private Gray's sentry box. Sentry Gray, a 'quiet and inoffensive man'[14], said nothing, didn't call out to ask his comrades what was going on. Intrigued, Gray simply watched as the guns were manhandled down a slope to the powder magazine a little to the south of their firing position. Both cannon were loaded with gunpowder and cannonball then wheeled back up to their original positions. There, Private Gillard, following the orders of Lieutenant Minchin[15], trained the guns to the east, directly at Government House. The gun crews then stood to attention by their weapons, and waited.

There were also two cannon down at Government House. One of them had been out of commission for months, but several days earlier, while the officers had been enjoying their mess dinner, Private Gillard, in the darkness, had removed the elevating screw from the other Government House gun, to prevent its effective use. Gillard would later testify that he had also done this on Lieutenant Minchin's orders.[16]

While all this activity was taking place up on Church Hill, down at an inn by the public wharf in the Rocks district, settler

George Suttor was thinking about the business he had to transact in the town the next day. Thirty-three-year-old Suttor had come out from England in 1800. He was 'an honest, hardworking, industrious, ingenious lad', in the words of his patron, Sir Joseph Banks, President of the Royal Society.[17] Like Banks, Suttor was a botanical expert, and had an excellent orangery on his 186-acre (75 hectare) farm at Baulkham Hills in the Hawkesbury district, sixty kilometres inland from Sydney.

Suttor, who had left his wife Sarah and five young children back at his farm, was chatting with other patrons of the public house over a jug of Cape wine when the drums of the Corps began to beat 'To Arms'. Getting to his feet, Suttor followed other patrons from the bar-room outside into the street, and looked up to the barracks. The sun was low in the western sky, but it was still possible to see soldiers streaming toward the Old Parade. Something was up, but no one around Suttor seemed to know what it was. Several people began to hurry toward the Old Parade to see what all the fuss was about, and Suttor joined them.

From his sentry post, a bemused Private Gray watched as Captain Anthony Fenn Kemp and Lieutenants William Moore, William Lawson and Cadwallader Draffin tramped arm-in-arm from the Old Parade, then past Mr Simeon Lord's mansion in Bridge Street, and across the brick and stone Tank Stream bridge that gave Bridge Street its name. The four officers, wearing swords and in black 'round hats' – the military version of the civilian top hat, scarlet tunics with a single gold-braided epaulette on the right shoulder, and black trousers, were gaily making their way toward Government House, with the setting sun casting long shadows in front of them. Then Gray noticed Adjutant Minchin hurrying to join his comrades, one hand on the sheathed sabre at his side and the other holding his hat in place.

On the Old Parade, the drums were still rolling, and the men of the Corps were falling in by company. The colour-sergeant was unfurling the Corps' colours. The members of the regimental fife band were assembling. Regimental Sergeant-Major Thomas Whittle, a veteran of forty-two years in the army and close to sixty years old, totally illiterate but 'not the worse man for that' in his own opinion,[18] was walking up and down the lines, exhorting the troops. The word that soon washed through the ranks was that Governor Bligh was about to throw six of the Corps' officers in jail, and the Corps was acting to save them.

Three doors along from Government House in Bridge Street, at his government cottage, Acting Principal Chaplain Henry Fulton had also heard the drums rolling. Originally sent out from Ireland as a political prisoner for involvement in Wolfe Tone's 1798 uprising against British rule, Fulton, an Anglican minister, had been pardoned and appointed chaplain of the penal settlement on Norfolk Island, 1500 kilometres out in the Pacific, before being transferred to Sydney in 1806. Now, coming out onto his front veranda, the chaplain saw the activity up on Church Hill, and saw the group of armed officers coming up the slope of Bridge Street in his direction. Fulton, who was a magistrate, had been in conference with the Governor all day concerning the legal wrangle involving John Macarthur. A little before 5.00, he had gone back to his own house for supper with his household.

Now, immediately realising what was afoot, Fulton left his veranda and ran toward Government House. The soldier in the sentry box by the gateway must have blinked as the minister came up; he would never before have seen a clergyman running in such an indecorous manner. In through the open gates to Government House hurried Fulton with one hand holding onto his broad-brimmed, round-crowned minister's hat. Panting up the front steps to Government House, the chaplain dashed in the front door, slammed it shut, then bolted it and took up duty there as the door's self-appointed guardian.

At the Guard House, moments after the reverend had run by, the Officer of the Guard and twenty-nine enlisted men tumbled out into the street opposite the Government House gates. It was no accident that there were four sergeants instead of the usual two at the Guard House. When, around 4.30, sentry Private Gray had seen Lieutenant Minchin dispatch a pair of messengers around the town, the men in question had been Sergeants William Bremlow and Edward Johnston. Once the sergeants' messages had been delivered to several leading civilian residents of the town, Bremlow and Johnston had come to the Guard House. Lieutenant Minchin had told each sergeant to go there by different routes, so they wouldn't raise suspicion.[19]

Via these two sergeants, Minchin had sent orders for the Governor's Guard to remain indoors and off the Guard House veranda. The men of the Guard had promptly gone inside. They would have already guessed that something out of the ordinary was brewing for, some hours before, Guard commander Ensign Bell had ordered his senior sergeant, Robert Hall, to keep the Guard well together during the afternoon. Having delivered their messages, Sergeants Bremlow and Johnston had remained attached to the Guard at the Guard House, as per Adjutant Minchin's orders[20] and, unusually, had sat down to supper with the men of the Guard.

Now, as the Guard fell in two-by-two and the private from the sentry box joined them, Sergeants Bremlow and Johnston took their places armed with muskets from the Guard House armoury. Ensign Bell, thirty-four, a former schoolteacher and a devout Anglican with nine children, half-heartedly ordered his senior NCO to have the men fit bayonets to their muskets. Soft-centred Bell was following orders from his superiors but he didn't have much stomach for those orders, and his superiors knew it – that was why Sergeants Bremlow and Johnston had been sent to join the Guard, to make sure that Bell followed through with their officers' preconcerted plan.

'Fix bayonets!' bellowed Sergeant Hall.

The men slid the slender, forty-three-centimetre-long bayonets from the scabbards hanging at their left sides and fixed them to the end of the barrels of their Tower muskets. Once fitted, the bayonet, a cross between a dagger and a sword, turned a musket into a pike 190 centimetres long. It was sharp enough, and had enough weight behind it, to go right through a man. When the bayonet was first introduced into European armies in the seventeenth century, it had been considered such a barbarous weapon that it was predicted that it would be a deterrent to all future wars.[21]

Suddenly, from the direction of Government House, there came a piercing and totally unexpected female scream. The red-coats of the Governor's Guard looked up from their muskets and bayonets to see a petite young woman running toward the gateway from the direction of Government House. In her twenties, with a good figure, she wore a sombre black dress, and her dark locks were tied up in a neat, conservative hairstyle which left ringlets dangling down her cheeks. Awkwardly holding up her skirts with her left hand so she could run, she carried a parasol in her right hand, as though it were a sword.[22] The soldiers of the Guard immediately recognised the young lady: Mrs Mary Putland, the widowed daughter of Governor Bligh. By the fierce look in young Mary Putland's eyes, it was obvious that she knew what these men were about, and she was determined to stop them.

Governor William Bligh had already begun to react to what was taking place outside Government House when he heard his daughter's screams.

Bligh was by this time fifty-three years of age. The son of the Customs Officer of the naval city of Plymouth, he'd gone to sea at fifteen. In his youth, he'd had a cherubic face and sported golden curls. Now his hair was grey and much receded, his face was drawn, and a paunch sat over his waistband. His piercingly blue eyes were active, and he possessed a warm smile. But he wasn't smiling now. Over his white breeches and white waistcoat he wore, not his naval uniform, but an austere black jacket. He and his daughter Mary were in deep mourning. Only twenty-two days before, Mary's husband and Bligh's aide-de-camp, Royal Navy Lieutenant John Putland, had died from tuberculosis, here at Government House. But this was the least of Bligh's current woes. Foremost in his mind all day had been the matter that had been occupying much of the Governor's time for weeks now – the Macarthur affair. That affair had blown up into a face-off between Bligh and a number of his own military officers, who were refusing to do his bidding. It was an affair that had rude echoes of a past conflict with subordinates such as Fletcher Christian that Bligh would rather not think about.

The mutiny of Christian and twenty members of the crew of His Majesty's Armed Vessel *Bounty* had taken place in 1789, the year of the French Revolution. Bligh, the *Bounty*'s commander, had been a thirty-four-year-old lieutenant at the time, not the middle-aged captain later portrayed by Hollywood. Much had taken place in Bligh's life in the nineteen years since the mutiny. There had been the 6000-kilometre journey to Timor in the *Bounty*'s open launch without instruments, saving his own life and those of most of his eighteen companions after they had been cast adrift by Christian and the mutineers and left to die. The journey would be rated one of the greatest navigational exploits of all time.

Subsequently, with another ship, the *Providence*, Bligh had completed the *Bounty*'s mission, transplanting breadfruit from Tahiti to the West Indies. He had been promoted to Captain, had fought under Admiral Parker at the Dogger Bank and under Lord Howe at Gibraltar. In the 1797 Battle of Camperdown, Bligh, commanding the 74-gun man o' war HMS *Director*, had silenced and captured the enemy Dutch flagship. At the 1801 Battle of Copenhagen, prior to which Admiral Lord Nelson had famously put a telescope to his blind eye to say he could not see a signal from his superior calling on him to withdraw his squadron, Captain Bligh had commanded HMS *Glatton.* Keeping the *Glatton* close beside Lord Nelson's flagship, HMS *Elephant*, Bligh had been in the thick of the fighting, and following the battle, had been called on board the *Elephant* to be personally thanked and congratulated by Nelson for his role in the victory. William Bligh was no coward. Once he realised what the New South Wales Corps was up to in the twilight of 26 January, his first inclination was to resist.

Governor Bligh had dined at 5.00 pm. Among those sharing his table in the Government House dining room at the front of the house had been his twenty-six-year-old daughter, Mary. Bligh's wife Elizabeth, his 'dear Betsy', had been too ill to travel when Bligh prepared to take up his appointment as Governor of New South Wales in early 1806. So Mary, the petite second eldest of his six daughters, had volunteered to serve as her father's 'First Lady' in the colony. She could be seasick on a millpond but, despite this, she had made the four-month voyage to Australia with her father and her new husband, Lieutenant Putland. Ever since their arrival in August of 1806, she had been the cultivated and well-liked hostess of Government House. Mary had her mother's small chin and long, hooked nose but she also had Betsy Bligh's large, beguiling eyes and could charm almost everyone she met. Playing the pianoforte well, credited with excellent taste and dress sense, well-spoken, and refined, Mary had even impressed John Macarthur, who considered her an accomplished young lady.

Also dining with the Governor on the evening of the 26th were several senior civil officials of the colony. There was Commissary-General John Palmer, who was in charge of government stores, provisions and livestock. Known popularly among the common classes as 'Little Jack', the friendly, cheerful Palmer was a short, dark and handsome man of forty-eight.

He had come out to New South Wales as the purser of HMS *Sirius* in the First Fleet, in 1788. Three years later, Governor Phillip, the colony's first governor, had appointed him to his present post, which he had held for close to seventeen years through several governors. In both government and private business affairs, Palmer had a reputation as an honest, ethical man. Commissary Palmer was accompanied this evening by his forty-six-year-old American wife Susan, whose family, the Stilwells, had supported the losing royalist side during the American War of Independence. Susan Palmer was a good friend to the Governor's daughter, being something of a cross between a mother figure and a lady in waiting to her.

Short, overweight, tousle-haired Scotsman Robert Campbell was another Bligh dinner guest. Thirty-eight-year-old Campbell was Little Jack Palmer's brother-in-law – he'd married Sophia Palmer, the Commissary's younger sister, in 1801. Born at Greenock, Scotland, Campbell had arrived in Sydney from India in 1796 to set up a branch of Campbell and Company, the business he and his brother had established at Calcutta. Campbell's business had soon flourished in New South Wales, becoming the colony's largest commercial concern. Its ships filled Campbell warehouses with imported goods and brought in large numbers of livestock from India to meet snowballing colonial demand. Known as a fair trader who reduced prices and offered generous credit when the colony was suffering after severe floods, Campbell had been given an address of thanks by 200 settlers in 1804. A Sydney magistrate for several years, for the past seven months Campbell had also been serving as New South Wales' Naval Officer – as the colony's superintendent of customs, collector of taxes, and treasurer was called.

Also enjoying the meal served by George Jubb, the Governor's liveried steward, were forty-nine-year-old Deputy Commissary James Williamson, who had been in government service in the colony for many years; and Edmund Griffin, Governor Bligh's loyal secretary. An intelligent and diligent young man, Griffin had come out to the colony with Bligh in 1806 and lived at Government House with the Governor and his daughter.

The party had finished eating. The two ladies had retired to Mary's boudoir, a small sitting room off her bedroom. In the dining room, as the gentlemen were downing their second glass of after-dinner port wine, a message was brought to the Governor by his servant, John Dunn. The message informed Bligh that the prisoner John Macarthur had been illegally released from the County Jail, and that there was much activity outside the military barracks, where 'To Arms' was being drummed and the Corps was assembling with its weapons.

As his companions looked at him in shock at the news, the Governor thought for a moment, then came to his feet. He guessed what was in the minds of his adversaries up on Church Hill, realised they were launching military action against him, and had decided on his course of action. He was hoping that gentle Ensign Bell and the Governor's Guard might remain loyal to him and keep other troops out of Government House, or at least delay them. Time was what he needed – for he planned to gallop to the Hawkesbury district and raise a force to oppose the Corps.

Only twenty-five days before, on New Year's Day, Bligh had received a loyal address from the citizens of the Hawkesbury, signed by 833 settlers, thanking him for his good government and assuring him of their loyalty and support. In Bligh's estimation, there were only fifteen or sixteen soldiers stationed at the Hawkesbury, with not a single officer. At this moment, as the Corps was assembling under arms, the Governor's plan was to escape from Sydney and raise a citizens' militia at the Hawkesbury and march at their head against the troops. The people of the Hawkesbury would, he believed, 'flock to my standard'.[23] As would later be proven, Bligh's confidence in the loyalty of colonists at the Hawkesbury was not misplaced.

But before Bligh departed Government House there were two tasks he needed to perform upstairs. Above all, he was determined to prevent his confidential papers from falling into the hands of enemies such as John Macarthur. As he strode from the dining room into the entrance hall, he called loudly to his Orderly Sergeant, the dragoon Whalley, who was stationed in the house. 'Whalley! Have the horses ready!' The Governor's anxious servant John Dunn now appeared in front of him. 'Dunn,' said Bligh, 'bring me my sword. Upstairs. Hurry, man!'[24] Bligh turned for the stairs, Dunn turned for the drawing room, where the Governor's sword was apparently kept in a cabinet.

Sydney's Government House of 1808 no longer exists. The Museum of Sydney now stands on its location, where some of the foundations are preserved. Few illustrations of the exterior remain, and of the interior we have only a basic floor plan. Begun by Governor Phillip, and added to by Governor King, the two-storey house was not grand, except for a modest ballroom with a gently curving south-facing wall, which Governor Bligh used as a drawing room. Behind the entrance hall, stairs zigged and zagged to the upper floor. The Governor now hurried up those stairs to his bed chamber, and Commissary Palmer and magistrate Robert Campbell followed after him.

In his first-floor bedroom, Bligh quickly removed his black jacket and, with Campbell's help, pulled on the blue and white uniform jacket of a commodore of the Royal Navy. Whatever happened next, Bligh was determined to meet his fate in the King's uniform. He then threw open a trunk, which was filled with documents, and began to rifle through his bureau, which consisted of a chest of drawers with a separate section on top containing smaller drawers and shelves. Urgently, he grabbed letters from both trunk and bureau, quickly reading a few words to determine their value, then stuffing a number of them inside his ruffled white shirt. At this point, William Gore, Bligh's Provost Marshal and Superintendent of Police, who had slipped into Government House via the rear entrance, hurried into the room, having been directed there by those downstairs.

Gore, a lean, bony Irishman of forty-two, had come out from England with Bligh in 1806 to take up his present duties. Efficient to the point of officiousness, and incorruptible, Gore was not well liked by any class in the colony. The soldiers particularly disliked him because he had schooled his constables not to be intimidated by the military when they had to arrest a friend or relative of a soldier. But he performed his duties legally and effectively, and for that the Governor was grateful, even if Gore's zealousness extended to battering down a locked door to serve a warrant.

Flush-faced now, Gore handed the Governor a slip of paper, informing him that it was a letter to the keeper of the County Jail, Barnaby Riley, a subordinate of Gore's. Written by Major Johnston of the New South Wales Corps, the letter ordered the jailer to hand John Macarthur over to his bailsmen, Nicholas Bayly and Garnham Blaxcell. Bligh read the brief letter of just a dozen lines, and bristled when he saw that at the end Johnston had given himself a title – 'Lieutenant Governor'.

Those two words told Bligh everything he needed to know. Under British law, if the governor of New South Wales were to die or be absent from the colony, a lieutenant governor could fill in for him. In such circumstances, the British government had stipulated, the most senior officer of the New South Wales Corps should occupy that position. That officer was Lieutenant-Colonel William Paterson, commander of the Corps, who was based in Van Diemen's Land, 1000 kilometres to the south. Major Johnston had assumed the title of Lieutenant Governor, and was issuing orders as though he were the colony's Governor. With a snort and a curse, Bligh handed the note to John Palmer to read. This seditious note, to Bligh's mind, was enough to see Johnston hanged. But more immediate matters had to be attended to before he could worry about that.

Having delivered the note, Provost Marshal Gore hurried back down the stairs. He then strode along the corridor at the rear of the house which led to the back door and the separate kitchen building and numerous other outbuildings. From the open back door, Gore was able to look to his right across a brick-paved expanse (later walled in) to the distant Government House gates to the north-west. At that moment he saw that Ensign Bell had formed up the Governor's Guard outside the open gates, and the soldiers of the Guard appeared to be priming and loading their muskets. Shocked by the sight, Gore ran back along the corridor, to the foot of the internal staircase.

'Governor! Governor Bligh, sir!' yelled Gore up the stairs. There was a hint of panic in his voice. 'The Main Guard is out, and priming and loading!'

Bligh appeared on the landing at the top of the staircase. 'Keep yourself cool, Gore,' he called down, himself sounding calm, 'and observe what goes forward.'[25]

'Yes, sir.'

Bligh, not knowing whether the Governor's Guard was preparing to protect him or to defect from him, disappeared back into his room. The Provost Marshal turned again for the rear door, intending to make for his own house. As he reached the door it opened, and in hurried elderly Thomas Arndell, looking worried. Formerly a New South Wales Corps Assistant Surgeon, Arndell had retired on half pay. With a small property at the Hawkesbury, he continued to serve as a civil magistrate, and he had been among the officials consulted by the Governor during the day. Arndell had a reputation for poor judgment, for being easily swayed one way or another – so much so that the common people of the colony had nicknamed him 'Foolish Tom'. He would live up to that nickname before long. There at the back door, Provost Marshal Gore and Foolish Tom Arndell propped, apprehensively discussing the situation and what they should do.

Upstairs, meanwhile, Commissary Palmer had read the

Johnston letter. Unimpressed, he made several comments to Bligh about its contents, then handed the letter to Robert Campbell. Campbell had barely finished reading it when they all heard Mary Putland scream downstairs.

Bligh momentarily froze at the sound of his daughter's terrified cries. He then told Campbell to look to the ladies. Campbell hurried from the room, leaving Palmer to help Bligh vet the official correspondence. After running down the stairs, Campbell looked into the entrance hall and saw Chaplain Fulton resolutely standing guard at the front door. At the end of the rear corridor, he saw Provost Marshal Gore deep in conversation with magistrate Arndell at the back door. Campbell now entered Mary Putland's sitting room where he expected to find the Governor's daughter and his own sister-in-law, but the room was empty. The door to Mary Putland's adjoining bedroom stood open; Campbell hurried through it. This room at the north-western corner of the house, later used as an office, had originally been the bedroom of the governors of the colony, but Governor Bligh had given it up to his daughter and son-in-law while he himself took a smaller bedroom upstairs. It had been from this downstairs bedroom that the screams of Mary Putland had first come.

Mary's bedroom was also empty. But a west-facing French door which opened onto the veranda stood ajar, and through it Campbell could see Susan Palmer standing out on the veranda looking toward the front gates. Campbell crossed the room and emerged via the French door onto the veranda. He found his sister-in-law in a petrified state. Following her gaze, he saw that forty metres away the plucky Mary Putland had pushed the cast-iron Government House gates shut. Now she stood there, refusing to allow Ensign Bell and his men to enter, waving her parasol at the ensign as she told him what she thought of him. Instructing his American sister-in-law to stay exactly where she was, Campbell ran toward the gates and Mary Putland.

According to one account, at this point Mary Putland was calling to the soldiers, 'Stab me to the heart, but respect the life of my father!'[26]

The soldiers had hesitated, unsure of how to handle this unexpected form of female resistance, until one of the sergeants gruffly told them to put their shoulders to the gates. Before Robert Campbell could reach the gateway, a number of soldiers had pushed the gates open, forcing slight Mary Putland back to one side behind a gate. As Ensign Bell and his men then marched in through the gateway, Campbell reached young Mrs Putland. Taking her arm, he pulled her from behind the gate and, telling her it was no use getting herself hurt, led her back to the veranda.

The men of the Governor's Guard were separating into five groups. One, led by Ensign Bell, was securing the main gate. The others, under Sergeants Bremlow, Johnston, Hall and Sutherland, formed up and waited for the five officers who were coming up Bridge Street to join them. Robert Campbell, observing these machinations, left Mary Putland, by one rebel account sobbing[27], but more likely dry-eyed and fuming, with Mrs Palmer on the veranda. Campbell told the pair that if they stayed there together, no one would harm them. He then dashed along the veranda to the front door. Rapping urgently on the door, Campbell called for Chaplain Fulton to let him in. There were two narrow windows at eye-level on either side of the door. Fulton looked out one of the windows, recognised Campbell, then unbolted the door and let him in. There, with Provost Marshal Gore and Foolish Tom Arndell stationed at the back door, the pair stood guard over the front entrance. Not one of them was armed.[28]

At the double, the men of the Governor's Guard were now spreading around the house. One group of six formed up outside the front door to Government House, where they were joined by Captain Kemp and Lieutenant Lawson. Another section of six trotted to the gubernatorial mansion's rear door, accompanied by Lieutenant Draffin. Lieutenant Moore led two sections whose objectives were to secure the outbuildings and rear gate. The Irish adjutant, Lieutenant Minchin, and one section advanced onto the veranda, to where the two women stood in terror of them. Minchin's task was to prevent anyone leaving the house via the French door to Mary Putland's bedroom. All entrances were quickly covered – the assault on Government House had obviously been planned down to the smallest detail.

By their own account, within two minutes of Campbell's retreat inside Government House, Captain Anthony Fenn Kemp and Lieutenant William Lawson stepped up to the front door, with their swords drawn. They saw Chaplain Fulton peering defiantly out the glass at them. 'Open the door, Chaplain!' commanded Kemp, a slender, narrow-faced man of thirty-four. In 1789, when Fletcher Christian was mutinying against Bligh and the French were ejecting Louis XVI and Marie Antoinette, sixteen-year-old Kemp, in England, had received a large inheritance. Within two years he had spent it all. Incapable of managing his finances, he had been in debt ever since. He had taken a commission in the New South Wales Corps to leave England and escape his creditors.

'Yes, open the door, sir!' echoed thirty-three-year-old Lieutenant Lawson. He had trained as a surveyor before buying his commission in the New South Wales Corps for £300. Unlike Kemp, Lawson came from a solid military family; his Scottish father had served as a surgeon in General Howe's Corps during the American War of Independence, and his maternal grandfather had been a senior officer in the same Corps.

'I will not open the door!' returned Fulton, the former Irish freedom fighter. 'You may drive your bayonets into me, if you choose, but I will not open the door.'

Kemp and Lawson looked at each other. Then Lawson said, more moderately, 'Captain Kemp would be obliged if you would tell the Governor that he wishes to speak with him.'[29]

Again Fulton refused their request, and for a time there was a stand-off at the front door.

At the rear entrance, Provost Marshal Gore and magistrate Arndell found the door being forced open from the outside by a party of half-a-dozen soldiers of the Governor's Guard commanded by Lieutenant Cadwallader Draffin. Lieutenant Minchin and others would later describe Draffin as 'not fit for duty' and 'mad' at this time[30], and there would be times that he would display signs of mental instability before eventually being declared insane. But Draffin was apparently considered fit enough to command one of the Government House storming parties on 26 January. Even so, it was his men who took the lead. Thomas Arndell shrunk back at the sight of the armed band, but Provost Marshal Gore found his courage and stepped into the insurgents' path.

'Get out of the way!' one soldier snarled, putting the tip of his bayonet to Gore's chest.

Gore folded his arms and stood his ground.

'He said, get out of the way!' growled another soldier. To emphasise his point, he crashed the butt of his musket into Gore's chest.

Gore staggered back and, with a victorious cry, Draffin's party surged in the door and pushed the Provost Marshal aside.[31] A grinning Cadwallader Draffin brought up the rear, sword in hand.

Upstairs, Bligh and Palmer had heard yelling at the front and rear doors. Bligh, impatient to have his sword in his hand, came out onto the first-floor landing to find out what was keeping his servant Dunn and to see what was happening downstairs. Dunn, it seems, was having trouble finding the key to open the cabinet containing the Governor's sword. It is unlikely that Dunn deliberately failed to produce the sword, for he was to perform a valuable service to the Governor before the evening was over.

Hearing Draffin's men come in the back way, the thud of their heavy boots resounding on the brown-painted cedar floorboards, Bligh realised that he would be seized if he stayed where he was. Sending Palmer downstairs to try to delay the invaders, the Governor withdrew. Palmer had just reached the bottom of the stairs when Lieutenant Draffin's party appeared in front of him. Pushing the little Commissary-General to one side, the soldiers charged upstairs. Palmer now saw Fulton and Campbell at the front door and, through the side-window glass, the faces and flashing bayonets of the troops with Kemp and Lawson outside. The soldiers were yelling at Fulton with increasing impatience.

At the same time, a party of soldiers led by Lieutenant Minchin poured into Mary Putland's bedroom via the French door. Mary had left the French door unlocked when she'd ventured out onto the veranda on her mission to bar the gates, and Robert Campbell had failed to lock it when he'd also gone out that way. Showing initiative, Minchin had tried the door, found it would open, and led his group of six soldiers into the house via that entrance. From the bedroom they'd entered Mary's sitting room, and from that reached the rear corridor.

Commissary Palmer heard Minchin's troops cheer as they gained access to the house via Mary's bedroom. Appreciating that resistance was pointless, and stupid, Palmer called out to the stubborn Reverend Fulton, 'I think you had better let them come in, Chaplain. They're coming in the end way, through Mrs Putland's room, anyway. Someone will do you a mischief by driving a bayonet through the glass, if you don't.'[32]

Looking around and seeing Minchin's men in the house, Fulton realised that the Commissary-General was right; the castle had been stormed. The unhappy Fulton unbolted the front door, then he and Campbell stepped back and stood to one side. With a cheer, the six soldiers there crushed in through the front door. Swords in hand, Kemp and Lawson strolled in after them.

'Where is Governor Bligh?' Captain Kemp pompously demanded of Fulton, Campbell and Palmer. When none of them replied, Kemp scowled at Palmer, whom he believed, with good reason, to be Bligh's closest friend and ally in the colony. 'I asked you, sir, where is Governor Bligh? I wish to speak with him.'

'I could not say,' said Palmer, eyeing the gleaming Sheffield steel blade of Kemp's sabre. 'The last I saw of His Excellency, he was putting his uniform on.'[33]

The New South Wales Corps was on the march. With colours flying and its fifes and drums playing 'The British Grenadiers' – a marching tune suggested, it would be rumoured, by John Macarthur[34] – the companies of the Corps were coming down Bridge Street from the rise of Church Hill three men abreast. At the head of the Corps marched Major Johnston, sword in his left hand because his right was in a sling. With him were Lieutenants John Brabyn and Thomas Laycock, and Corps Surgeon Dr John Harris and Assistant Surgeon Dr Thomas Jamieson. The number of troops on the march on the 'Glorious 26th', as the day would be dubbed by the coup's more ardent supporters, was estimated at around 300 by those who took part that day.[35]

The soldiers, most of them clean-shaven apart from thick 'mutton-chop' side-whiskers, marched with muskets on their shoulders and looking smart in their scarlet 'coatee' tunics. Red had been the colour of most British soldiers' uniforms for centuries, initially because red cloth was cheap. Several regiments had changed to green during the American War of Independence to make them less conspicuous in North American forests. Transverse white belts formed a cross over the chests of the men of the Corps, their brass central clasps shining brightly. From the right belt hung a black leather ammunition pouch. From the left swung an empty bayonet scabbard. The scarlet and white plumes at the front of the black shakos of the men of the Corps nodded as they marched. The thick woollen uniforms made marching on a summer's day sticky work for a British soldier. But now the sun was going down. And the men of the Corps didn't have far to tramp before they reached the day's field of battle.

At the very rear of the long lines of redcoats marched Sergeant-Major Thomas Whittle, ensuring there were no stragglers. Immediately behind Whittle came a group of half-a-dozen civilians of the officer-settler cartel, headed by John Macarthur and his friends, Bayly and Blaxcell. As the procession gained momentum, it gathered followers from the town, growing like a snowball, but many townspeople stayed indoors, frightened by the sight of the fully armed troops and fearful of what might happen next.

Thomas Tait, a former convict, was one of those frightened townspeople. He worked as a clerk in the Commissary-General's office next door to Government House, but had gone home for the day by this time. Tait would later say that he had seen the Corps march on Government House, but did not see it later return to barracks.[36] Made so afraid by the sight of the Corps on the march and the dread that he might be included in a round-up of the Governor's employees, it seems that Tait bolted his door, closed the curtains, and cringed.

The more curious and adventurous townspeople flooded along behind the marching red lines. A shipwright from the Rocks district by the name of James Dowse Harris was in that crowd. He had come out to the colony in 1800 as a convict and had since been given his freedom. He was to estimate that the civilians who followed the Corps that day numbered 200.[37] George Suttor, the visiting Baulkam Hills farmer, was also now in that throng. He was near the forefront, close enough to hear Sergeant-Major Whittle call out to the troops ahead of him, 'Men, I hope you'll do your duty, and don't spare them!'

'Aye, never fear [doubt] us,' a soldier replied from the ranks.

Several excited children were running along beside the rear ranks. 'Get out of the way, children,' the Sergeant-Major now called, 'for some of you I expect will be killed.'

This brought a cautionary note from one of the settlers just behind him. 'Hush! Hush!' It was the voice of John Macarthur. At which Sergeant-Major Whittle held his tongue and refrained from any further similar outbursts.[38]

After crossing the Tank Stream bridge, Bridge Street climbed with increasing elevation to the east until it terminated at Government House. A high brick wall stood across the end of the street, with the double cast-iron gates of Government House running parallel to the street on an east–west alignment. Anyone standing inside the gates looking out would see a track running down to the government wharf, then Sydney Cove and the harbour, and its forested northern shore beyond. Up the Bridge Street slope now toiled the lines of troops, in step to 'The British Grenadiers', played continuously by the band during the five minutes it took to march from the Old Parade to Government House.

To the rattle of the drums, the squeal of the fifes, and the coordinated tramp of hundreds of marching feet, the column passed the Bridge Street homes and offices of the Surveyor-General, the Principal Chaplain, the Judge Advocate, and finally the premises of Commissary-General Palmer. When the lead elements arrived outside the open Government House gates and opposite the Guard House, an order rang out: 'Column, halt!' The troops came to stop, the band fell silent.

By this time, the men of the Governor's Guard had forced their way into Government House via three different access points. Outside, company sergeant-majors ordered their newly arrived troops to surround the house. On the double now, soldiers passed in through the gateway. Some companies swung left and swept along the gravel path at the front of the house. Others kept on going straight ahead, their hobnailed boots clattering over a brick-paved yard on the town side of the house. Moving to extend a cordon around the rear of the building, these troops trotted by a row of single-storey Government House offices and servants' quarters.

Mary Putland and Susan Palmer still stood where Robert Campbell had left them, on the veranda. As Major Johnston came through the gate, he ordered Surgeon Harris to attend to the ladies, and Dr Harris hurried to take up the role of their guardian. Harris and the women would remain there on the veranda for the next two hours. According to Harris, a self-important man, Mary Putland 'clung' to him throughout.[39]

Major Johnston himself, sword in left hand, took up a position on the path opposite the front door to Government House as his troops flooded along behind him. There, Johnston would wait in expectation of the news that Governor Bligh had been taken prisoner by the men of the Governor's Guard now inside the building. There too, in the twilight, Johnston was joined by Assistant Surgeon James Mileham, Surveyor-General Charles Grimes, and several settlers and merchants – John Macarthur, Nicholas Bayly, Garnham Blaxcell, Simeon Lord, John Blaxland and his younger brother Gregory, Robert Townson, and Sydney flour-miller and baker James Badgery.

The members of the crowd that had followed the column found themselves facing a line of troops outside the gate. They had to be satisfied with standing in Bridge Street, craning their necks and cocking their ears in an attempt to find out what exactly was taking place. In the crowd, shipwright James Dowse Harris asked those around him if anyone knew what was going on but, while everyone seemed to have an opinion, no one had a definitive answer for him. Contrary to later rebel claims that the invasion of Government House was the result of a popular uprising by the majority of the people of the colony, Harris was to say that the crowd would remain ignorant of what was taking place at Government House for some time yet.[40]

At the rear of that crowd, two hundred paces from the Government House gates, stood Francis Oakes, the mild-mannered Chief Constable of the Parramatta district, whose attempt to arrest John Macarthur on 15 December had set this whole drama in motion. In Sydney on official business, Oakes, a former missionary who had been appointed to his post by Governor King, had been at the head of Pitt's Row, today's Pitt Street, south-east of the Parade Ground, when he had seen and heard the Corps on the march. Warily he had followed the procession, and now he lingered on the fringes of the throng in Bridge Street, hoping to learn what was happening at Government House without becoming personally embroiled. In Oakes' estimation, the people around him were 'much alarmed' by the sight of the armed troops.[41]

Inside Government House, all of the Governor's officials who had been captured were herded into the drawing room, at the back of the house, opposite the dining parlour. The Governor's servant, John Dunn, was sent out onto the veranda to join Surgeon Harris and the ladies. In the drawing room, with Corps sentinels on the door, Palmer, Campbell, Gore, Fulton, Arndell, Williamson, and Secretary Griffin waited unhappily, some sitting, others standing, while men of the Guard ranged throughout the house, upstairs and down, looking for Governor Bligh.

Despite the troops' best efforts, William Bligh could not be found anywhere. It was as if the Governor had vanished into thin air. So, a party under Lieutenant Thomas Laycock was dispatched to search the outbuildings. Lieutenant Moore, who had earlier conducted a search of the first floor of Government House, led another group of soldiers with orders to put a fine toothcomb through all the government buildings stretching back along Bridge Street. It seemed unlikely, but the Governor may have managed to slip out the back way, to find a hiding place in one of these buildings. After a time, Moore came back to report he'd had no success.

Rangy Lieutenant Thomas Laycock, the tallest man in the New South Wales Corps at a reputed six feet six inches (198 centimetres), was the son of Thomas Laycock Senior, a former sergeant and quartermaster with the Corps. Thomas Junior had played a leading role in putting down the rising of hundreds of Irish convicts at Vinegar Hill outside Sydney in 1804. He'd also made a name for himself a year back as an intrepid explorer. Dispatched by Captain Kemp, who had then commanded at Patersonia, Laycock had led four soldiers across mountainous Van Diemen's Land, an island the size of England, to Hobart Town, the principal settlement in the south, in eight days.

Lieutenant Laycock was not as successful on his mission today, as he searched through the row of Government House service rooms and offices that lined the brick-paved yard behind the house. One of these rooms contained the printing press used to irregularly produce the *Sydney Gazette*, the colony's government newspaper. In quest of the Governor, Laycock climbed up into the loft above the print room where paper was stored, only to lose his footing and tumble to the floor below. It seems Laycock dislocated his hip in the fall. It was a painful price to pay for no reward – no trace was found of Governor Bligh.

With the rebels growing frustrated, Sergeant-Major Whittle had gone into the house to join the search, and now he was heard to exclaim, 'He's gone down to Palmer's, I'm sure.'[42]

So Sergeant Johnston of the Governor's Guard was ordered to take Commissary Palmer to his house and thoroughly search it again. This second search of the Commissary's quarters, right next door to Government House, would continue for some time. At Government House, Sergeant-Major Whittle was nearing the end of his patience. It was now approaching 7.30. An hour had passed since the invasion of Government House. Deciding to make another search of the mansion, Whittle collected one of the six-man sections from the Governor's Guard, dividing it into two teams of three. He would lead one, the other would be led by Sergeant John Sutherland.

Apparently thinking there must be some secret door, hidden trapdoor or other hideaway in the house, Whittle dragged Secretary Edmund Griffin from the drawing room and brought in the Governor's servant John Dunn from the veranda. Both were men who should know the house intimately. Whittle took Griffin with his search party and gave Dunn over to Sutherland's group. Equipped with these 'guides' and lanterns, they began the fresh search.

This second scouring of the ground floor produced nothing. Whittle was furious. 'Damn my eyes!' the Sergeant-Major exclaimed loudly when the two empty-handed groups met up again in the hall. 'I will find him! Soldiers, come upstairs again.'[43]

The search parties then climbed the stairs. At the first floor they divided, Whittle taking his men and Secretary Griffin to the right, Sutherland and his party going to the left with servant Dunn. Sergeant Sutherland's search eventually brought him to a closed door. He asked John Dunn what room lay beyond the door, and Dunn answered that it was his own bedroom. Sutherland then asked him, 'What's in there?'

'There is nothing in there but for my bed and some lumber,' Dunn replied.[44]

Sutherland opened the door. The dusty, gloomy room was long and thin, with a sloping skillion-style roof dropping from high by the door to quite low at the back. A wooden partition partly divided the space. With Private William Wilford, a tall, solid man, holding a lantern high, Sergeant Sutherland, Corporal Michael Marlborough and Wilford advanced into the room. On the other side of the partition they found, as Dunn had described, a bed, and lengths of dressed timber piled up on the floor at the end of it – for what purpose remains unclear. The pile of timber was so high that no one could easily pass over it to reach the far side of the bed. There was a small window in the back wall. Unlike the four-poster beds elsewhere in Government House, Dunn's bed possessed neither curtains nor a wooden top rail. The bedcover hung almost to the floor. The only other item in the austere room was a bag containing clothing which sat on the bare wooden floor.[45]

Sergeant Sutherland bent and, using his rifle like a pike, ran the end of his bayonet around the space between the underside of the bed and the floor. Feeling nothing, he decided to repeat the action one more time for luck. As he did so, he heard the sound of a boot scrape on the floor on the far side of the bed.

'Come out! Come out!' Sutherland commanded.

Marlborough and Wilford, suddenly both excited and anxious at the same time, were also yelling. Marlborough, a short man with a moustache and neat goatee beard and sideburns shaved to a point that made him look like a Spanish grandee, was waving his musket as if it were a wand. Then, slowly, the unhappy face of Governor Bligh emerged in the low light, on the far side of the bed.

'Here he is! Here he is!' Sergeant Sutherland yelled at the top of his voice, so that others elsewhere in the house would hear him.[46]

Sergeant-Major Whittle was in a room to the right of the first-floor landing when he heard Sutherland's shout. Whittle hurried from the room and across the landing. By the time he reached the doorway to John Dunn's room, it was crowded by the three men of his own search party including Private William Hutton, all looking delighted. Servant John Dunn and Edmund Griffin, the Governor's secretary were also there, both stricken with concern.

The word was quickly relayed to the troops waiting outside Government House: 'The Governor is found!' A cheer went up from the troops lined up all the way around the house. This was Major Johnston's cue to make his entrance.

At that moment, Adjutant Lieutenant Minchin, standing down in the entrance hall, heard a voice calling from upstairs. Moving to the foot of the stairs, Minchin looked up and saw a terrified Edmund Griffin. Secretary Griffin begged Minchin to come at once and wrest the Governor from the troops who had located him, as he feared for his safety. Minchin dashed up the stairs. When he arrived at Dunn's room, Minchin found his way barred by the five men who crowded the doorway.

Inside the room, Governor Bligh had come to his feet and Sergeant Sutherland had reached out his hand to him, to help him climb over the bed. Initially hesitating, Bligh soon realised he had no other alternative, so he took Sutherland's hand and climbed unsteadily up onto the bed. As he did, he felt the papers concealed under his waistcoat and shirt begin to move. Letting go of Sutherland's hand, and still standing on the bed which sagged beneath his weight, Bligh put his right hand inside his waistcoat to stuff the papers back inside his shirt.

'Man, take care of yourself!' yelled Corporal Marlborough in warning to Sutherland. 'He's going to take a pistol out of his bosom!'[47] With that, Marlborough took a step forward and thrust his bayonet up at Bligh's throat. 'Damn your eyes, if you don't take your hand out of there,' he threatened the Governor, 'I'll whip this into you immediately!'[48]

It must have occurred to Bligh that the troops had orders to kill him and make it appear that he had been resisting arrest. And this brute Marlborough looked as though he was about to carry out his threat to use the bayonet. Remaining perfectly still so he didn't provoke the corporal, Bligh called to Sutherland, 'Sergeant, keep the man off! I have no arms. Stand off!'[49]

Lieutenant Minchin, meanwhile, had resorted to crawling on hands and knees through the legs of those in the doorway. As he emerged into the room, Corporal Marlborough called to him, 'Take care, he has a pistol!'[50]

'I have no arms,' Bligh repeated, now slowly removing his hand from his waistcoat to show that it was empty.

'Sergeant, keep the men off,' Minchin ordered, as he pulled himself to his feet. 'The Governor is not armed. I will answer for it. The Governor is not armed.'[51]

Sergeant Sutherland called Marlborough off and, begrudgingly, the corporal took a few backward paces and lowered his weapon. The sergeant then commanded all the soldiers to withdraw from the room. As Corporal Marlborough went to depart with the others, he pointed under the bed. 'We found him there, sir,' he told Minchin.[52]

Now, Lieutenant Minchin reached his hand to Bligh. The Governor took it and allowed the officer to help him down from the bed. There the Governor stood, brushing dust from his white lapels and coat-tails.

'I'm extremely sorry you suffered yourself to be found in this manner, Governor,' said Minchin. 'You should have come forward in the first instance to meet the officers when they came to your door.'[53]

Bligh, buttoning his shirt and waistcoat, did not reply. He glared at the lieutenant.

'Major Johnston wishes to see you below, sir,' said Minchin. 'I will safely see you downstairs, if you will allow me.' He offered the Governor his left arm.[54]

Bligh, realising he had no choice and that he would have to put a brave face on his 'capture', took Minchin's arm. Together they walked from the room, as a leering Sergeant-Major Whittle and the soldiers with him parted to make way for the pair. Bligh spotted John Dunn hovering worriedly behind the soldiers. Bligh was confident he could trust Dunn implicitly, for the man had been in his service for years. Like Bligh's steward George Jubb, his secretary Edmund Griffin, and his daughter's maid, Dunn had come out from England with the Governor in 1806. Bligh made a movement with his eyes toward Dunn's room, and hoped that the man would get the hint and check his room when the troops weren't looking, there to find and destroy the shredded documents that Bligh had hidden beneath the mattress on Dunn's bed.

Secretary Edmund Griffin was waiting on the landing. Relieved that the Governor was unharmed, Griffin moved to Bligh's left side and said, 'Will you take *my* arm, sir?'

Bligh smiled faintly. 'No, I am perfectly safe with Mr Minchin.'[55]

As he and Lieutenant Minchin reached the top of the stairs, Bligh hesitated. Below, the hall was a blaze of scarlet uniforms. Officers of the Corps and men of the Governor's Guard all looked up at him with a mixture of delight and scorn. The scene, like this entire episode, would have reminded William Bligh of another warm summer's night nineteen years before when men he commanded had risen up against him. Steeling himself for what lay ahead, Bligh proceeded down the stairs with the lieutenant.

2

The Night of the Inquisitors

Slowly, with all the dignity he could muster, the Governor descended the stairs holding Lieutenant Minchin's arm. Close behind them came young Griffin, Bligh's anxious secretary, followed by a triumphant Sergeant-Major Whittle and his men. As Bligh and Minchin reached the ground floor, soldiers of the Governor's Guard in the entrance hall made way for them, and the lieutenant guided his captive toward the drawing room.

Bligh had been very close to evading capture. If Whittle had not been determined to conduct a second search of the upper floor, it's likely the rebels would have assumed that the Governor had escaped and withdrawn most of their men from Government House to scour the town for him. Later that night or early the next morning, under cover of darkness, Bligh might have made his escape into the shrubbery to the east of Government House. Beyond a four-storey white windmill on the Domain owned by Commissary Palmer, Bennelong Point – the home to Sydney's famous Opera House today – was then rocky, barren ground. Beyond that to the east lay fertile farmland around Farm Cove and Garden Island Cove. Once into the farmland, Bligh might have made for Woolloomooloo Farm, Commissary Palmer's 100-acre (40 hectare) property at Garden Island Cove. Acquiring a horse there, Bligh would have dashed for the Hawkesbury as he had originally planned, on a ride just as daring as Paul Revere's, to declare that a revolution had taken place at Sydney and to raise a citizen's army in the King's name.

Bligh had no idea what had happened to his orderly, Sergeant Whalley. At no point would Bligh later suggest that Whalley had betrayed him. So, it seems that the sergeant had hurried out to the wooden stables just to the south of Government House, as Bligh had ordered, only to be found there by Lieutenant Moore in the process of saddling two horses.

Knowing that Lieutenant Draffin's men had been just moments behind him as they burst in the rear door and headed for the stairs, Bligh, in desperation, had chosen John Dunn's room as his hiding place. The sight of the lumber piled at the end of the bed had suggested that no one would look around the other side of the bed, and he had dived over there. Draffin's men had been far from thorough in their search and had missed him. A little later, Lieutenant Moore, conducting his own perfunctory search of the upper floor, had come into the room. 'Poo! Poo!' Moore had loudly exclaimed. 'He is not in here. The Governor is not here.'[56]

After Moore's departure, Bligh, on his knees behind Dunn's bed and in increasing darkness as the sun went down outside the room's window, had set to work tearing into small pieces many of the documents he had salvaged from his room. Some he was determined to keep. The others were downright dangerous – copies of his reports to London on a variety of people in the colony. It would be a disaster for him if they were to fall into the hands of the very people about whom he had written confidential and sometimes uncomplimentary reports. He had subsequently gone to great lengths to stuff the pieces of paper up between the bed's straps and the sagging feather mattress. Servant Dunn would find the torn documents hidden under his bed – he must have looked for them, for the soldiers never spotted them. Dunn subsequently burned these papers, probably in the kitchen fire.

All the while he'd been hiding in Dunn's room, Bligh had been able to hear much of what was going on in the house and, around 7.30, he had heard with sudden concern the declaration by Sergeant-Major Whittle that he would find the Governor. Then he had heard Whittle's two search parties come upstairs, and had pressed himself to the floor when Sergeant Sutherland and his two companions came into the room. To this day, Bligh's critics have described the fact that he hid in the bedroom as an act of cowardice. But Bligh, from bloody naval battles to navigating the *Bounty* launch to safety against impossible odds, had shown more than his share of courage. His attempt to evade capture and defend his governorship had been no less courageous than Bonnie Prince Charlie dressing as a woman to escape Scotland after his failed attempt to win the British throne sixty years earlier.

On the evening of 26 January, as Lieutenant Minchin conducted Governor Bligh across the crowded hall toward the drawing room, they passed Surgeon John Harris. Harris studied the captured Governor with satisfaction, noting the grubby state of his uniform, then followed him and Minchin into the drawing room.[57] Bligh would later say, 'I found troops stationed all round the walls' of the drawing room, 'just like a Robespierrean party, or a revolutionary tribunal'.[58] Only one of the Governor's advisers remained in the room – Robert Campbell. Commissary Palmer was still at his own quarters while Gore, Fulton and Williamson had all been taken away under guard – where, or why, none of them had been told. Behind the Governor, Griffin and Dunn were herded back into the room.

At that moment, Mary Putland appeared in the doorway that led to the adjoining dining room. If she had indeed been sobbing earlier, she had composed herself by this point and looked relieved that her 'Papa' was unhurt. Bligh hurried to her. Taking his daughter's hand, he guided her to one side of the room, assuring her that he was unhurt and that all would be well. There the pair stood, talking in lowered voices. It's probable that Bligh urged his feisty daughter to remain calm, to not provoke the military, and to allow him to deal with the rebels his own way. They were interrupted by Lieutenant Moore, who came in from the dining room and handed the Governor a letter. As Bligh opened it, Moore retreated the way he had come. Bligh read:

> *William Bligh, Esq.*
> *Sir,*
> *I am called upon to execute a most painful duty; you are charged by the respectable inhabitants of crimes that render you unfit to exercise the supreme authority another moment in this colony; and in that charge all the officers serving under my command have joined.*
>
> *I therefore require you in His Majesty's sacred name to resign your authority, and to submit to the arrest which I hereby place you under by the advice of all my officers, and by the advice of every respectable inhabitant in the town of Sydney.*
>
> *I am, sir, Your most obedient humble servant*
> *GEORGE JOHNSTON*
> *Acting Lieutenant Governor, and Major Commanding*
> *New South Wales Corps*[59]

Bligh had only just finished reading the letter when Lieutenant Moore returned to say that Major Johnston wished to speak with him in the adjoining room. Moments later, Johnston himself appeared in the doorway to the dining room, surrounded by officers and enlisted men, and with his sword still in his left hand as though he might yet have need of it.

Of medium height and build, with grey sideboards and thick

grey hair swept back rakishly, George Johnston was a smart figure in his cocked hat and tailored uniform, despite the tunic's tight fit, which could not disguise bulges at the waist. He had an impish mouth and his nose glowed red, a sign that Major Johnston enjoyed a tipple or two. Born in Scotland, Johnston had been a soldier for more than thirty years. His father had also been an officer, and with the help of the family's patron, Lord Percy, young George had taken an ensign's commission in the Royal Marines when just two weeks short of his twelfth birthday. Johnston himself was to remark that this was 'an early age'[60] for such responsibility, but it was common for ensigns and midshipmen to enter the army or navy so young – the sons of officers could go to sea at eleven. At twelve and thirteen, Johnston was leading men twice and three times his age in Britain's struggle against America's revolutionaries, serving at New York and Halifax in 1776–77. Promoted to Lieutenant, he had subsequently been involved in various actions at sea and on land. Seriously wounded in a 1786 battle against the French in the East Indies, he had taken six months to recover.

Assigned to the Royal Marines contingent sent out to New South Wales with the First Fleet, on 26 January 1788, Johnston had been the first British officer to step ashore at the future site of Sydney. Two years later, when the Marines were withdrawn, Johnston transferred to the New South Wales Corps. Apart from two brief visits home to Britain, Johnston had spent the last twenty years in New South Wales. On land granted to him by the government, he had created the comfortable life of a country squire at Annandale, his estate just outside the capital. Named by Johnston for his home town in Scotland, Annandale would in time become the inner-Sydney suburb of that name. Becoming less and less interested in military and public life, especially once Governor Bligh had taken charge in the colony, Johnston had come to lead what many colonists were to describe as a 'retiring' way of life.

Here in the drawing room at Government House, Bligh noted that the right side of Johnston's face was bruised. The bruising, and the arm in a sling, were consistent with the Major's story that he had been unwell and unable to write. Johnston had genuinely taken a tumble from his gig after leaving the officers' dinner the previous Sunday evening – a drunken tumble. The extent of his injuries was questionable, as was the excuse Johnston had given Orderly Sergeant Whalley when he had turned down the request to come and see the Governor. Johnston had claimed to have been too unwell to come into Sydney to present himself at Government House, yet he had been well enough to lead the New South Wales Corps on a march to seize Government House and arrest the Governor.

Bligh handed the Major's letter to Robert Campbell, then strode across the room to Johnston and confronted him. 'You are to be congratulated, Major,' said Bligh, 'on the handsome manner in which you have carried the wishes of "the inhabitants" into effect.' He was referring to the Major's letter in which, to Bligh's mind, 'the inhabitants' referred to John Macarthur. 'Had I known I was so much disliked, I would have left the colony by the first available ship!'[61] Bligh was being facetious. But his words, meant as jibes, would later rebound on him, being given an entirely different connotation by his enemies.

Johnston was not going to be baited. He was soft-spoken at the best of times, which made it difficult for fellow Scot Robert Campbell, on the other side of the drawing room, to hear all that Johnston now said to the Governor. Bligh could hear him well enough, as the Major repeated the 'request' contained in his letter, that Bligh resign and submit to arrest. Then, said Johnston, who continued to brandish his sabre, 'I have put you under arrest, sir, by the advice of my officers, and I therefore command you to remain under the arrest that I have placed you.'[62] Johnston then turned to his officers and issued instructions regarding the disposition of Bligh and his officials.

Bligh now said, 'Major Johnston, I suppose you will not take my secretary away?' Of all the men who served Bligh in the colony, Griffin was his most intimate confidante, and Bligh was worried that the rebels would put pressure on the young man, perhaps even torture him, to make him divulge the Governor's secrets. 'He may remain with me?'

Johnston turned back to the Governor and said, 'Oh yes, certainly, Mr Griffin may remain.' But then he suddenly had second thoughts. 'But stop.' He called to one of the civilians in the next room. 'Mr Bayly.'

Nicholas Bayly hurried to the Major. Welsh-born, husband of Lieutenant Laycock's sister Sarah, thirty-seven-year-old Bayly had resigned as a lieutenant in the Corps in 1802. He was one of John Macarthur's closest friends.

'Mr Bayly,' said Johnston, 'go and ask the inhabitants outside whether they approve of Mr Griffin's remaining here.'

Bayly jogged outside. He hadn't been away a minute before he returned, and advised, 'It is *not* approved of.'[63]

Bligh felt sure that 'the inhabitants' referred to John Macarthur who, unlike some of the other civilians, had made a point of remaining outside Government House, as if to exonerate himself from what was going on inside. Major Johnston now ordered Ensign Bell to take Edmund Griffin under guard to the Guard House.

While this was taking place, Commissary Palmer was returned to Government House by Sergeant Johnston. Escorted into the dining room, Palmer was briefly reunited there with Susan, his terrified wife. As he comforted her, he saw the Major in conversation with Bligh in the next room, and realised that the Governor had been apprehended. Lieutenant Minchin now spotted Palmer, and came to him.

'Consider yourself under military arrest, Commissary,' Adjutant Minchin said to him. 'You must give up the keys of the public stores, and of your office where all your books and papers are.'

'I understand that you people are in possession of my office and the stores already,' Palmer coolly replied. 'The storekeeper has the keys.'[64]

Minchin ordered Palmer taken back to his house under guard, with sentries posted at the Commissary-General's office. Minchin then returned to the next room. As Palmer was led away, Bligh was now accompanied by just his daughter, his servant Dunn, and Robert Campbell. Minchin went to Campbell. 'Mr Campbell,' he said, 'as a friend of the Governor, Major Johnston requests that you go upstairs to see his papers searched.'[65]

The seizure of the Governor's papers were as crucial to John Macarthur and his fellow rebels as the seizure of the Governor himself. They hoped that those papers would provide evidence to be used in the local courts to clear Macarthur and to condemn the Governor, to turn Bligh's supporters in the colony against him, and more importantly, to substantiate the rebels' claims to the authorities in London that Bligh had been guilty of acting tyrannically and corruptly.

Campbell glanced at Bligh, who nodded his approval for Campbell to be present when his papers were searched. Minchin then told servant John Dunn to lead the way to the Governor's room, and the lieutenant and Campbell followed him upstairs. They found John Macarthur's friend, Surveyor-General Grimes, and Robert Townson, formerly a captain in the Corps, already in the Governor's room, trying to force open locked drawers.

Grimes looked around and said to John Dunn, 'Where are the Governor's keys?'

'I don't know where they is, sir,' the servant replied.

Townson, possessor of a 2000-acre (800 hectare) land grant, was unique among the settlers of New South Wales, being the holder of a doctorate in philosophy. He frowned at Dunn and demanded, 'Where are the Governor's papers, public and private?'

'I don't know where they is,' Dunn repeated.

Grimes came to Dunn and glowered at him. 'Damn me! You know where they are. If you choose to tell us.'

Dunn only shrugged, and tried to look dumb.

Then Grimes said, 'Never mind, gentlemen. I know where the Governor's papers are.' He led Townson to a chest of drawers at the far end of the room. 'They are here. For I have seen the Governor, when I have come on business, put them here.'[66]

Someone, possibly Minchin, suggested that the locked bureau in the room was also a likely place for the Governor's papers. So Grimes and Townson lifted up the bureau and carried it to the door, saying they would take it downstairs before returning for the chest of drawers. As they were carrying the bureau out the door they caught it against the door-post, to John Dunn's horror, breaking off the ornate top section containing small drawers and shelves. The damaged bureau, the chest of drawers, the Governor's desk and his tools of office including the Great Seal of the colony, were all carried into a room downstairs. The two doors to the room were then locked and sealed, and a soldier put on guard at each. In the meantime, Campbell was taken back to his house under guard and locked in, with sentries stationed front and back.

Bligh was left with his daughter and Susan Palmer. Mrs Palmer would have to spend the night at Government House separated from her husband, Commissary Palmer. Outside, the men of the Corps were falling in by company. Johnston, about to depart, informed Bligh that, although he was declaring martial law, Bligh could remain living at Government House and would be able to retain his servants, his horses, carriage and so on. But he was to always consider himself under house arrest.

Bligh said, 'I hope you would have no objection if I have a few friends to Government House to eat a bite of dinner with me now and then?'

Johnston, surprised at Bligh's apparent acceptance of his lot now that he was a prisoner, replied, 'Certainly not, sir.'[67]

Bligh now held out his hand. Both Lieutenant Minchin and Surgeon Harris would later testify to having been astonished that the Govenor would do such a thing after Johnston had just deposed him.[68] But it's obvious that, by seeming to be acquiescent, Bligh was hoping to catch Johnston off-guard. Johnston's right hand was in a sling and supposedly so damaged he couldn't even hold a pen, while his sword was in his left hand. In theory, there was no way he could shake anyone's hand at that moment. But if there was nothing wrong with his right hand, as Bligh suspected, in an unguarded moment Johnston might remove it from the sling and reach for Bligh's outstretched hand, thereby giving himself away.

But Johnston didn't fall for it. Ignoring the Governor's hand, the Major mumbled a good-night and left the house, finally sheathing his sword as he went. Minchin, Harris and the remaining officers and the civilian leadership of the coup also departed. Sentries from the Governor's Guard were posted outside the doors. Orders rang out. The Corps assembled in three lines once again. Johnston and his officers took their place at the head of the column, John Macarthur and his fellow rebel leaders took theirs at the rear. The regimental band struck up 'Britons Weep'. Company sergeant-majors bawled 'Quick march!' And the Corps marched back the way it had come, with the crowd in Bridge Street quickly parting to allow the soldiers to pass through their midst. Lieutenant Laycock was limping as a result of his fall in the office of the *Gazette*, but otherwise the Corps was retiring without casualties. It was 8.20 pm. The coup had been carried out in just under two hours.

Up Bridge Street the troops marched, with John Macarthur and the other rebel leaders at the rear in buoyant mood. With the Government House gates clanging shut behind them, and manned by sentries of the Governor's Guard, the crowd wrapped around the rear of the column and followed it back to the Old

Parade. Baulkham Hills settler, George Suttor, was still in the throng. He had at last worked out that the Corps had invaded Government House and deposed Governor Bligh, a man he liked and respected. Suttor, and others of a like mind in the crowd, were not at all happy with this business. In Suttor's opinion, and according to others he spoke to, the Governor would have been justified in shooting the first man who came through his door.[69] Not that such a step would have guaranteed an outcome any different from that which had eventuated. And it would have put others inside Government House, in particular the women, in danger.

As Suttor watched from the perimeter of the Old Parade, the Corps reformed in neat ranks by company on the parade ground, and then the men gave three hearty cheers. 'Hurrah! Hurrah! Hurrah!' They followed this by calling out something else – Suttor could not make out precisely what. He thought it was either, 'Johnston forever!' or 'Macarthur forever!'[70]

The troops were then dismissed and, as the men dispersed to their quarters talking animatedly among themselves, the officers retired to the Major's barrack, where they were joined by Macarthur and several other gentlemen. Suttor slipped back to the inn where he was staying. He had an ominous feeling about the future now that the colony was in the hands of the military. The tune played by the Corps as it marched away from Government House, 'Britons Weep', could well, he thought, be prophetic. He made up his mind that the next day he would complete his business in Sydney as quickly as he could and then head home. There was no telling what the rebels would do next.[71]

Chief Constable Oakes was also still in the crowd when it broke up. As people went this way and that, deep in conversation about the evening's incredible events, some excited, others looking worried, Oakes lingered in the centre of town. Perhaps he might pick up a piece of useful intelligence, or perhaps he would see a senior Bligh administration official who would advise him what he could do to help His Excellency. By 9.00 o'clock he had decided that there was no point waiting around any longer. Fetching his horse, he mounted up and rode along High Street to the west. When he reached the outskirts of the town and drew opposite a spot where a gallows sometimes stood, he received a fright. In the fading light he could make out several soldiers with fixed bayonets manning a checkpoint in his path.

There was a fierce challenge. 'Who comes here?'

For all Oakes knew, the troops may have had orders to arrest the Governor's officials, including police officers, but Oakes decided to risk toughing it out. 'Francis Oakes, Chief Constable of Parramatta,' he announced, as officiously as he could.

'Pass, friend.'

A relieved Oakes urged his horse forward, rode on by the soldiers, and settled into the saddle for the ninety-minute ride through the night to his home.[72]

Five or ten minutes after Oakes rode out of town, in a cell at the Guard House opposite Government House, a glum Edmund Griffin looked up as the cell door opened. Lieutenant John Brabyn ordered the Governor's secretary out. Fearful of what would happen to him, Griffin rose up. Outside the cell, Brabyn took him by one arm, and the settler John Blaxland took the other.

Thirty-nine-year-old Blaxland was a former captain with the Duke of York's Cavalry, and very much of the officer class and mindset. The son of the mayor of Fordwich in Kent, Blaxland had followed younger brother Gregory to the colony eighteen months back with a promise from the government of land, convict servants and cattle. Gregory Blaxland had received 4000 acres (1600 hectares), forty convicts, and seventy cattle, so John was affronted when Governor Bligh would only give him 1300 acres (520 hectares), twenty-one convicts, and sixty cattle. Bligh had said that Blaxland had not fully met the government's requirement of investing £6000 in the colony. Blaxland, a petty, difficult man, had been bitter ever since, and had been quick to jump on the rebel bandwagon once it was rolling down the road to revolution.

Blaxland and Brabyn hustled Griffin out of the Guard House, along Bridge Street and over the bridge, across the Old Parade, and into Major Johnston's quarters. Sitting at a table in one of the barrack rooms were Lieutenant Draffin and Robert Townson, the doctor of philosophy who, with Surveyor-General Grimes, had taken such an interest in the Governor's papers at Government House. Settler Blaxland joined the other two at the table, and Griffin was made to stand in front of the committee of three.

Major Johnston then arrived with a Holy Bible in his hand and required Griffin to give his oath that he would tell the truth, the whole truth, and nothing but the truth to the committee. Secretary Griffin objected to taking the oath, but Johnston said that martial law had now been officially proclaimed and he must follow military commands. 'This committee is agreeable to the Duke of York's order,' he added. The Duke of York was the commander-in-chief of British armed forces, and under his name the rules for the enforcement of martial law had been published. Under martial law, civilians had to obey the military. Griffin must either obey Major Johnston's command, or face jail. Griffin took the oath.

John Macarthur then ambled into the room. 'With your permission, Major,' he said, 'I will join the committee.'

Johnston said he had no objection, and left the committee to do their business. Macarthur took his seat with the others, and proceeded to take charge. Griffin was grilled by Macarthur for half an hour, with Lieutenant Draffin noting down the prisoner's words. 'I was in a very agitated state of mind,' Griffin would later say. 'Mr Macarthur proceeded to put a variety of questions to me.'[73] After years of squabbles in the courts of the colony,

Macarthur had come to consider himself quite the lawyer. He had no legal training, but that also went for virtually everyone else in the colony. He did have an agile mind, could speak at length on any subject, and had a small library of legal books at home at Parramatta.

Macarthur's questions to Secretary Griffin mostly related to Macarthur himself and his trial in the Criminal Court, the catalyst for the revolution. Macarthur also put it to Griffin that Governor Bligh had taken items out of the government stores for his own use while charging them to the government. Griffin may have been in an agitated state of mind but he quickly realised that the committee was looking for evidence against the Governor, to justify the coup. Griffin didn't oblige them with the answers they wanted, and denied every proposition put to him. In fact, Griffin became quite defiant. Even though he was 'expecting every moment to be murdered'[74], he reprimanded Macarthur and his colleagues for staging an armed coup against His Majesty's representative.

This brought a faint smile to the lips of his chief inquisitor. 'Never,' Macarthur said, with considerable pride, 'was a revolution so completely effected, and with so much order and regularity.'[75] When Macarthur realised that the young secretary was too bright and too loyal to Bligh to be of help to the junta, he dismissed him. But Griffin was not yet off the hook. He was taken by Lieutenant Moore to the lieutenant's house, where he was given a bed but kept under arrest.

Earlier, William Gore, the Provost Marshal, had been sent home from Government House by order of Lieutenant Minchin, with an escort of two soldiers. At his Bridge Street home, he fretted about his future until, at 10.30, there was a knock at his door. When he opened it, he found a Corporal Henry Hughes of the Corps on his doorstep together with Barnaby Riley, keeper of the County Jail, and Gore's subordinate.

'You're under arrest,' the corporal abruptly announced. 'You're to come with us to the County Jail.'

'Where's your warrant?' Gore demanded, looking from Hughes to Riley.

'We have none,' said jailer Riley, an Irishman, with a shrug.

'You are to be taken to jail by order of Mr Macarthur,' said Hughes, grabbing Gore by the arm. So it was that Provost Marshal Gore, the man who had arrested John Macarthur and taken him to the County Jail that morning, was himself led off to the same jail.[76]

Around the time that Gore was being locked away, an exhausted Chief Constable Oakes arrived home at Parramatta, twenty kilometres away. He had hardly walked into his government barrack and told his wife about the uprising in Sydney before there was a knock at his door. Apprehensively he opened it, to find a soldier of the Corps who informed him that Parramatta's military commandant, Captain Edward Abbott, wished to see him at once. Abbott's barrack was only a short distance away, so Oakes walked there with the soldier.

Edward Abbott had been born at Montreal, Canada, to Scottish parents. He had transferred to the New South Wales Corps from the 73rd Regiment. A long-time friend of John Macarthur, Abbott was nonetheless a reasonable man who very much played by the book, so Oakes had no idea how the captain would receive the news of the overthrow of the Governor. As soon as he was ushered into Abbott's presence, Oakes gushed out what he had seen take place in Sydney.

Captain Abbott nodded. 'Very well,' he remarked, 'it must be for the better.' He then revealed that, ninety minutes earlier, a dragoon had arrived with a dispatch from Major Johnston in Sydney which had informed him of the arrest of the Governor and that martial law was now proclaimed. 'Put an extra constable or two upon the town watch tonight,' he instructed Oakes, 'and report to me if anything out of the ordinary course takes place.'[77]

While Oakes waited, Abbott wrote a short proclamation

to be posted for the attention of everyone in the Parramatta community: 'Major Johnston having arrested His Excellency Governor Bligh and having taken upon himself the charge of the Government, no orders are to be obeyed unless they come from him. Martial Law is proclaimed.'[78] Oakes took his leave of the captain and hurried away to rouse two of the fifteen constables of his local force to reinforce the night's watch as instructed by Abbott.

Back in Sydney, John Macarthur had retired for the night to Captain Abbott's Sydney house, in High Street, west of the Parade Ground. Macarthur's pregnant wife Elizabeth was also staying at the Abbott house, as was their sickly fifteen-year-old daughter, also named Elizabeth. Twelve days later, Mrs Macarthur would write to tell family friend, Captain John Piper, the Norfolk Island commandant, 'I had come from Parramatta about a month ago with our dear Elizabeth, who has been exceedingly ill ever since the month of May last, in order to try what change of air might do for her, little dreaming of a revolution'.[79]

It's likely that it was Elizabeth who had sent son Edward after Chief Constable Oakes on the night of 15 December to attempt to retrieve Macarthur's note, the note that denied the legitimacy of Oakes' arrest warrant. It's equally likely that Macarthur had kept his wife in the dark about the tactics he was planning to employ against the Governor. Elizabeth Macarthur was the most level-headed of women. Half-a-dozen years before, when it appeared that Captain Piper would face a court martial for acting as Macarthur's second in his duel with Lieutenant-Colonel William Paterson, Commanding Officer of the Corps, Elizabeth had written to Piper, 'Avoid all offensive in your defence. It is useless, my good friend, to add fuel to the fire that has been blazing for too long already.'[80] Had she known what her husband had been planning for 26 January, it is advice she would surely have given him too.

On the night of the 26th, when Macarthur gave Elizabeth

his version of the events of the rebellion, she was astonished. 'Although the excessive despotism of the ruling power called aloud for a reform,' she soon after wrote, 'it never entered my head to imagine that the inhabitants would so effectively rouse themselves from the despairing lethargy they had fallen into.'[81]

At Government House, just across town from the Abbott house, Governor Bligh was coming to terms with his situation. He had given up the idea of escaping to the Hawkesbury. On reflection, this would have meant abandoning his daughter Mary to the rebels. He now had two plans in mind. One of the colony's warships would return to Sydney before long and their officers were, like Bligh, Royal Navy, not British Army. He could not imagine them going against him as the New South Wales Corps had; he was confident he could rely on their support in a bid to regain power. In the meantime, he would secretly gather as much evidence against the coup leaders as possible and work toward the day the rebels were brought to trial for mutiny and High Treason.

Bligh had already begun to formulate a list of coup leaders he would wish to see tried for their part in the crime. Throughout his career, Bligh was extremely thorough, showing an exceptional eye for detail. Following the *Bounty* mutiny, he had noted in his journal the details of every one of the mutineers – their height, hair colour, deformities, and distinguishing marks – to help the authorities eventually track them down and bring them to justice. A number of the members of the *Bounty*'s crew, including Fletcher Christian, had been tattooed while the ship spent many months at Tahiti, and Bligh had remembered and noted down the individual tattoos of every man, describing them in detail. Of mutineer Edward Young, for example, he had written, 'A small mole on the left side of the throat, and on the right arm is tattooed a heart and dart through it with E Y underneath, and the date of the year 1788 or 1789'.[82]

Bligh's list of the Sydney coup leaders would also be

comprehensive. Johnston and the six officers who had been sitting on the Criminal Court that day were, of course, included, along with the others who had participated in his overthrow. But the name that topped the list was that of John Macarthur. From Bligh's first realisation earlier in the evening that a coup was being mounted against him, there had been no doubt in his mind that Macarthur had engineered the whole affair.

While it would have given Bligh some satisfaction to contemplate the arrest of the men who had arrested him, there was the matter of surviving the coup long enough to see his enemies brought to justice. Fletcher Christian had consigned him to a seemingly certain death in an open boat in 1789. In the same way, Bligh genuinely believed that, having committed treason in overthrowing the British Crown's legitimate governor, the coup leaders might decide that they may as well, as the saying went, be hung for a sheep as a lamb, and kill Bligh. It would be easy enough. He might be shot 'while trying to escape'. Then again, he might be smothered in his bed, just as the Roman emperor Tiberius had been, after which the rebels would claim that the Governor had died in his sleep.

With Bligh out of the way, the coup leaders could manufacture a case against him without the fear of the Governor countering their version of events. With Bligh dead, the Governor's supporters in the colony might be so intimidated and so fearful for their own lives that they wouldn't oppose or testify against the coup leaders. Perhaps, having murdered Bligh, the rebels might also line up his officials against the wall of Government House and shoot them. A musket ball to the brain, or a pillow in the night – either would provide an elegantly simple solution to what Bligh believed was the rebels' dilemma. For Bligh could not imagine what case they could put for deposing him – after all, he had acted within the law at all times, and had been following orders from London. That night, Bligh genuinely suspected that his murder and that of those close to him was being contemplated by hard-liners among the revolutionaries. 'Nothing but calamity upon calamity was to be expected,' he later wrote, 'even massacre and secret murder.'[83] Undoubtedly, after Bligh eventually went to bed that night of the 26th he slept poorly, with his bedroom door barricaded from the inside.

Late that night, after the lights had gone out at Government House, a weary Private John Gray up at the sentry post on the Parade Ground was relieved of duty by the next watch. Gray had witnessed the coup from afar. The soldier taking his place at the sentry box would have told him that the Corps had arrested the Governor. All that Gray had seen unfold during the evening now made sense to him. His Excellency the Governor arrested? The peaceful scene that now met Gray's eyes seemed to deny that such a monumental event had taken place. Private Gray had watched as the gunners rolled the guns back down to the magazine, unloaded them, then manhandled them back to their original firing positions, aiming them out over Sydney Cove once more. By the time Lieutenant Minchin had later come by Gray, heading home to his house in the town, it was as though the guns had never been moved.

With a yawn, and his musket on his shoulder, Private Gray tramped toward his quarters, deep in thought. Like other soldiers of the Corps and a number of people of the town, Private Gray was not sure he agreed with the overthrow of Governor Bligh.

3

Celebrating the Revolution

At 7.00 am on Wednesday, 27 January, the day after the coup, the Governor's Guard paraded outside the Guard House. Previously, the task of the soldiers of the Guard had been to protect Governor Bligh. Now they were his jailers.

Isaac Champion came on duty with the Guard that morning following the coup. A sergeant ever since the formation of the Corps more than twenty years before, Champion was now pay sergeant to two companies and an acting Sergeant-Major. As he stood in line with the other men assigned to the Guard this day, he heard Ensign Bell read a general order from Major Johnston. The men of the Guard were to keep Governor Bligh closely confined at Government House, said the order. Bligh could take the air in the garden, but the sentries were not to let the Governor out of their sight, following him at a distance of not less than seven or eight paces.[84] The guardsmen were given their dispositions. A number were stationed at the front and rear gates, but a sentry box was now set up at the eastern end of the house, with one sentry posted close by on the path that ran along the front of the house. A second sentry was stationed further west along that path, near the bottom of the steps leading to Government House's front door. Visitors to the house would be made to wait on the veranda until admitted by the guards who were posted indoors.[85]

Inside Government House, William Bligh had risen early. He habitually rose with the cock every morning. Had this been a normal day, by 7.00, like the convicts of the Jail Gang and their guardians, Bligh would have been at work. Some mornings, he had mounted up and ridden around the town to inspect public works, with Sergeant Whalley and another dragoon riding close behind. Other mornings he would attack paperwork with his secretary. But this was not a normal day. This was the day after the reins of government had been forcibly taken from his hands and assumed by a junta of officers and former officers.

On the morning of 27 January, the first thing Bligh had done when he rose from his bed was go to the front of the house to look out a window. His eyes went beyond the sentries on the path outside Government House, his jailers, to Sydney Cove. With no sign as yet of the colony's warships, Bligh focused on the government schooner, *Estramina*, to see if his broad pennant still hung from her mainmast.[86] He must have cursed out loud. The *Estramina* had once been a pirate ship; she had been confiscated from a Scottish pirate who had taken her from a Spanish crew in South American waters. Now Commodore Bligh's broad pennant had been pirated from her mainmast. The rebels had not waited long to remove that visual symbol of Bligh's rule – Major Johnston had sent a written order to the schooner's master, John Apsey, requiring him to lower the pennant.

Bligh's breakfast with his daughter Mary and Mrs Palmer would have been a sombre affair. All were worried about the fate of Mrs Palmer's husband and brother-in-law, and likewise fearful for the others who had been arrested and taken away in the night. This day would drag by for Bligh. He had just one visit from a representative of the revolutionary leadership – Lieutenant

Moore came, with written orders from Major Johnston to search the house for weapons. He took away Bligh's sword and another he found in the house – no doubt the sword of Lieutenant Putland, the Governor's late son-in-law. Moore also confiscated several pistols which he located after a search of the premises. Left alone again, Bligh could only guess at what was taking place in the town.

Around noon, Bligh heard cannon firing up on the Parade Ground. There were no invading French ships out on Port Jackson, as Sydney harbour was called. Bligh could only assume that the Corps was firing a salute in honour of his overthrow, especially as, according to what he was told later, the two guns up there fired a total of twenty or twenty-one times. Commissary Palmer, under house arrest over at his Garden Island Cove residence, also heard the dull thud of cannon firing in the distance that day.[87]

Throughout the day, the rebels were far from idle. At the barracks and around the town, enthusiastic members of the Corps' rank and file were making preparations for a celebration of the Governor's overthrow which was to take place that evening. Their officers, meanwhile, were busy taking a firm hold on the government and building their case for initiating the revolution and overthrowing King George's representative in the colony. Three separate revolutionary committees were set up by the junta at the military barracks. One sat at the quarters of Major Johnston, one at Lieutenant Minchin's barrack, and the third at the commodious quarters of Surgeon Harris. Throughout the day, various residents of Sydney were sent to the barracks to be interviewed by the committees.

In many cases it was the police of Sydney who were knocking on doors and instructing people to report to the committees. The constables, who were mostly Irish croppies, former crop farmers from tenanted farms in Ireland, had quickly fallen into line with the rebel administration once their chief William Gore had been thrown in jail. Apart from being outnumbered and outgunned by the military, the constables had no affection for Provost Marshal Gore. Besides, the Chief Constable of Sydney, John Redman, had quickly sided with the rebels; his men had followed his lead. Redman's lack of loyalty to the Governor and the Provost Marshal had a personal root – he was nursing a grudge against Governor Bligh. The previous year, Redman had made an addition to his house in High Street, opposite the County Jail, without seeking official permission. Governor Bligh had ordered the addition pulled down and Redman, feeling that a man in his position should not be embarrassed in this way, had bitterly resented it.

Some citizens who were rounded up and sent to appear before the revolutionary committees were required to give statements about their dealings with Governor Bligh and his officials. All were told to sign two handwritten documents. One document had been drawn up the previous evening by John Macarthur shortly after his release from the County Jail. This was a requisition to Major Johnston, calling on him to arrest Governor Bligh. It read:

> *Sir,*
> *The present alarming state of this Colony, in which every man's property, liberty, and life is endangered, induces us most earnestly to implore you instantly to place Governor Bligh under an arrest and to assume the command of the colony. We pledge ourselves, at a moment of less agitation to come forward to support the measure with our fortunes and our lives.*[88]

When Johnston and the Corps had marched on Government House the previous evening, that document had carried just nine signatures. Macarthur's was the first. The others were those of settlers John Blaxland and his brother Gregory, Assistant Surgeon James Mileham, wealthy merchant Simeon Lord,

James Badgery the baker, Assistant Surgeon Thomas Jamieson, and Macarthur's bondsmen Bayly and Blaxcell. Later that same evening, at 11.00 pm, after Bligh had been deposed, Surveyor-General Grimes had become the tenth signatory. He signed in Major Johnston's barrack, and then encouraged several others who were present to also put their signatures to the list. Now, Grimes and others urged and cajoled the people of the colony to add their names.

The second document in circulation this Wednesday was an address drawn up that morning, thanking Major Johnston for having taken the action he did the previous day in overthrowing the Governor. Those people finding themselves before the committees were also told to sign this, but a number refused to put their names to either this address or the Macarthur requisition.

In his County Jail cell on High Street, Provost Marshal William Gore, imprisoned without a warrant by order of John Macarthur the previous night, was in fear for his life. Jailer Barnaby Riley had lodged him in the two-metre by three-metre basement cell reserved for men condemned to hang. During this morning of the 27th, Gore had a visitor, Major Johnston's orderly sergeant, who showed Gore his orderly book, in which was written an order for the suspension of Gore from the offices of Provost Marshal and Superintendent of Police. That order likewise suspended most other senior civil officials who had served under Governor Bligh. Having delivered the news of the Provost Marshal's removal from office, the sergeant left Gore to mope. Gore's biggest fear was for his wife and four little children, the eldest of whom was just eight years of age. With Gore a prisoner, his family would have to rely on his friends to survive.

At 2.00 pm, Bligh's treasurer Robert Campbell answered a knock at his guarded door, to be greeted by a grim-faced orderly from the Corps, who instructed Campbell to accompany him to the barracks. Once they reached the Old Parade outside the barracks, Campbell was made to stand there, under the blazing sun, as the revolutionary committee convened to examine him busied itself with another of the Governor's men, Commissary John Palmer. Palmer had earlier that afternoon also been brought to the barracks under guard, and placed before a committee made up of Nicholas Bayly, Garnham Blaxcell and Assistant Surgeon Thomas Jamieson.[89] Major Johnston briefly appeared in the room where the committee was sitting, produced his Bible and made Palmer swear to tell the truth, and then withdrew to allow the committee to do its work. The committee demanded that Palmer tell them all he knew about Governor Bligh's administration.

Palmer was so stressed by the grilling he received, ever conscious of the soldier at the door armed with musket and intimidating bayonet, and fearful for his future and that of his family and friends, that when he was later taken back to his house he found it hard to remember precisely what he had told the inquisitors. He had done his best not to say anything that reflected badly on himself or the Governor, but for the life of him he was not sure if he'd been successful.

Toward 3.00 pm, while Palmer was still being questioned and Campbell was being made to stand on the Old Parade in the heat of the day, Captain Edward Abbott rode into town from Parramatta. In early January, Major Johnston had sought Governor Bligh's permission for Abbott to take leave from his post as commandant of the Parramatta district from 11 January and come into town, where he might sit on the bench of magistrates. This would have made Abbott, a well-known friend of John Macarthur, the senior military officer sitting at Macarthur's trial. Bligh had declined the request, instead granting Abbott leave from 27 January. So, now officially on leave, Abbott travelled no further this Wednesday afternoon than his Sydney house in High Street, where he joined his house guests, John and Elizabeth Macarthur.

At four o'clock, after standing for two hours under the sizzling January sun, Robert Campbell was led into Major Johnston's barrack to face the same committee that had quizzed Commissary Palmer. Campbell's mind was in turmoil, his head ached, he was harangued by committee members and, he would later say, 'I certainly expected some bodily harm.'[90] But Campbell was determined not to be badgered into saying anything he would later regret. Always a stickler for the truth, he was confident that if he stuck to the truth now he should have nothing to fear, as he had nothing to hide. So, when he was asked to detail what had taken place at Government House on 25 and 26 January in relation to John Macarthur's court case, he gave a quite detailed account of the consultations that he and the other civil magistrates had had with Governor Bligh over those two days. His statement was noted down as he spoke.

The committee members listened with keen interest. So far, while the inspection of the Governor's papers and interrogation of scores of civilians had produced some useful information, the rebels had been unable to find any evidence that would damn Bligh in London. But now they learned what had gone on behind the doors of Government House while the six officers of the Criminal Court had been waging their campaign against Judge Advocate Atkins. They were particularly interested to hear from Campbell's own lips that George Crossley, an ex-convict who had once been a lawyer in London, had been a key legal adviser to the Governor over the previous few days. It was John Macarthur's contention that Bligh's use of Crossley was illegal. Campbell, who didn't share that view, told the committee that Crossley had urged the Governor to immediately summon the six officers to Government House to answer to the civil magistrates. But, said Campbell, he himself had counselled a milder measure – the six officers should be ordered to see the Governor alone the following day – and that was how Bligh had proceeded. When Campbell finished making his statement, realising that he had pleased his questioners, he quickly regretted having been so candid, and declined to sign the written statement.[91]

By the time that Campbell was taken under guard back to his house, many townspeople had eaten their supper, and there was considerable activity around Sydney. Directed by Sergeant-Major Thomas Whittle, soldiers were carting wood to a location on Church Hill, and building a huge bonfire. The spot Whittle had chosen for the bonfire was almost on top of the two-week-old tomb of Lieutenant Putland, Governor Bligh's late son-in-law. Before darkness fell, Sergeant Bremlow hurried to Whittle and the soldiers working with him to say that Major Johnston wished the bonfire moved away from Lieutenant Putland's gravesite, and Whittle begrudgingly complied.[92] Elsewhere around the town, other smaller bonfires were being built on open ground. To create these bonfire stacks, soldiers directed townspeople to bring barrows and handcarts laden with firewood. Meanwhile, a thousand gallons of brandy and rum were landed from the American brig *Jenny* by order of the new administration.

During the afternoon, the *Sydney Gazette*'s printing press, in the service wing attached to Government House, was inked up and put to work. It was soon churning out a single-sheet proclamation for distribution throughout the town in the early evening. Issued by order of 'His Honour the Lieutenant Governor', the proclamation was signed by Nicholas Bayly, who had been appointed Johnston's secretary. It announced the end of martial law, and declared Johnston's approval of the way 'the whole body of the people' had supported his overthrow of the Governor with their 'manly, firm and orderly conduct'. In terms that rang with echoes of the French Revolution, Johnston reserved his highest praise for the men of his regiment: 'Soldiers! Your conduct has endeared you to every well-disposed inhabitant in this settlement! Persevere in the same honourable path, and you will establish the credit of the New South Wales Corps on a basis not to be shaken.'[93]

Also that afternoon, settler George Suttor departed the inn by the wharf, to head home to Baulkham Hills. In his account of his movements during this period, Suttor did not identify the inn where he stayed, or its proprietors, but this was almost certainly the inn of rebel sympathisers, Isaac and Rosanna Nicholls, who were related to Major Johnston. As Suttor set off, those proprietors were preparing to hang a large double-sided painting outside their door. It was something of a work of art. Suttor saw, on one side, a Highland soldier [Johnston] standing with a snake [Bligh] under his feet, while the Genius of Liberty presented the Major with her cap. The other side bore the message, 'The ever-memorable 26th of January 1808'. Suttor would see the painting still hanging there several weeks later, on his next visit to Sydney.[94]

Once night fell, the large bonfire on Church Hill was lit and the smaller bonfires around the town were also soon blazing. They acted like beacons, drawing thousands of Sydneysiders out into the streets of the capital. Soldiers in their uniforms; men, women and children from the town; convict servants; and seamen from the ships in port including the Americans off the *Jenny*; all came to admire the raging fires, whose flames soared high into the night sky, and to gratefully drink the grog unloaded from the *Jenny* that afternoon. They perambulated the streets, looking in the windows of shops, inns, taverns, bordellos and private houses, to see paintings and signs hastily created during the day, all illuminated by burning lamps.

The paintings had revolutionary themes. The most popular showed Governor Bligh being found under a bed. Corporal Marlborough had been quick to claim credit for the discovery of the Governor. In Marlborough's version of events, his rival, Sergeant Sutherland, didn't figure in the Governor's capture. According to Marlborough, only he, Private Wilford and Lieutenant Minchin had been in the room at the time, and Marlborough, finding Governor Bligh under the bed, had grabbed him by the coat collar and dragged him out. The less artistic window displays comprised signs with pro-rebel messages: 'No Tyranny'. 'No Gore'. 'Johnston Forever'.[95]

Walking the streets in the mild summer air with thousands of others, taking in these 'illuminations' as they were being called, was Charles Walker, a sea captain. Previously in the employ of John Macarthur as master of a trading brig, Walker was planning to shortly leave the colony aboard the *Jenny* and try his luck in China. For the moment he was living at a Sydney brothel kept by a lady friend who would later become his wife. During the day Captain Walker had seen soldiers and some of their rough friends among the townspeople going about the town coercing locals into preparing illuminations for their windows. Walker had witnessed a Reverend Shelly, a missionary, being threatened that if he didn't illuminate his window that night, his house would be pulled down.[96]

According to another contemporary source, the stand-over men were chiefly a group of soldiers led by Sergeant-Major Whittle; their officers had given them the job of making the townspeople illuminate.[97] Some shopkeepers had direct links to the Corps – Sergeant-Major Whittle's wife, for example, ran a shop at the hospital wharf – and they didn't have to be encouraged to participate in the celebrations. Others who refused to illuminate, said another witness, had their windows broken.[98]

Several times in the past, sea captain Charles Walker had heard his then employer John Macarthur complain bitterly about Governor Bligh. Once, Walker remembered, Macarthur had suggested that perhaps Bligh would get another voyage in his launch if he was not more generous toward Macarthur and his friends. Another time, only recently, Macarthur had said, 'The colony has suffered Governor Bligh to reign long enough. There will soon be an alteration.'[99] Now, Walker marvelled that Macarthur had actually achieved that very change of government, but not in any way that Walker had imagined, or approved of.

Sergeant-Major Whittle was the master of ceremonies up on Church Hill, but his house down in Spring Row in the town was also a popular attraction. His children were welcoming passersby into the house, to the parlour, where Whittle had set up a painting of Governor Bligh's capture, with a lamp either side of it, creating an altar to the revolution. Sergeant-Major Isaac Champion was one of the hundreds who went in to see the Whittle display. His colleague Whittle had told Champion that afternoon on the Parade that he would have displayed the painting on his roof had not Major Johnston told him that would hurt him (Johnston) back in England.[100]

Thomas Tait, Commissary Palmer's frightened clerk, also saw the painting in the Whittle parlour. He hadn't heard how the Governor had been captured, so couldn't make out exactly who the figure being dragged from under the bed was supposed to represent. Several of the Whittle children delighted in informing Tait that it was Governor Bligh.[101] Private Thomas Finnegan was another who viewed the display in Sergeant-Major Whittle's house. A year earlier, Finnegan had joined in a vote of thanks to Governor Bligh from the enlisted men and NCOs of the New South Wales Corps. Personally, Finnegan still had no reason to be unhappy with Governor Bligh. 'I was very well satisfied with his conduct,' the little Irish private would later say.[102]

Edmund Griffin, Governor Bligh's secretary, also took in the illuminations. While still under military arrest, he was allowed to walk the streets that evening in the company of Lieutenant Moore. It seems that Moore, who was of a similar age and background to Griffin, had been given the task by the rebel leadership of winning the confidence of the Governor's secretary and convincing him to make statements detrimental to Bligh. But Griffin was on his guard, and was careful what he said.

As Griffin came up to the main bonfire on Church Hill with the amiable Moore at his side, he saw the principal leaders of the revolutionary junta out on parade, walking along Church Street past the bonfire and giving the celebrations their seal of approval. Sergeant-Major Champion and Sergeant Bremlow also saw the new regime's leadership pass by with their ladies, walking two by two. The unmarried Major Johnston led the way, accompanied by Captain Abbott, whose wife Louisa was back at Parramatta. Strolling along behind them came John Macarthur, with his very obviously pregnant wife Elizabeth on his arm. Adjutant Minchin and his wife Ann came next. Champion and Bremlow would remember that there were several other officers in attendance, but not who they were – probably Captain Anthony Fenn Kemp and Lieutenant Lawson, who had proven to be the two junior officers of the Corps most committed to the revolution.

Under Sergeant-Major Whittle's direction, two giant effigies were brought to the main bonfire, amid much excitement from drink-soaked soldiers and convicts and wide-eyed children. The figures, made of canvas stuffed with straw, were painted and dressed to look like Governor Bligh and his unpopular Provost Marshal, William Gore. The two effigies were consigned to the fire, and as flames consumed the bodies the crowd gave three mighty cheers. The regimental band struck up a popular song, 'Silly Old Man', and there in the firelight the delighted and increasingly drunken crowd sang along as the straw figure of silly old man William Bligh contorted in the flames.

While the celebrations raged in the town that night, the work of the revolutionary committees also continued. One of the government functionaries now examined was Commissary Palmer's deputy, James Williamson. Taken by his military escort to Major Johnston's barrack while the celebrations carried on into the late hours of Wednesday evening, Williamson was sworn by Johnston and quizzed by a committee made up of Nicholas Bayly, Surveyor-General Charles Grimes, and Isaac Nicholls. Nicholls had been sent out to the colony in 1790 for petty theft. Later pardoned, he had served as Superintendent of Convicts at Parramatta. He was now farming 1400 acres

(560 hectares) to the west of Sydney, operated a shipyard at the Rocks, and had a large house and an inn on a leased half-acre (.2 hectares) of government ground in Sydney's Rocks district, near the government wharf.

To some, Nicholls would have been an unlikely choice for a junta committee. He and Macarthur were bitter enemies – Macarthur had once instigated a prosecution against Nicholls that had seen him sentenced to fourteen years on Norfolk Island. It was a trumped-up charge, and the Governor at the time had set the sentence aside after Macarthur's hearsay evidence was discounted. After an appeal to London, Nicholls had won a pardon. To counter Macarthur's antipathy, Nicholls had the support of Major Johnston. In 1805, Nicholls had married Rosanna, eldest of the four daughters of Johnston's beautiful 'housekeeper' of the past twenty years, Esther Julian, making Nicholls the Major's de facto son-in-law. This relationship, together with an enthusiasm for the revolution and certain talents – he was described as 'a zealous, active and useful man'[103] – qualified Nicholls for rebel committee work despite his bad blood with Macarthur. It seems that Johnston spoke for Nicholls' involvement, perhaps at the insistence of Esther Julian, and Macarthur acceded to his request to keep Johnston happy.

The Bayly–Grimes–Nicholls committee tried unsuccessfully to press Deputy Commissary Williamson to divulge useful information about Governor Bligh's administration and the Macarthur court case. When Williamson proved unhelpful, Nicholls pushed a sheet of paper across the table toward him and instructed him to sign. Williamson saw that the paper already contained a number of signatures and recognised it as one of the two documents then being circulated by the rebels. Williamson didn't attempt to read the document, and refused point blank to sign it. Then, to his astonishment, Williamson was shown a General Order from Major Johnston in which he, Williamson, was directed to take over the post of Commissary-General from his boss, Little Jack Palmer, who was suspended by the same order.[104]

Williamson was one of the few members of Bligh's 'old guard' retained by the rebel administration. In other appointments announced on or shortly after the 27th, William Gore was replaced as Provost Marshal by Nicholas Bayly, who would at the same time continue to serve as Major Johnston's secretary. Lieutenant Lawson was appointed Johnston's aide-de-camp. Richard Atkins was suspended from the post of Judge Advocate and replaced by Captain Edward Abbott. Garnham Blaxcell was appointed government auctioneer. D'Arcy Wentworth, who had been removed from the post of Assistant Surgeon by a Corps court martial the previous year for insubordination to Captain Abbott, and publicly admonished by Governor Bligh, was reinstated to that post. All the civil magistrates under Bligh were replaced by civilians Charles Grimes, Garnham Blaxcell and John Blaxland, and by the Corps' Captain Kemp, Lieutenant Minchin, Ensign Bell, Surgeon Harris, and Assistant Surgeon Jamieson. In this way, the junta infiltrated its people into the colony's top jobs. Remaining office-holders would find that they either came around to the rebel way of thinking or forfeited their positions.

Around 10.00 pm on the 27th, one of those existing office-holders, Nicholas Divine, the Superintendent of Convicts, was brought before the committee. Lieutenant Minchin was present for this interview, and would note that Divine was a far from reluctant participant.

'I have come to tell His Honour everything I know,' Divine informed Major Johnston as he prepared to take the oath. When someone in the room expressed surprise at Divine's cooperative attitude, the Superintendent of Convicts shrugged and said with a wry smile, 'Self-preservation is the first law of nature.'[105]

Divine was the brother-in-law of George Crossley, the convict lawyer who was particularly in the junta's sights, and when Isaac Nicholls subsequently pushed a paper across the table at Divine, saying it was the previous night's requisition for a revolution, Divine signed without even reading it, becoming the fortieth signatory. He would later explain, 'I knew that if I did not sign it I should incur the displeasure of the then existing government.' Besides, Divine thought the document wasn't worth the paper it was written on. How, he was to reason, could a document seek to have done that which had already been done? That, as least, was his excuse as he put his name to it. Nicholls then pushed the second document over to him; this was the address to Major Johnston praising him for overthrowing the Governor. Again, Divine signed without reading a word.[106]

That same night, from the windows of Government House, Governor Bligh, his daughter Mary, and Susan Palmer saw the houses of the town ablaze with light, and noticed the orange glow of the bonfires. And they heard the cheering of the crowd, the playing of the band, the singing, and increasingly drunken cries. When the three of them turned in that night, it was with the hope that grog and wild talk would not turn the crowd into a mob that decided to make Government House their symbolic Bastille and tear it down brick by brick. The entire Governor's Guard hadn't protected Bligh the previous night, so there was no guarantee that the few soldiers of the Guard now on duty would stand between the occupants of the Governor's residence and that potential mob if some among that throng took it into their heads to storm, loot and burn Government House and kill its occupants.

4

The Rebel Net Spreads

Francis Oakes awoke with a start. Someone was bashing loudly on the door to his Parramatta barrack. It was the early hours of the morning of Thursday 28 January, and it was still dark. Telling his wife and young children not to be concerned, Oakes rose, threw on a coat, and answered the door. Two soldiers stood there, both wearing supercilious grins. One held a lantern, the other thrust a document at Oakes. In the light of the lantern, Oakes read that the new administration of Major Johnston had dismissed him from office as Chief Constable at Parramatta, and that Barnaby Riley, jailer at the County Jail in Sydney, had been appointed in his place. To replace Riley as jailer, the rebels had appointed Daniel McKay, who had previously been dismissed from that same position by Provost Marshal Gore.

This all came as a blow to Oakes, especially after the initial indications that Johnston would leave him in his post. He was not surprised that Riley had been given his job. Provost Marshal Gore had personally appointed Riley jailer, considering him trustworthy, but Francis Oakes knew that around Parramatta it was common knowledge that Riley was in John Macarthur's debt.

It would later emerge that when Macarthur was being lodged in the County Jail on the morning of the 26th, jailer Riley had whispered to Macarthur, 'There is a cutlass hidden in the cell for Your Honour.'[107]

As Oakes read the notice of his dismissal from the post of Chief Constable, he 'received great insult from the persons who brought it'.[108] Now, not only was the mild-mannered Oakes out of a job, he and his family would have to give up his rent-free government quarters. He was also concerned for his life and limb. The previous night, there had been illuminations in the windows of several houses around the streets of Parramatta. These illuminations had not been on the same scale as those in Sydney, but to Oakes' consternation the insults on the few signs in the windows had been directed at the Chief Constable of Parramatta – at him. Francis Oakes was paying the price for having attempted to arrest John Macarthur on the night of 15 December, just as the illegally imprisoned Provost Marshal Gore was paying the price for arresting Macarthur on 26 January.

In Sydney, when the Corps paraded at 7.00 that morning of the 28th, the rank and file looked surprisingly orderly considering the amount of drinking they had been doing during the celebrations the night before. The town itself was littered with the detritus of the biggest party the twenty-year-old settlement had ever seen. But at least no one had run riot, and Government House was still standing.

At 11.00 am, a rebel delegation arrived at Government House. Leading the group was the haughty Nicholas Bayly, revelling in his new roles as Provost Marshal and Secretary to Major Johnston. Governor Bligh knew that Bayly was the son of a Welsh member of the House of Commons, was a nephew of the Earl of Uxbridge, and had an elder brother who was a general, all of which caused Bayly to consider himself rather grand. Bligh also knew of Bayly's reputation for brutality against convicts in his charge, for which he had faced a court martial when in the Corps. He was also aware of Bayly's close connection to John Macarthur.

Behind Bayly came his rebel colleagues Garnham Blaxcell, Assistant Surgeon Thomas Jamieson, and Captain Edward Abbott from Parramatta. Bayly informed Governor Bligh that 'His Honour the Lieutenant Governor' had appointed his companions and himself as a committee, under the chairmanship of Captain Abbott, to examine the Governor's papers and to retain all documents that related to the public concerns of the colony and its dependencies.

Bligh folded his arms and glared at Bayly, whom he considered the principal motivator of this particular committee.

'During the examination of those papers,' Bayly went on, 'you may be present and have any friend or other persons present you may choose to appoint.'

Bligh shook his head. 'By frequent private communications with His Majesty's principal Secretary of State for the Colonies, before I left England,' he said, 'I was ordered to inquire into particular circumstances, to which I have made answers.' Considering these documents to be secret government communications, Bligh objected to giving up the public papers of the colony to any person other than Johnston, and even then, he said, they must be sealed.[109]

Bayly was not happy with this, so Bligh put his objection in writing, addressing his note to 'Major Johnston'. A fuming Bayly scurried back along Bridge Street to the barracks, carrying the Governor's brief note, while the remaining members of the committee kicked their heels around the hall of Government House. Bayly soon returned. Scrawled on the back of Johnston's original direction for the examination of the Governor's papers, in Johnston's own handwriting, was the reply: 'I hereby command you to the execution of my orders, as expressed on the other side of this paper.' Bayly also advised that Johnston would refuse to accept any future communications from Bligh unless they were addressed to him as 'Lieutenant Governor'.[110]

Bayly, who would not be put off any longer, instructed Bligh to nominate those he wished to have present for the examination. Bligh, seeing an opportunity to learn the welfare of his closest advisers, nominated Griffin, Palmer and Campbell. This would not have pleased Bayly, who would have preferred to have just a single witness apart from Bligh present, but as Johnston's offer had not limited the number of witnesses, Bayly sent soldiers hurrying around the town to collect the Governor's three most senior men.

With great relief, Bligh was soon able to greet Griffin, Palmer and Campbell when they were brought to Government House from their places of arrest, satisfying himself that they were unharmed. Palmer was also able to briefly speak with his wife Susan. The seal on a door of the room where the Governor's papers were being held was broken, and the committee began its work. Over the next two hours or so, Bligh and his three colleagues had to sit and tolerate the reading of the official papers in front of them. As Captain Abbott was nominally chairman of the committee, if something was found which was considered of interest to the rebels, Abbott showed it to Bligh before placing it in a pile of documents to be taken away. Several times, Abbott scribbled notes on one document or another. When Bligh demanded a list showing every document that was removed from Government House, Abbott, who seemed uneasy about this whole process, promised that such a list would indeed be provided.[111]

Once the committee members left for the day, taking their chosen documents with them, the room was again sealed and the guards once more took up their places at the doors. The committee would resume its work the next day. As Griffin, Palmer and Campbell were escorted away, Bligh was left to mull over what had taken place. On the evening of his overthrow, with John Dunn's help, he had been able to destroy a number of important documents that he knew would be of great interest to the rebels. Just the same, he knew that several of the documents singled out by the committee during their examination could prove to be valuable ammunition for them.

During that morning and afternoon, more loads of wood were carted to bonfire sites in Sydney. The previous night's revels had proven so popular with some people in the town that the soldiers planned to repeat the celebration again that night. Out at Parramatta, sacked Chief Constable Francis Oakes, who remained in his quarters all day with his frightened family, saw that preparations were being made for a major celebration there as well. From his front window he watched as government carts brought loads of wood to the barracks from the town's public lumberyard. Several bonfire stacks were set up outside the barracks. One of those bonfires and another fire for a spit-roast were set up right outside Oakes' door.

Further west, at the Hawkesbury district's principal settlement of Green Hills (today's town of Windsor), local surgeon Martin Mason was unhappy about what was taking place in his community that day. Previously the surgeon aboard the transport *Britannia* and later aboard HMS *Buffalo*, Dr Mason had arrived in New South Wales from England in 1798. He had later served as an Acting Assistant Surgeon and had also been a magistrate for a time. On the night of 27 January he'd slept badly, kept awake by the fourteen soldiers of the local garrison who, while their sergeant was away, had become uproariously drunk in their barracks as they celebrated the colony's revolution.

During the morning of the 28th, Mason had two visitors, who came to his door together. One was Thomas Hobby, a former lieutenant in the New South Wales Corps who had been called on to resign for sleeping with convict women. Hobby was now a Hawkesbury settler with close links to junta member John Blaxland, who had loaned him a considerable sum of money the previous year. Dr Mason's other visitor was Robert Fitz, Deputy Government Commissary for the district and a local magistrate. Thirty-nine-year-old Fitz had also formerly been an army officer, serving as paymaster of a regiment in Ireland before coming to New South Wales. In addition to his government job, which entailed running the Crown's storehouses at Green Hills, Fitz kept a chandler's shop in the town.

Hobby was anxious to keep on the right side of the junta, and Fitz wanted to keep his government job. Encouraged by Sydney rebel sympathisers, John Brannen and James Badgery, who had property in the district, Hobby and Fitz had drawn up an hyperbolic address to Major Johnston, congratulating him on overthrowing Governor Bligh and vowing the support of Hawkesbury colonists for his rebel regime. They now showed this address to Dr Mason, and asked him to sign it. But Mason refused. Mason had not only been one of the 833 Hawkesbury settlers who had signed the loyal address to Governor Bligh just twenty-seven days earlier, he had been among those who had gone around the district collecting the signatures on that address. He doubted that many locals would be prepared to put their names to a document like the one Hobby and Fitz were promoting.

'I know the disposition of the settlers towards Governor Bligh,' Dr Mason told the pair.[112]

That disposition was strongly in favour of Bligh. In fact, so strong was the support among Hawkesbury settlers for Governor Bligh that during the period of the rebel regime many of them would name their newborn sons after Bligh. One such colonist was John Turnbull, who had come out to New South Wales from Scotland as a free settler aboard the *Coromandel* in 1802. To register both his support for Governor Bligh and his disgust with the rebel regime, he named his youngest son William Bligh Turnbull. It subsequently became the tradition in the Turnbull family to give their sons the middle name of

Bligh. This tradition has continued down to present day – Malcolm Turnbull, MP, renowned in Australia as the defence lawyer in the 1988 Spycatcher trial and more recently as a minister in the Howard Liberal government, is himself Malcolm Bligh Turnbull, and he continued the family tradition by giving his own son the middle name of Bligh.[113]

'I'll make five hundred sign by night!' Hobby declared to Mason that day on the Green Hills doctor's doorstep, before turning on his heel and heading off to the local tavern of Andrew Thompson with the address flapping in his hand.[114]

Sure that his judgment of the local mood was correct, Mason followed Hobby and Fitz to the Green Hills tavern. In the bar-room, Hobby called for silence, then read the address aloud to tavern patrons. Mason saw many of his neighbours there, among them Thomas Bigers, who kept a grog shop in the town, and young William Cox Junior, son of the Captain William Cox who had been paymaster of the New South Wales Corps after Macarthur, and who was now back in England facing court martial for financial improprieties. Dr Mason knew for a fact that young Cox supported Governor Bligh because both Cox and his mother had signed the loyal address to Bligh on 1 January along with Mason and 830 others.

Most of the men in the tavern were looking at each other uncertainly. Fitz proceeded to sign the address, Hobby followed. Then Hobby called on others to step forward to sign. No one did. Hobby, growing increasingly frustrated, then turned to Mason who, as the local doctor, was considered a leading member of the community. For the second time that day Hobby urged him sign, and for the second time Dr Mason declined.

'If you don't sign it,' Thomas Bigers warned Mason in a whisper, 'you will be in the body of Sydney Jail within twenty-four hours.'[115]

This possibility had no effect on Mason, nor on anyone else at the time. So, Hobby and Fitz bought wine and gin for everyone in the bar, and sent for their staff and friends. 'When they were heated up with wine and spirits,' Mason would later say, 'they sallied out to solicit signatures.'[116]

During the remainder of the day, Mason was approached by a number of settlers, all worrying about how they might avoid putting their signatures on the Fitz–Hobby address. None wanted to sign, but they were being threatened by Hobby and Fitz. When threats of physical violence failed to work, those who refused to sign were menaced with the loss of convict labour from their farms. Mason advised his neighbours to simply stand on their principles and refuse to sign. In the early evening, Mason ran into Hobby again, this time on the road. For a third time, Hobby called on Mason to put his name to the address. And for a third time Mason declined.

Hobby was furious. Using strong and insulting language, Hobby demanded Mason's reasons for not signing. 'Is it timidity or temerity that induces you to refuse?'

'I have no complaint to make of Governor Bligh myself,' Mason returned. 'And I am fully convinced the settlers generally are well satisfied with his administration.'[117] Dr Mason continued on his way.

Several days later, this Hawkesbury address, dated 30 January, would be sent to Major Johnston in Sydney. There would be four signatories: Fitz, Hobby, James Badgery, and Thomas Arndell – Foolish Tom, the former magistrate under Bligh. Another 280 names would follow the four signatures, but without the actual signatures of those people. Rebel sympathisers would later claim that the names had been written out in this way because the signatures of those 280 had become too blotted to be legible. Even if all 280 of those named had genuinely signed, and even if they had done so without threat or inducement, the total number [284] didn't compare with the 833 who had signed for Governor Bligh four weeks earlier.

In reality, probably only four Hawkesbury men signed

the Hobby–Fitz document, and one of those soon recanted. Before long, Foolish Tom Arndell would live up to his name by disavowing his support for the address, declaring that he had been in terror of the military at the time. 'By this same terror I was, through weakness, induced to sign a paper which my heart and better judgment abhorred,' he was to tell Governor Bligh.[118]

That night of the 28th, as the soldiers stationed at Green Hills became rolling drunk once more, bonfires and illuminations lit up Sydney for the second evening in a row, and Parramatta had its big revolutionary celebration. From his Parramatta house, Francis Oakes watched with growing fears as the party outside his window became increasingly rowdy. A crowd milled. The bonfires raged. Two sheep were being roasted on spits, one right outside his door. Grog flowed. And then a large effigy was borne around the streets, by men previously arrested by Oakes for petty crimes in the district. The effigy was not of Governor Bligh, nor of Provost Marshal Gore. It was an effigy of former Chief Constable Oakes. Taken to the bonfire outside his quarters, the effigy was thrown into the flames, to the approving cheers of the mob.

The previous day, Oakes had seen looks of concern on the faces of locals when, summoned by fife and drum, they had heard Captain Abbott's declaration of martial law publicly announced at Parramatta. Unlike Sydney, which had a large population of ex-convicts, at Parramatta four in every five residents were free settlers. Here, if anywhere, Oakes would have expected people not to have become infected by the rebellious spirit of the convicts. But grog and anti-authority rhetoric combined to turn the mood of the crowd ugly. 'The people who were concerned in this seemed to be very much enraged with me,' a surprised Oakes would say. Shocked and disbelieving, and with his family now terrified, he hustled his wife and children out the back door of his quarters and hurried them through the darkness to the house of a friend in the town.[119]

The Oakes family spent the night in dread of the crowd tracking them down and murdering them.

5

The First Split in the Junta

The rebellion was not yet three days old, and already a senior member of the rebel leadership was having second thoughts about the whole affair.

On the morning of Friday the 29th, Captain Edward Abbott and his fellow committee members returned to Government House to again take up their examination of the Governor's papers. Griffin, Palmer and Campbell were once more brought under guard to join the Governor and witness the assessment of the documents. But Captain Abbott was having his doubts about this revolution. Or, to be more precise, he was having doubts about the way the revolution was being conducted.

Two weeks later, Abbott would confess that he had known that the rebellion was being planned well in advance of the event, and that he had encouraged it. In a 13 February letter to former governor King in England, he would write, 'I certainly gave my hearty concurrence to the matter of arresting the Governor.' Abbott said, of Johnston, 'Had he followed the advice I gave him previous to taking the step, that, in that case, to send for Colonel Paterson [the Corps' commander, who was in Van Diemen's Land] immediately afterwards, and to go home with the Governor to account for his conduct, it would have shown that he had not done so to obtain the command, instead of oversetting everything and styling himself Lieutenant Governor.'[120]

Since coming into Sydney from Parramatta, Abbott had found that Johnston was resisting the idea of sending for Paterson, his superior and the only man who could legally run the colony as its Lieutenant Governor in the absence of the Governor. At the same time, behind closed doors, the more rabid rebels would have been advocating some very unpleasant retribution against old foes. As Abbott's committee continued to rummage through papers at Government House, it must have become apparent to Abbott that the hard-line Bayly was determined to ferret out every piece of information that could embarrass Bligh, to turn his supporters in the colony against him and to sway the unhappy majority in favour of the rebel administration. Abbott had been under the impression that the committee had been created to find evidence to support the case for Governor Bligh's prompt return to England. But it had become clear that Abbott's objective and that of Bayly were quite different. One was about having Bligh removed and a new governor sent out from England. The other smacked of a grab for power.

In the light of his growing disillusionment with Johnston and suspicions about his motives – and surely also the motives of the lynchpin in this business, his own friend Macarthur – Abbott quickly lost his taste for this style of revolution. 'In short,' Abbott would write to his friend Captain Piper, of the work of the committee, 'I did not like it.'[121] After an hour or so, he could take no more of this hunting for ammunition for scandal at Government House, and bid his colleagues good-day. Abbott walked out of Government House and went directly to the barrack of Major Johnston and demanded a private interview. 'I apologised to Major Johnston, and begged he would excuse me, which he did,' said Abbott.[122]

Captain Abbott not only withdrew from the committee, he decided not to take up the appointment of Judge Advocate in place of Richard Atkins that Johnston had announced. Abbott wanted out of the rebellion, full stop. This was a major blow to the rebel leadership; Abbott, well-respected throughout the colony, was something of a poster boy for the uprising. That afternoon, washing his hands of the revolution, Abbott rode out of town and headed back to Parramatta.

The immediate reaction of John Macarthur, who was living at Abbott's Sydney house at the time, to his good friend's desertion of the rebel ship is not recorded. Intriguingly, it is probable that Abbott had company on the road back to Parramatta that Friday – Macarthur's wife Elizabeth. By the next day, Elizabeth was back at Elizabeth Farm at Parramatta. It is likely that the two successive nights of drunken revelry in the streets of Sydney had been enough for her. Worried about her children, and with her husband happy to have her out of town while the rebel leadership got down to its unpleasant business, she withdrew with daughter Elizabeth back to the family home.

That night at the Hawkesbury, rebel sympathisers Thomas Hobby, Robert Fitz and their adherents enjoyed the district's own bonfire night. The military commander for the district, Sergeant George Lowther, had returned during the day and had given orders for a gallows to be erected fifty paces from Dr Martin Mason's door. Private John Butcher had spent a number of hours hauling cartloads of firewood to the site and erecting a bonfire beneath the gallows. Sergeant Lowther must have been in Sydney for the 27 January illuminations because, no doubt inspired by and in emulation of the effigies he'd seen burned there, he had two effigies made, one of Governor Bligh and another of Provost Marshal Gore. His men weren't as creative as the effigy-makers in the capital; the Green Hills effigies were merely a pair of tarred hides in the shape of Bligh and Gore. These were suspended from the gallows with ropes around the necks.

After dark, the bonfire was lit, the locals were summoned by Thomas Hobby and Sergeant Lowther to watch the Governor and his Provost Marshal burn, and quantities of wine and spirits were consumed. Dr Mason didn't stray from his house, spending the evening in a courtyard from where the partying crowd could be observed at a safe distance. There he was joined by magistrate Foolish Tom Arndell, whose conscience was by this time bothering him. Another magistrate also spent the evening with Dr Mason in his courtyard, keeping well away from the drunken crowd – none other than Robert Fitz, co-author of the Hawkesbury address to Major Johnston. That night, and over the next two nights, the soldiers of the Green Hills detachment and a number of locals drank themselves insensible in the name of revolution.

In Sydney, the celebrations were tapering off by the time the weekend arrived, as the grog supply ran out and the rebel leadership decided that it was time to put a respectable face on their assumption of power. On the Saturday, a General Order was issued commanding all military and civil officers to attend a thanksgiving service at the New Church the next day, to express gratitude for the change of government and for the peaceful way that it had been achieved.

This same day, most of the restrictions on Bligh's former senior officials were relaxed. The previous evening, Edmund Griffin had been allowed to dine at the house of Robert Campbell, and now he was given permission to move out of Lieutenant Moore's house and take up residence with the Campbells. Despite this concession, Griffin would not be permitted to return to Government House, and his access to the Governor would continue to be restricted. At the same time, Campbell and John Palmer received formal notice from Johnston's ADC, Lieutenant Lawson, that their arrest was now at an end, and Palmer and his wife were reunited. William Gore was not so fortunate; he remained lodged in the County Jail, locked in the condemned cell for thirteen-and-a-half hours each day and prevented from receiving visitors even when allowed, alone, into the exercise yard.

Nor was there any lessening of the restrictions placed on Governor Bligh. His around-the-clock guard was maintained, and access to him continued to be very limited. If anything, the screw was tightened on Bligh. On the Friday he had received written notice from Johnston that he would now be expected to pay for all provisions that he and his household consumed. Up to this point, the Governor's expenses had naturally been covered by the government. On the Saturday, just as the arrest of most of Bligh's people was being terminated, Bligh must have said something to Nicholas Bayly that caused Bayly to lose his temper. Bayly told Bligh that, as a result of confessions obtained from the Governor's former magistrates during their examination by the committees, and from other evidence, very serious charges would soon be preferred against him. Bligh promptly wrote to Johnston, still addressing him merely as 'Major Johnston', demanding to know if that meant the rebels intended trying him in a court in the colony.

On the Sunday, a chastened Bayly returned with a written reply: no, the charges against Bligh would be sent to the home government. Major Johnston, said Bayly, just wished to give the Governor notice of that intention. Always one for wanting the last word, Bayly ended with another warning that Johnston would refuse to accept any further correspondence from Bligh unless he was addressed as Lieutenant Governor. Bligh was left with the satisfaction of having annoyed the annoying Bayly, and some relief in knowing that the junta had no plans to haul him before a kangaroo court in Sydney. Just what they really planned to do with him he didn't know. As it happened, the rebels didn't themselves know what to do with him. For the moment, their attention was focused on their own concerns.

John Macarthur had been keeping a comparatively low profile since the 'Glorious 26th', but he had been behind every important act since the overthrow of Bligh. In between writing all the proclamations, letters and notices of appointment which went out under Johnston's name, late on Saturday the 30th Macarthur took a moment to write a quick note from Sydney to his wife Elizabeth, who was by then back at Elizabeth Farm. She had just sent him two letters she had penned – 'admirably written' in Macarthur's opinion – to be forwarded to family in England in which, no doubt, she gave the Macarthur version of the overthrow of Governor Bligh. Telling Macarthur that she was suffering from a severe headache, Elizabeth was sounding depressed by current events. In his reply, Macarthur urged her, 'Be cheerful. Your headache will go off then.' His note, which their son Edward would carry to Elizabeth out at Parramatta in the coming days, said, in part:

> *I have been deeply engaged all this day in contending for the liberties of this unhappy colony, and I am happy to say I have succeeded beyond what I expected. I am too much exhausted to attempt giving you the particulars . . . The Tyrant is now no doubt gnashing his teeth with vexation at his overthrow.*[123]

Unlike his wife, Macarthur seemed not the slightest bit worried. Just the contrary, he was very pleased with himself, like a victorious general after a battle. But if he thought the war was won, he was to be greatly disappointed.

6

The Macarthur Doublecross

On the first day of February, a bright ray of hope shone into Government House. Governor Bligh looked out his window that Monday morning and, to his delight, saw that the warship HMS *Porpoise* was dropping anchor in Sydney Cove. He had been expecting the frigate back in port any day, after he had sent her off the previous 26 November to transfer settlers from Norfolk Island to the settlements on the Derwent and Tamar Rivers in Van Diemen's Land, on orders from London. To Bligh's mind, no matter what action the rebel junta took on land, and no matter what justification they gave, they had no authority to deprive him of the command of a Royal Navy ship.

Bligh immediately wrote a letter to Johnston, enclosing his King's Commission appointing him captain of the *Porpoise*, plus the Admiralty order authorising him to fly his commodore's pennant from the ship – having succeeded in hiding both these documents in his shirt on the evening of 26 January. He informed Johnston that he planned to take command of the vessel and return to England in her. Bligh had no intention of returning to England in the ship, as Macarthur and his colleagues suspected.

Some members of the junta feared that, as soon as he was on board, Bligh would attempt to retake control of the colony by turning the ship's guns on Sydney. But Bligh was hopeful that the rebels would be so glad to get him out of the colony and out of their hair that they would let him board the *Porpoise*. It also gave him considerable pleasure to enclose the two documents with the letter. It must have rocked the rebels' proverbial boat just a little when they discovered that the Governor had somehow kept important papers from them. It also suggested that he had other documents up his sleeve.

The following day, Nicholas Bayly replied to the Governor on behalf of Major Johnston, acknowledging receipt of the letter and documents and advising that, 'He cannot permit you, sir, to return to England in His Majesty's Ship the *Porpoise*'.[124] Bligh, who never saw his commission or the Admiralty order again, then decided to try to slip a message to the master of the *Porpoise*, Acting Lieutenant James Symons, via surreptitious means.

Bligh's covert messenger, probably a member of his domestic staff such as Dunn or Jubb, was caught in the act. For, two days later, Bayly wrote to Bligh again, this time to tell him that Johnston 'cannot allow you to hold any communication with the officers of His Majesty's Ship *Porpoise*; and that he shall consider any attempt to do so, either by letter or otherwise, as a breach of your arrest'.[125] Bayly was threatening to lock Bligh away in close confinement if he tried the same thing again. The allegiance of Lieutenant Symons, meanwhile, had already been pirated away from Bligh – a member of the junta would have gone aboard the *Porpoise* as soon as she arrived back at Sydney. Symons was convinced to obey Major Johnston's orders in preference to those of the Governor.

While Bligh was plotting, unsuccessfully, to board the *Porpoise*, his adversary John Macarthur was occupied with the next stage of a plot of his own. On 30 January, the same day that Macarthur had written to his wife saying that he had been busy all day on revolutionary business, he had composed a General Order which went out under Bayly's signature and in Johnston's name. At first glance it was just another piece of rebel housekeeping: the Reverend Fulton, one of Governor Bligh's magistrates and advisers, was dismissed from his office of Acting Principal Chaplain; Surveyor-General Charles Grimes was appointed to act as Judge Advocate, the post vacated by Atkins by rebel decree and recently declined by Captain Abbott; the military and civil officers were commanded to attend Sunday's thanksgiving service. And, almost as a throwaway line, it was announced that a Criminal Court consisting of the Acting Judge Advocate and six officers of the Corps would sit on the upcoming Tuesday, 2 February, 'for the trial of such offenders as may be brought before it'.[126]

When 2 February arrived, while Governor Bligh was considering the rebel leadership's refusal to allow him to board the *Porpoise,* the court case that had been the catalyst for the overthrow of Bligh, that of Macarthur himself, was resumed in the assembly hall of the King's Orphan School, which then served as Sydney's temporary court house. The same six officers as before sat on the bench – Captain Kemp and Lieutenants Minchin, Lawson, Moore, Laycock and Brabyn. Now Charles Grimes took his seat at the Judge Advocate's table for the first time. Grimes had no training or background in law. He had been a surveyor in the colony for the past seventeen years, and was complaining of severe rheumatism which he put down to years of sleeping on wet ground while out doing his job in the colonial wilds.

The courtroom was packed on 2 February, mostly with soldiers. The soldiery had been alerted to the trial's resumption, but Macarthur's own wife had not. Macarthur didn't tell Elizabeth that he was going back into court. She learned of it second-hand, and even then she was uncertain of the charges her husband was facing. On 5 February, Elizabeth wrote to her best friend in the colony, Captain Piper at Norfolk Island, of her husband's situation: 'The Criminal Court is now sitting and he is before it as a prisoner, but I trust it will be for *no serious offences.*'(Her emphasis.)[127]

That same day, as the Macarthur case dominated public attention, the brig *Speedy* slipped out of Sydney heads and turned south for Van Diemen's Land. Chartered by the rebel government, she carried a dispatch from Major Johnston to his superior, Lieutenant-Colonel Paterson, at the Yorktown settlement on the Tamar River, informing him of the arrest of Governor Bligh on 26 January. The dispatch, almost certainly written by Macarthur, was limited in its detail. It was, according to Paterson, 'somewhat wanting of explanation'[128] as to why Johnston had taken on the removal of Governor Bligh himself without even consulting Paterson, his commanding officer. As we know, Captain Abbott had urged Johnston to send for Paterson to come and assume charge at Sydney as soon as Johnston had deposed Bligh, but Abbott was the only member of the junta who wanted to see Colonel Paterson in Sydney. The majority of the rebel leaders were perfectly happy for the agreeable Johnston to remain in nominal command.

Shortly after the *Speedy* departed, the brig *Harrington*, which was part-owned by John Macarthur, also set sail for Port Dalrymple, carrying as passenger Walter Davidson, a twenty-three-year-old Scot from Aberdeen. Davidson was the nephew of Sir Walter Farquar. Sir Walter, who was physician to the Prince of Wales, was a patron of John Macarthur, and when Macarthur had returned to the colony in 1805 after charges related to his duel with Colonel Paterson had been dropped, he brought young Davidson with him as a rather young but well-connected immigrant settler.

Davidson, on the instructions of the British Government, had been granted 2000 acres (810 hectares) of prime grazing land at the Cowpastures, later renamed Camden, south-west of Sydney, by Governor King. That Camden grant was located right next door to one of Macarthur's properties and, instead of operating it himself, Davidson had permitted Macarthur to run his sheep on it while the young man captained a ship on trading ventures in the Asia-Pacific region. By the beginning of April 1808, Davidson had just returned to Sydney after a successful voyage to India and China. That voyage had been financed by several New South Wales businessmen – John Macarthur, the Blaxland brothers, and Robert Campbell. It would be said of Davidson's now sudden and unexpected trip to the penal settlements at Port Dalrymple that he had been briefed by Macarthur to convince Paterson not to come up to Sydney.[129]

What was Colonel Paterson, the Commanding Officer of the New South Wales Corps, doing hiding away down on the Tamar River in remote Van Diemen's Land? Sad to say, he was drinking heavily and pottering in an extensive garden hacked out of the wilderness at the poorly chosen Yorktown site. For the inoffensive William Paterson was a broken man, of no use to the Crown or the colony. In late 1803, when the Secretary of State had ordered Bligh's predecessor Governor King to establish settlements in Van Diemen's Land, Paterson, recovering from the serious gunshot wound he had received in his duel that year with John Macarthur, had convinced King to give him command of the settlement to be established on the Tamar in the north of the island. King had gladly rid himself of the alcoholic colonel, and Bligh had obviously come out to New South Wales well-briefed on Paterson's condition, for he never recalled him to Sydney; he left him where he was, out of harm's way.

Paterson was an amateur naturalist and, based on the examples of native flora and fauna which he collected in the colony, the Royal Society had made him their first Fellow in the colony – Bligh was the second FRS in New South Wales. There, on the Tamar River, Paterson had remained, with his wife Elizabeth, his longtime secretary Alexander Riley, 100 convicts, and thirty soldiers, contentedly living the secluded life. When the site of the settlement at Yorktown had proven totally unsuitable, Paterson had sent most of the troops and convicts of his little command upriver to form a new settlement at Patersonia, the later Launceston. But Paterson had remained at Yorktown, treating it like his private estate, collecting botanical specimens by day and drinking himself into oblivion by night, while subordinates at Patersonia did his job for him as Commandant.

Governor Bligh had not only followed King's example, he had formalised Paterson's exile, in 1807 sending Surveyor-General Grimes to survey the north of Van Diemen's Land and draw a line on the map at the 40th parallel where it cut the island in two. Paterson was named Lieutenant Governor of all of Van Diemen's Land north of that line, while Lieutenant-Colonel David Collins, the Royal Marines officer who commanded at Hobart Town, became Lieutenant Governor of all of Van Diemen's Land south of the line. Both were answerable to Governor Bligh in Sydney. Physically and mentally intimidated by Macarthur, and with no hankering for the responsibilities of command that would fall to him in Sydney, Paterson was perfectly happy to live a quiet life in the southern backwater. It was Walter Davidson's job to make sure he stayed there, and out of John Macarthur's hair. None of the rebels wanted Paterson back in Sydney where, they feared, the weak and indecisive colonel might cave in to William Bligh's demands to reinstate him as Governor.

As Davidson sailed south, in Sydney, the illegally constituted Criminal Court sat for five days in the continuation of the *Parramatta* case against Macarthur, the case that had brought on the coup against Bligh, the case resumed on Macarthur's orders. During those five days, with Macarthur in the dock, the court listened to testimony from six witnesses. One after the other, former Judge Advocate Atkins, Governor Bligh's secretary Edmund Griffin, ex-Commissary 'Little Jack' Palmer, ex-Chief Constable Francis Oakes from Parramatta, Robert Campbell's nephew Robert Campbell Junior, who had been working in the customs office, and John Glenn, master of the schooner *Parramatta*, took the stand.

Each was asked several questions by Acting Judge Advocate Grimes, and then Macarthur, acting as his own defence attorney, cross-examined them in depth. Captain Kemp had passed on to Macarthur the papers that Judge Advocate Atkins had left behind at the court house on 25 January. From these, Macarthur knew exactly what evidence the Prosecution, now conducted by Grimes, would present, and what questions it would ask. Macarthur was additionally armed with both the statements taken by the revolutionary committees during interrogations at Sydney between 26 January and 1 February and the Governor's confidential papers seized at Government House.

Macarthur's disillusioned friend Captain Abbott, now back at Parramatta, threw his hands in the air when he heard what was going on. He would tell former governor King in his 13 February letter that Macarthur's resumed trial 'appeared like a mock trial more than anything else'. In his view, 'The Governor could nor would not appear in any shape against him now,' because Bligh was a prisoner at Government House. 'The advantages were all on Macarthur's side, and there were none left on the other.'[130]

In the dock, but holding all the cards, Macarthur, who was in his element now, was able to assault the Governor's former officials with a barrage of questions that had little to do with the original charges against him. They were mostly about Governor Bligh's actions, tactics, and intentions. For hours on end he 'audaciously browbeat and interrogated'[131] the witnesses, without restraint from Acting Judge Advocate Grimes or the military magistrates, as he strove to force incriminating and embarrassing admissions from them. It swiftly became apparent that, as Bligh himself was to conclude after he learned of what transpired, 'They were trying the Governor, and that Macarthur, instead of being prisoner at their bar, directed the prosecution.'[132]

Apart from the testimony of the witnesses, there was the documentary evidence, which Macarthur took full advantage of. He produced the Governor's letter book, which contained copies of every letter going in and out of Government House, 'out of which he read such passages as suited his designs'.[133] The most damning testimony had come from Richard Atkins, and the Governor's letter book was also a catalyst for his startling turnaround. Friends of Bligh were surprised that Atkins had switched sides and changed tune so quickly, until it was learned that Atkins had been shown letters about him that Bligh had sent to England.

In a letter to Sir Joseph Banks in which he expressed the view that the colony should have its own attorney-general as well as a proper judge and a trained lawyer, Bligh had described Atkins as 'a disgrace to jurisprudence'.[134] Writing a report to London, Bligh had said that Atkins' knowledge of the law was poor, his determination weak and his opinion infirm, and he could not be trusted. Worst of all, he said Atkins was a drunkard who was 'a disgrace to the community', even delivering death sentences while drunk. Bligh had asked that London appoint a suitably qualified replacement for Atkins as soon as possible.[135]

Bligh's predecessors as Governor had expressed similar concerns to London about Atkins, and Governor King had also sought his replacement. But Atkins had never seen their letters. Once Atkins had read the Bligh letters, he needed no persuading to change camps. Even though he was to admit that he occasionally drank a little heavily, the haughty Atkins – whose father was a baronet from a noble line, and whose elder brothers, a general and an admiral, were also both baronets – would not acknowledge his weaknesses or accept criticism. Atkins joined the attack on the Governor, claiming in the witness box that he had always been in fear of Bligh and that the Governor had admonished him if he delivered a verdict that Bligh disliked.

Macarthur, after making a great impression on his audience with his five days of theatrical interrogations, resumed his seat without even offering a defence. On Saturday, 6 February, the court delivered its verdict in what a twentieth-century Australian chief justice was to call 'this caricature of a criminal trial'.[136] The court found that Macarthur's past behaviour had not been seditious and the warrant of 15 December had been illegally issued and served, and therefore his trial in relation to the *Parramatta* matter could not be proceeded with. They unanimously and fully acquitted him of all the charges, and set him free. His own friend Captain Abbott considered this mock Macarthur trial 'shameful', as he wrote to former Governor King a week after Macarthur had been cleared. Abbott added, 'And there are several of my way of thinking.'[137]

But at the moment of his acquittal, Macarthur seemed invincible. Certainly his supporters in the ranks of the Corps thought so. Sergeant-Major Whittle had made a platform with a chair nailed to it, and when Macarthur emerged from the court house he was carried around part of the town on this victory litter by Whittle and several brawny soldiers. Other soldiers streamed along beside and behind cheering, 'Huzzah! Huzzah! Huzzah!' Some people they passed applauded, others looked bemused. At the same time, the bells in the New Church's round tower, only recently installed by Governor Bligh, began to peal. That night, illuminations again lit many Sydney windows, and a fresh supply of free liquor appeared from out of nowhere to quench the thirst of all who wanted to share in Mr Macarthur's joy.

The next day, it was announced that the Lieutenant Governor was generously allowing officers and respectable inhabitants to purchase a moderate supply of spirits for their domestic use. But a number of those officers and respectable inhabitants could not be bought by a few litres of brandy, gin or rum. In just one week, they had tired of citizen Macarthur's behind-the-scenes power plays and courtroom antics. They had hatched a plot of their own, without consulting Macarthur. And it seems they caught him off-guard.

On Monday morning, two days after Macarthur's acquittal, the town crier went about the streets of Sydney ringing his bell and announcing that a public meeting would take place at the New Church at 8.00 o'clock that evening, to discuss the colony's affairs. Quite a large gathering turned out at 8.00, although the church was by no means full. Many of those present were soldiers. Macarthur was there. His expressionless face hid his inner concern. For Macarthur had not called this meeting. He had received an invitation to attend, from Nicholas Bayly, but he had no idea what it was about.

When the meeting got underway Bayly rose and addressed the audience. The Welshman, one of Macarthur's closest friends and considered along with Macarthur one of the fathers of the revolution, proposed that a subscription be raised to send Macarthur to London as a delegate of the colonists. In London, said Bayly, Macarthur could lay before His Majesty's Government the many grievances the colonists had with Governor Bligh. The crowd roared its approval.

Now Macarthur knew what Bayly was up to – he was trying to get rid of him, so that Bayly could profit more freely from the revolution with Macarthur out of the colony. Macarthur, who had no desire to leave New South Wales just as he was getting into his dictatorial stride, not only quickly recovered from the surprise of this move by his closest ally, he countered it with a stroke of brilliance. Instead of exploding with anger, Macarthur came to his feet and addressed the crowd as if the proposal was the finest idea he had ever heard. He didn't criticise Bayly or his proposal. He wholeheartedly endorsed the idea, and accepted the nomination as the colony's delegate to London.

'I thank the populace for the honour they have conferred on me,' he said. 'However repugnant it is to my wishes to embark for England at this time, and not withstanding my want of capacity to fulfil the arduous task imposed on me, yet in gratitude to my friends I will devote the last hour of my existence to their service.'[138] Amid cheers and applause, Macarthur announced that he would immediately settle his business affairs in the colony, proceed to England, and lay before His Majesty's ministers the heavy grievances the colonists had with Governor Bligh.[139]

Macarthur's business partner, Garnham Blaxcell, who, like Bayly, had gone bail for Macarthur, now proposed that a public subscription be raised to cover the cost of their delegate's trip to London. This was agreed, and a document was quickly produced, with members of the audience lining up to put their names down for particular amounts, depending on their circumstances. John Macarthur, smiling tightly and shaking hands, noted the identity of each person who put their name on the list. Yorkshireman Simeon Lord and his two business partners, the illiterate, redheaded merchant Henry Kable and the enterprising young shipbuilder James Underwood, all three of them wealthy ex-convicts, jointly promised the largest amount, £500. The Blaxland brothers put up £200, Blaxcell £100, Bayly £100, and Isaac Nicholls £50. There were a number of lesser amounts promised, including £10 each from jailer McKay and Chief Constable Redman, with the smallest being a pound from ex-convict John Miller. The total came to £1154 and 2 shillings.[140]

The smaller donors – the likes of McKay, Redman, and the businesswomen Elizabeth Driver, Rosetta Marsh and Mary Skinner – no doubt genuinely believed that they were acting in support of Macarthur. But Macarthur saw the men who promised the larger amounts as actually identifying themselves as his foes; clearly, these were men who wanted him out of the way. To Macarthur, who never forgot a slight and always held a grudge, they became marked men, former allies who could no longer be trusted: Bayly, Blaxcell, the Blaxlands, Lord, Kable and Underwood. Nicholls he had never trusted. And then there were those who promised nothing, and the majority of those present fell into this category, for only thirty-one people promised money to the fund.

Of the military officers who attended the meeting, Minchin, Lawson, Moore, Harris and Jamieson did not subscribe a penny. Neither did their civilian junta colleague, Townson. This could have been taken one of two ways. These men were either no longer supportive of Macarthur, or they were alert to the motives of Bayly's group and were not going to play along. As it turned out, just one man out of this latter group of six, Lieutenant Lawson, would still be loyal to Macarthur three months later.

The meeting further proposed that a sword be purchased and presented to Major Johnston, and silver dinner plate be given to the six officers who had sat at Macarthur's trial, by way of thanks for the overthrow of Governor Bligh. This suggestion was unanimously endorsed. Yet another motion was then put by the meeting's convenors, proposing an address of thanks to Macarthur, 'as having been chiefly instrumental in bringing about the happy change which took place the said day [26 January]'.[141]

This motion, which was also enthusiastically carried, would have been considered a masterstroke by its creators, Bayly and Blaxcell. On the surface it praised Macarthur. But at the same time, it offered irrefutable proof that the inhabitants of Sydney acknowledged the overthrow of Governor Bligh to have been chiefly Macarthur's doing. When shown to His Majesty's ministers, the record of this motion should get Bayly, Blaxcell, the Blaxlands, Lord and Nicholls off the hook when London apportioned blame for the rebellion. Or at least, that was their plan. Few in the New Church audience would have recognised this motion for what it really was, but John Macarthur certainly did.

Macarthur departed the meeting leaving Bayly and his cronies with the impression that they had won, that Macarthur would meekly sail off to England, and that he would cop the blame for the rebellion while leaving them to share out the spoils in his absence. They should have known Macarthur better than that. He went directly from the meeting to Major Johnston. It is probable that he urged Johnston to immediately dismiss Bayly as his secretary and Provost Marshal, but Johnston would not break with Bayly. As for the matter of sending Macarthur as the colonists' delegate to London, it was about to be elegantly scuppered, by a scheme that Macarthur now put to Johnston.

Four days after the New Church meeting, Johnston created a brand new position, that of Secretary to the Colony. The office holder would be the most senior civil administrator in New South Wales. The appointment was announced on 12 February in a brief General Order which began: 'John Macarthur, Esq, is appointed a Magistrate, and Secretary to the Colony.'[142]

7

Enter the Dictator

The attempt by Nicholas Bayly and Garnham Blaxcell to double-cross John Macarthur had failed, spectacularly. Macarthur was now the so-called Secretary to the Colony, and by Johnston's General Order of 12 February all communications concerning the government of the colony that would have previously been addressed to the Lieutenant Governor had now to be sent to Macarthur.

Major Johnston retired to his country seat, as colonists called Annandale, his farm outside Sydney, to play very little active part in the affairs of the colony. All orders and decrees still went out in his name and were signed by his secretary Bayly, but they were written by Macarthur. Johnston was now merely the figurehead of the rebel administration, the puppet president of this new Antipodean republic of New South Wales, while Macarthur was its unelected prime minister. Or, as both Bligh supporters and Macarthur's own former allies would soon be labelling him, its dictator.

Later, when Johnston attempted to justify the creation of the post of Secretary to the Colony and his appointment of Macarthur to fill the position, he would say – in words written for him by Macarthur – 'I requested Mr Macarthur to assist me in the arduous undertaking. As there was no office vacant to which I could appoint him, and as it was necessary he should have some public character, I created an office which has never before existed here.'[143] He was to stress that Macarthur would receive no payment as Secretary to the Colony. Macarthur was trying to make it appear that he was not in it for the money, that he was driven purely by public spirit. But public spirited or not, Macarthur was now in a position of total power in the colony, a position from which he could further his interests and the interests of those he favoured. There would be, it would turn out, countless ways to fleece both the British Government and the colonists of New South Wales, and Macarthur would exploit every one of them.

Obviously, now that Macarthur was officially engaged in running the colony, he could not very well leave and go home to England. The proposal that he head off to London as the colonists' delegate promptly sank without trace. No alternative delegate was suggested, and this would have only confirmed Macarthur's belief that Bayly, Blaxcell and company had been trying to get rid of him. The money subscribed at the 8 February meeting was never collected.

Now that he was Secretary to the Colony, Macarthur took a New South Wales Corps military orderly for himself. That orderly was Corporal Hughes, the same Corporal Hughes who had hauled Provost Marshal Gore off to jail on the night of 26 January on Macarthur's orders. And Macarthur was now accompanied everywhere he went by an armed dragoon as bodyguard. Quickly getting down to the business of running the colony his own way, Macarthur attempted to cement cracks in junta solidarity by distributing some of the spoils of victory. He began by dismissing three government storekeepers, Wiltshire, McGowan and Baker, accusing them of mishandling the stores in their charge. To replace them he appointed men of his own choosing, and in doing so gained direct control over the issuing of government stores.

It would later be alleged that Macarthur now personally profited by taking numerous items from the government stores. These included thirty stand of muskets from the armoury, to be sent to the South Pacific in his ship *Parramatta* and exchanged for pork that would be sold in the colony. He was said to have also appropriated fresh beef, clothing and millstones, among other things, from the government stores, and to have fitted out the trading ship *Pegasus* with Royal Navy sail canvas. A six-oared boat belonging to the government was sold. And ship owners such as Macarthur, who had previously carried government stores to Newcastle in their ships as ballast, free of charge, were now paid to do so by the colony's treasury.[144] This was just the beginning.

Macarthur dismissed the Superintendent of Livestock, John Jamieson, and replaced him with Hawkesbury rebel sympathiser, Robert Fitz, after Jamieson had protested that 'Mr Macarthur wanted the whole government stock removed' from the prime grazing ground at the Cowpastures 'to Broken Bay, amongst the rocks and barren ground'. The reason that Macarthur ordered the transfer of the stock from the Cowpastures, said Superintendent Jamieson, was 'that he might have the whole range of land where they now graze for his own stock to run in'.[145] At that time, Macarthur had 3000 to 4000 sheep and several hundred cattle.

The government cattle herd was quickly reduced, as the new administration distributed cows and bullocks to members of the junta and their friends, 'for which it is *said* they are to pay in grain'. (Superintendent Jamieson's emphasis.)[146] Grain receipts would be manipulated to make it look as if the cattle had been paid for. In this cattle carve-up, officers received between six and seventeen cows each plus bullocks. Sergeants received between one and three cows each, while Sergeant-Major Whittle received five. 'Mr Fitz, Deputy Commissary, who has been so officious in the Cause, Mr Macarthur has rewarded him with seventeen picked cows, and some bullocks.'[147]

Another junta member who was able to snap up a share of the government herd was Dr Townson. Parramatta clergyman the Reverend Rowland Hassall, a close friend of Robert Campbell – a teenaged son of Hassall was employed in Campbell's Sydney office as a clerk – wrote in a covert letter to Governor Bligh in February that Townson was well pleased with the deal. Townson, said Hassall, 'thought the revolution was good because he got his cows'.[148] Nicholas Bayly, meanwhile, received no government stock.

Governor Bligh's prohibition of the unrestricted importation of wine and spirits was now lifted by Macarthur. Officers of the Corps, including Captain Anthony Fenn Kemp, resumed their previously profitable activities as grog traders – Kemp kept a store in High Street. An estimated 40,000 gallons of wine and spirits would be distributed by the rebel government to military and civil officers during the coming months.[149]

Just as had been the practice prior to Governor Bligh's arrival, the purchase of all imported goods was once again monopolised by members of the officer cartel, and merchants such as Robert Campbell were squeezed out. Meanwhile, farmers were required to sell their grain to the administration. Macarthur undervalued the grain at three shillings a bushel. He then forced the farmers to accept wine or spirits in payment, valuing it at fifty shillings a gallon, many times more than the few shillings the administration had paid for it and ten times the price that Macarthur had charged soldiers of the Corps for the wine, from the same shipment, that he'd sold to them in late January. Macarthur also let stocks of salt pork sit in the government stores to rot, and sold his own pork and that of his favourites to the government. Another dodge was for the rebel government to buy rundown houses owned by members of the junta, at inflated prices.[150]

Then there was the matter of convict labour. Macarthur promptly diverted 300 convicts previously engaged on public works to the service of friends of the revolution. It was not as if the colony was swimming in excess free labour at the time. Within a decade the colony would be receiving more convicts than it knew what to do with, but during the period of Captain Bligh's governorship only a trickle of new convicts arrived from Britain and Ireland. In an April dispatch to the Secretary of State for the Colonies by Major Johnston, Macarthur, the author of the dispatch, would justify his reallocation of convict labour in typical style. It was an act of economy worthy of praise, he reckoned, because it had removed 300 people from the list of those receiving government food and clothing.[151]

Again, Bayly, like several of his cohorts, was not included among those who benefited from this distribution. Former allies such as Bayly, Blaxcell and Abbott whom Macarthur felt had turned against him received little more than a cold shoulder. Captain Abbott noted, the day after Macarthur's appointment, that he, Abbott, was 'considered as dissatisfied by the present Ruler, because I disapproved of several things in the early stage of the business'.[152]

Macarthur, in Johnston's name, also doled out land grants to those who remained faithful to him. Governor Bligh, during his seventeen months in office, had approved grants totalling 2180 acres (880 hectares). Macarthur would give 5660 acres (2260 hectares) of the British Crown's prime land to the chosen ones in a third of that time.[153] Those whom Macarthur did not trust received little or no acreage – Corps Adjutant Lieutenant William Minchin, for one, was granted a measly 100 acres (40 hectares).

Excluding powerful former allies was not the ideal way to make friends and influence people. All this did was make new enemies for Macarthur and make existing enemies all the more bitterly opposed to him.

8

Rebel Versus Rebel

Governor Bligh had watched the skirmishes between the junta members steadily grow into a war. Now allowed visits from his former officials, and receiving secret letters from unwavering supporters among the colonists, and from converts such as Thomas Arndell and John Jamieson, Bligh was being kept up to date with the resistance that Macarthur had been facing since engineering his own appointment as ruler of the colony. Life at Government House was still difficult; Bligh was watched like a hawk. Whenever he took a walk in the garden with daughter Mary on his arm, the two guards posted on the path outside the house fell in behind them and walked just six paces to their rear. If Bligh and Mary put their heads together and tried to talk privately, the guards would coarsely call for them to speak loudly enough for them to overhear.

Bligh had been informed that the rebel administration wanted to send him home to England. This was the last thing that he wanted. His plan was to regain control of the colony and put the rebel leaders on trial for High Treason. His best means of achieving this, he judged, would be through gaining control of HMS *Porpoise*. So, recently, he had told Nicholas Bayly when he came to deliver messages that he would agree to go home to England if allowed to do so on the *Porpoise*, as this was the only vessel in the colony that could provide comfortable accommodation for his daughter, who suffered from chronic seasickness.

Macarthur didn't trust Bligh; there was no way he would allow the Governor to set foot aboard the warship, which he might try to take control of. Just the same, he wanted him out from under his feet, so, in February, Macarthur made a verbal agreement with the owners of the large cargo ship *Pegasus* for Bligh, his daughter, his servants and any Bligh adherents who wished to accompany them to go home to England in that ship. Bligh, determined to remain in the colony, stalled by demanding that the *Pegasus* be surveyed to prove she was seaworthy. Bligh's later critics, such as Macarthur biographer M. H. Ellis, would claim that the *Pegasus* charter fell through because of Bligh's obstinate objections. This was not the case. Major Johnston would declare, in Macarthur's words, that 'her owners for some private reasons considered it expedient to decline the bargain'.[154]

Those owners were merchant Simeon Lord (whose share of the ship was clandestine, for reasons that will be explained shortly), Surgeon Harris and settler Thomas Moore. Even though the rebel government fitted out the *Pegasus* with government sails, the three owners backed out of the deal at the last minute. Lord had already shown that he had joined Bayly's opposition rebel camp, while Harris' support for Macarthur had clearly begun to waver. If they hadn't been in John Macarthur's black book before, all three of these gentlemen were well and truly in it now.

Another ship, the *Brothers*, was due to sail for England soon, and Macarthur apparently considered using her to take Bligh home, but a series of legal wrangles involving the *Brothers* that began in February seemed to rule her out. So, in desperation, Macarthur wrote to Bligh in Johnston's name suggesting that he make the trip in the *Dart*, a South Sea sealer owned by Macarthur. The *Dart* was a tiny vessel with just a single below deck, and her hold would be filled with reeking salted seal hides. Bligh dismissed the proposal out of hand, and again pushed for the *Porpoise*.

Macarthur, influenced perhaps by his wife, who would have considered the *Dart* a totally unsuitable vessel for a lady such as the Governor's daughter, discarded the *Dart* proposal and began to reconsider the *Porpoise* as the best mode of transport for Bligh and his daughter. But he would only countenance this on condition that Bligh gave his word as an officer that he would not attempt to take command of her and would continue to consider himself under arrest until he reached England. Bligh readily agreed to this condition, but Macarthur still didn't trust the Governor to keep his word to men he considered mutineers and rebels: 'His whole conduct left me without doubt that he designed to take command of His Majesty's ship the moment he put his foot on board her'.[155]

So, it seems that Macarthur attempted to do a deal with young Lieutenant Symons, commander of the *Porpoise*. If Symons agreed to keep Bligh under lock and key throughout the voyage, then it would be safe to allow the Governor aboard the warship. But as February continued, Macarthur found the naval lieutenant pulling back from him. Symons wasn't the only one resisting Macarthur's wishes. With each passing day, Macarthur was encountering increasing opposition from men who had been his revolutionary allies only weeks before. No member of the junta wanted to reinstate Governor Bligh, but few of them were happy with Macarthur at the helm of the rebel ship of state. As the end of February approached, an opportunity arose for Macarthur to assert his authority and to put several of his most vocal opponents in their place.

John Blaxland and his brother Gregory, by now firmly in the opposing rebel camp, jointly had an interest in the appropriately named ship the *Brothers*. The remaining half was officially owned by the London shipping firm Hulletts & Co, which was also in partnership with John Macarthur in three of his four ships. Hulletts' half share of the *Brothers* was actually mortgaged by the firm to Simeon Lord who, as an ex-convict, was not supposed to have a financial interest in any ship. The *Brothers* had just completed a successful sealing cruise in New Zealand waters and her skipper, Oliver Russell, was ready to leave Sydney to take his cargo of 40,000 seal skins to the English market where the price for seal skins was then at its peak. But Blaxland wanted to keep the ship in Australian waters, presumably shipping the cargo to Britain in another vessel. Russell said his orders from Hulletts were to sail for home, and a dispute erupted. Macarthur stepped in. Wearing his hat as Secretary to the Colony, he took the side of skipper Oliver Russell against the Blaxlands.

A complex series of skirmishes now took place in and out of the courts of the colony which lasted through March and April, with Macarthur determined to be the victor. (See Appendix, 'The *Brothers* Case', for a detailed account of those battles.) This vicious, drawn-out dispute between members of the rebel junta who had been one-time allies would certainly have amused and delighted Governor Bligh, who received accounts of the battle from his staff and supporters. And Bligh no doubt hoped that it was a precursor to the imminent internal collapse of the rebellion.

During the *Brothers* dispute, Acting Judge Advocate Charles Grimes and several rebel-appointed magistrates spoke or ruled against Macarthur. In response, Macarthur removed his former good friend Grimes from the post of Judge Advocate, and removed the obstructive Lieutenant Symons and Surgeon John Harris from the magistracy. Through Macarthur's intervention, Captain Russell won his case, and he prepared to sail for England in the *Brothers*. A furious John Blaxland determined to get to London, to take up the matter of the *Brothers* with Hulletts and, no doubt, to try to have Russell dismissed by them. He also wanted to stir up trouble for Macarthur and Johnston in the halls of officialdom. Blaxland arranged a passage in the *Rose*, a ship jointly owned by Robert Campbell, William Wilson, and the *Rose*'s master, Richard Brooks. The *Rose*, which was due to depart within a week or so of the *Brothers*, would be heading for Cape Town to pick up a cargo there. At Cape Town, Blaxland planned to find passage to England in another vessel.

As the *Brothers* would be the first ship to undertake the voyage from Sydney to England since the 26 January coup, it provided the first opportunity for Macarthur to send a dispatch to Lord Castlereagh, the Secretary of State for the Colonies in London, advising that Governor Bligh had been arrested, and explaining why. On 11 April, Macarthur wrote Castlereagh a letter running to many pages, which would go under Johnston's name. To excuse the overthrow of the vice-regal representative, Macarthur wrote that Governor Bligh had 'acted upon a pre-determined plan to subvert the laws of his country, to terrify and influence the Courts of Justice, and to bereave those persons who had the misfortune to be obnoxious to him, of their fortunes, their liberty, and their lives'.[156] He supported this astonishing claim in one short paragraph, saying that Bligh had dispossessed several inhabitants of their houses, while several who had 'become opulent by trade, were threatened with the Governor's resentment if they presumed to build upon or alienate their own land'.[157] Macarthur, who was one of those who had 'become opulent by trade', offered no proof of this claim.

Secondly, the Johnston letter advised Castlereagh that Johnston had ordered Superintendent of Livestock Jamieson; storekeepers Wiltshire, McGowen and Baker; and a servant of Commissary Palmer's to be questioned. Their statements, said the letter, 'although extremely incomplete', would convince

His Lordship of 'the various frauds that have been committed on the public property, and that His Majesty's interest has not been the first object of consideration with Governor Bligh and Mr Commissary Palmer'.[158] But no copies of these statements were sent with the dispatch. The dispatch also claimed that Andrew Thompson, who managed Bligh's properties in the colony, had made a confession which would 'disclose to Your Lordship the arrangements made by the Governor for the improvement of his private fortune, at the expense of the Crown'.[159] This 'confession', like the other statements, was not tendered to prove the claim.

Detailed supporting documents *were* provided for the issue at the core of the Johnston dispatch – John Macarthur's court case of 25–26 January. 'While they were trembling with apprehension for their own safety,' the dispatch said, 'the eyes of the whole were suddenly turned from the contemplation of the general danger to that of Mr Macarthur.'[160] There followed page after page justifying Macarthur's position in that court case. And he attached copies of the letters from the six officers of the Criminal Court to Bligh relating to the case.

In focusing so obviously and obsessively on his own dispute with Bligh, and then by following that up later in the letter with the information that Johnston had appointed Macarthur to run the colony, Macarthur was unwittingly telling London all they needed to know about the true villain and true cause of the rebellion. In this same dispatch, Macarthur also vented his spleen against the junta members who had been causing him so much trouble lately. 'Every obstacle that knavery or cunning could devise has been interposed to distract my attention' by 'several of the better class' who 'have been engaged in illicit or dishonest practices'. Here Macarthur held no punches. 'The two Mr Blaxlands,' he wrote, 'have been amongst the forwardest and most troublesome of my opposers.'[161]

He also mentioned the Blaxlands' partner, Simeon Lord.

'These gentlemen have, unhappily for themselves, formed a connection with an inhabitant by the name of Lord, who was once a convict, but now possesses a very extensive fortune, or at least the appearance of it.'[162] Lord, the former convict now made good, had more land in the colony than anyone else and a grand three-storey mansion in the heart of Sydney that had reputedly cost £10,000 to build. That mansion, according to one observer, 'would be an ornament to the most fashionable square in London'.[163] Macarthur's own residence at Elizabeth Farm was humble by comparison. Macarthur seems jealous of Lord's fortune, not the least because Lord had not long before been a convict.

Macarthur's unflattering opinion of Lord was not shared by even his closest friends. Captain John Piper, commandant at Norfolk Island, had used Lord as his business agent in Sydney since 1802, and would continue to do so until 1811. But there was a distinct motive behind Macarthur's attack on John Blaxland, in particular, in the Johnston dispatch. It was aimed at destroying his credibility, and countering anything that Blaxland might say against Macarthur and Johnston once he reached England.

In contrast to these attacks on Macarthur's former allies, the Johnston dispatch, written by Macarthur, also contained praise for Nicholas Bayly, and a request that London confirm his appointment as Provost Marshal. Yet privately, Macarthur was at war with Bayly. At the same time, Macarthur confided to his friend Piper that Bayly 'is become a violent oppositionist. The assigned reason, some information he received from Grimes of my finding fault with him – but the real one, because I would not advise Johnston to make Laycock a magistrate and police officer – with some other little disappointments respecting men, cows, etc. In short, I am of the opinion that had they been given way to, the whole of the public property would not have satisfied them.'[164]

That Macarthur supported Bayly publicly while reviling him privately suggests he was influenced by Johnston, who begged this favour of Macarthur in return for his continued compliance. Johnston had, after all, succeeded in having his son-in-law Nicholls appointed to the revolutionary committees despite Macarthur's longstanding antipathy toward Nicholls. Alternatively, it may have been through Elizabeth Macarthur's influence that Bayly retained his position. As it would turn out, she was the one person to whose will Macarthur bowed. Elizabeth, a conciliator by nature, had previously included Bayly along with Abbott and Piper in the close-knit Elizabeth Farm set, and she may well have convinced her husband not to outwardly abandon his closest friends when he needed them most. So, Macarthur lived with Bayly's continued presence in the junta hierarchy, and even refrained from publicly admonishing or punishing Abbott, who had disappointed him most by walking away from the junta.

Needing someone from the rebel side to carry this dispatch to London, Macarthur took the opportunity to kill more than one bird with the same jagged stone and rid himself of some troublemakers. Surgeon Harris, who had lost his magistracy as a result of the *Brothers* case, in which he had been seen by Macarthur to favour the Blaxlands, was instructed to carry a copy of this dispatch and its attachments home to England in the *Brothers*. Harris did not want to go. Originally coming out to the colony a poor young doctor, he had subsequently built a very comfortable existence for himself in New South Wales. The last thing he wanted was to take a year out of his life making the trip to England and back. Replying to Johnston's written command to go to England in the *Brothers*, Harris declared that of course he was prepared to go at once. But then he remarked, 'I trust I shall be able to explain to His Majesty's ministers many things which otherwise might never have reached them.'[165]

How times had changed since Macarthur and Harris had come out to the colony together on the *Neptune* in 1790. On that journey, the pair had become good friends; Harris, a raw Surgeon's Mate, had even acted as young Ensign Macarthur's second in the duel fought by Macarthur with the captain of the *Neptune* at Plymouth. Now, eighteen years later, the two men had become bitter enemies. In response to Harris' veiled threat, Macarthur wrote demanding an explanation of his meaning. Harris came back, 'It is very probable that I may be in possession of many transactions which may not have come' to Johnston's attention.[166]

In other words, Harris knew all about Macarthur's behind-the-scenes role in the coup. But Macarthur threw the final knockout punch. He sent a letter from Johnston which directed Harris to focus on telling His Majesty's ministers all about the tyranny of Governor Bligh, adding, 'You will naturally explain your own reasons for joining with the officers and inhabitants in calling upon me to assume command, and to put Governor Bligh in arrest.'[167] This succeeded in bringing Harris to heel, for the moment.

Harris' friend Charles Grimes was also being removed from the scene by Macarthur. The former Acting Judge Advocate was ordered to take a duplicate set of the same documents back to England in Macarthur's smelly little sealer, the *Dart*. Although he had 'the greatest cause to be dissatisfied' with Mr Grimes, said Macarthur in the Johnston dispatch, he hoped 'that his errors have been errors of judgement more than of design.' He added that he was confident that Grimes would provide His Lordship with all the 'many important facts' relating to Governor Bligh.[168] But, just to make sure that Grimes stayed true to the basic rebel dictum – that no matter what personal differences they might have they must all remain united against Bligh, for their own protection – Macarthur was sending his eldest son Edward on the voyage with Grimes, with orders to accompany him to see the Secretary of State once they landed in England.

By this time, Lieutenant-Colonel Paterson had sent a response to the 2 February letter in which Johnston had informed him of the coup. It had taken Paterson four weeks to write, but when he did send his reply back up to Sydney in the *Harrington* it was a surprising one. Shaking himself from his lethargy, on 12 March Paterson announced that he was coming to Sydney to take charge, without delay. He instructed Johnston to send him a suitable ship in which he and his family could make the journey from Van Diemen's Land, at the same time telling him to use that ship to send supplies, more troops and more male convicts to Port Dalrymple. Paterson also advised that he had written to London to let His Majesty's ministers know what he was planning to do. Paterson didn't seem to trust Johnston; he noted that if the Major failed to send a suitable ship within one month of receiving Paterson's letter, Paterson would instruct his agent in Sydney to charter a ship to come for him. If that wasn't possible, he would send an officer overland to Hobart to charter a vessel there.[169]

Macarthur would not have been overly concerned by Paterson's note. If Paterson did in fact make the journey north and take command in Sydney, Macarthur was confident of being able to easily control the weak-kneed colonel. Besides, tellingly, Paterson had remarked at the end of his letter to Johnston, 'I do not at present purpose making any change in the arrangement you have formed at Sydney until I may hear from His Majesty's ministers.'[170] This process, involving messages carried to England and back, could take a year or more; a year of continued rebel administration during which Macarthur could make hay while the sun shone in New South Wales.

Macarthur now drafted orders for HMS *Porpoise* to make the seven- to ten-day voyage to Port Dalrymple to collect Paterson and his family and then bring them back to Sydney. But Macarthur was in no hurry; he would delay Paterson's arrival for as long as reasonably possible. The *Porpoise* did not sail for another month – exactly the time limit stipulated by Paterson in his letter to Johnston – a month from the time his dispatch from Port Dalrymple arrived at Sydney before his agent would seek to charter another ship to come and fetch him. As in all things, Macarthur was pushing the limits of the restrictions placed on him.

During that month-long interregnum, the provisions that Paterson asked for were assembled and a small detachment of military reinforcements and a handful of convicts were assigned to the *Porpoise*'s mission. For Macarthur, the *Porpoise*'s southerly sailing would have the advantage of effectively taking the warship out of Governor Bligh's reach for a time. As for Bligh himself, Macarthur washed his hands of his prisoner – in the dispatch to London, Macarthur noted that Johnston would now leave all arrangements regarding Bligh's return to England for Paterson to decide when he reached Sydney.[171]

On 12 April, as Macarthur was completing the Johnston dispatch for their lordships in London, he received some disturbing news about HMS *Porpoise* from an informant – almost certainly Acting Lieutenant William Ellison, one of the junior officers aboard the ship, who would later prove to be firmly pro-rebel. Macarthur learned that the commander of the *Porpoise*, Lieutenant James Symons, who had displeased Macarthur during the *Brothers* case, was planning to put to sea in the warship, but without carrying out the junta's orders or taking Johnston's dispatches to Colonel Paterson at Port Dalrymple.

That same day, 12 April, Johnston ordered Symons ashore and Acting Lieutenant William Carlile Kent was ordered to transfer from HMAT *Lady Nelson* to take over the command of HMS *Porpoise*. To give Kent's appointment as captain of the *Porpoise* an official air, Johnston presented the young lieutenant with Captain Bligh's written commission from the Admiralty to command the ship, the same commission that Bligh had sent to Johnston months before in support of his claim to the *Porpoise*.

Young Symons obeyed Major Johnston's orders, and gave up the ship and came ashore. A week later, on 19 April, Lieutenant Kent sailed the *Porpoise* out of Sydney on the mission to resupply Port Dalrymple and collect Colonel Paterson and his party.

The *Brothers* was due to depart for England any day, but at the last moment Surgeon Harris claimed to be too ill to travel. 'Very conveniently,' thought Macarthur.[172] A replacement courier had to be found, and Macarthur chose Lieutenant Minchin for the job. 'Not from any confidence placed in him,'[173] so Macarthur was to reveal to Captain Piper. Like Bayly and his clique, the efficient adjutant of the Corps had also quickly fallen out with Macarthur since the coup. He too had generated Macarthur's displeasure during the *Brothers* case. Now Minchin was being dispensed with. The junta had become very shaky indeed.

The three outward-bound ships sailed from Sydney, starting with the *Brothers* on 1 May, removing some of Macarthur's rebel opponents from the long-playing coup drama – Minchin in the *Brothers*, Grimes in the *Dart* under the watchful eye of Macarthur's son Edward, and John Blaxland in the *Rose*. In May, Macarthur wrote to his friend Piper, 'I am sorry to report that some of your old acquaintances have behaved most scurvily – Abbott amongst the worst.' Macarthur went on to mention that Minchin and Grimes had been sent home with dispatches, and to detail his problems with Bayly. 'In short, if I exempt Kemp, Lawson and Draffin, there is not a man that affords Johnston the least support, and most of them oppose everything.' He lamented that all these men had given their pledge to support Johnston when they'd called on him to assume the government of the colony. 'Pretty pledge, you will say!'[174]

From Government House, William Bligh also watched the three ships set sail. He had reason to feel some satisfaction as he watched the last of them, the *Rose*, up anchor and sail with a May tide. The loyalty to Bligh of the ship's part-owner, Robert Campbell, had never wavered, even though the rebel administration did everything in its power to make business difficult for him. Via Campbell, Bligh had smuggled two letters to the master and co-owner of the *Rose*, Captain Richard Brooks. One letter, dated 30 April, just days after the nineteenth anniversary of the mutiny on the *Bounty*, was addressed to Secretary of State, Lord Castlereagh. It described Bligh's latest overthrow and his continuing arrest, and outlined his plans to gain command of HMS *Porpoise* to counter the rebels.

Governor Bligh's second letter concerned John Blaxland. As the *Rose* left the colony and headed for Cape Town, Blaxland, on board, had no idea that the ship's captain was carrying this letter. Addressed to the British commander at the Cape Colony, it asked for Blaxland to be placed under arrest for participating in his illegal overthrow. If Bligh's luck held, within a month the belligerent Blaxland would be under military arrest and in irons in the bowels of a Royal Navy ship at Cape Town. Blaxland would, Bligh hoped, be the first rebel of many to meet their comeuppance.

9

Enemies Within, Enemies Without

On 11 April, while Macarthur was composing the dispatch that would go to London in Johnston's name, other letter writers were also hard at work. At Green Hills, former magistrate Foolish Tom Arndell had rediscovered his courage, and with a group of other Hawkesbury settlers he penned and signed a letter addressed to Major Johnston calling for Macarthur's removal.

Quite accurately summing up the situation his letter said, in part: 'The whole government appears to be put in the hands of John Macarthur Esq., who seems a very improper person, he having been a turbulent and troublesome character, constantly quarrelling with His Majesty's Governors and other principal officers from Governor Phillip to Governor Bligh, and we believe him to be the principal agitator and promoter of the present alarming and calamitous state of the colony'.[175]

Six days later, two more letters were delivered to Johnston. Both denounced Macarthur, with one declaring, 'We believe John Macarthur has been the scourge of this colony by fermenting quarrels between His Majesty's officers, servants and subjects. His monopoly and extortion have been highly injurious to the inhabitants of every description.' It went on: 'We most earnestly pray that the said John Macarthur may be removed from the said office of Colonial Secretary.'[176]

Unlike the settlers' letter, both of these latest missives were unsigned, but Johnston and Macarthur knew from their wording that they had originated with Macarthur's opponents within rebel ranks. At this point, Harris, Grimes, Blaxland, Minchin and Symons had yet to set sail for England, and all but Minchin knew that they had been designated to make the trip. Some or all of these gentlemen had probably been behind these letters, together with Gregory Blaxland and his cohort, Simeon Lord. As Macarthur was to write to Piper, the only men he now could count on were Kemp, Lawson and Draffin, suggesting that a whole coterie of other military and civil officers could have been behind these letters. It was time for Macarthur to make a fresh stand against his opponents.

In February, Macarthur had managed to foil the Bayly–Blaxcell plot by using Major Johnston, and he turned to the same saviour to terminate this latest counter-revolution. Many historians through the years have puzzled at the hold that Macarthur had over 'Jack Bodice's tool', as Johnston was then being called in some quarters.[177] But it's not hard to imagine the conversations that passed between the persuasive Macarthur and the passive Johnston during these months. In his requisition to Johnston calling on him to overthrow Bligh, Macarthur had promised to support the Major with his fortune and his life. Now, he would have pointed to the likes of Harris, the Blaxlands and Lord, and asked Johnston if he thought those gentlemen would stay by their pledge to support the Major with their fortunes and their lives.

Difficult times might lie ahead for Johnston, the figurehead of the coup. Expensive times. Macarthur would have assured Johnston that if they stuck together, Macarthur would support Johnston to his last guinea – a phrase he was fond of using. Johnston's alternative, that of siding with the belligerent Blaxlands and their cronies against an unforgiving Macarthur, was suicidal, in more ways than one. Johnston had hitched his star to Macarthur's, and there was no turning back. On 26 April, nine days after the two latest protest letters had been delivered to Major Johnston, all the military and civil officers at Sydney were summoned to a meeting with him. There, Johnston read the assembled officers a very crafty letter – which was no doubt written by Macarthur. As they stood before him, Johnston issued Macarthur's opponents with a challenge.

'Those officers who have anything to allege against that gentleman [Macarthur] may come forward and distinctly state in writing what it is they have to charge him with. If he has committed any offence, it is not my intention to shut my ears against the proof of it. If anything improper in his conduct can be made to appear, he shall be immediately dismissed from his office.' He then proceeded to lavish praise on Macarthur for the job he was doing, without pay, including detecting 'the frauds and oppressions of the late Governor'.[178] Macarthur, said Johnston, had faithfully carried out his wishes to reduce the expenditure of public money and to prevent the improper distribution of public servants and property. 'Perhaps these are his offences' – to restrict the distribution of the spoils. 'If so, let me assure you that he has only obeyed my orders.'[179] Johnston suggested that the officers think about what he had told them.

The Major's challenge dared Macarthur's rebel opponents to put up or shut up. If they stood up, individually, and attacked Macarthur, the Johnston letter made it clear they would also be attacking Johnston, the military commandant and Lieutenant Governor. This entailed the clear risk of court martial for military officers and a civil court appearance for the others. They didn't have to think long. A written reply soon came back, to say that the signatories did not question Johnston's right to consult any person he liked, and declared that they would take pleasure in obeying his orders. This letter, possibly drafted in advance by Macarthur and quite probably proposed to the gathered officers by his ally, Captain Kemp, was signed by every military and civil officer in Sydney bar three – the doctors of the medical department, Harris, Jamieson and Mileham. The counter-revolution melted away before the Major's eyes.

The first letter of protest against Macarthur, from Foolish Tom Arndell and other Hawkesbury settlers, had even less impact on Johnston. George Caley, a Parramatta settler and noted naturalist who had not signed that protest because he feared being hauled into court by Macarthur on an invented charge, was to say, after Arndell and his compatriots failed to receive a response to their letter, 'Finding it would be at the hazard of a prosecution, they gave up their hopes as fruitless.'[180] Further attempts to remove Macarthur went underground.

As word spread through the colony that Lieutenant-Colonel Paterson was intending to come up from Van Diemen's Land to take charge at Sydney, at the Hawkesbury pro-Bligh residents Dr Martin Mason and George Suttor covertly put their heads together to draft an address to Paterson. They wanted to leave the Colonel in no doubts about the true feelings of the majority of settlers when he arrived in Sydney. Suttor had always been on good terms with Paterson who, being an avid naturalist, had given Suttor several orange trees that had become the foundation of Suttor's small orange orchard at Baulkham Hills. That connection, Suttor hoped, would help him win Paterson's ear when he arrived, and help him convince the Colonel to deal with Macarthur and restore Governor Bligh to power. As the months passed, Suttor and Mason continued to hone their address, waiting for the day that Paterson arrived. For all his faults, they felt, Lieutenant-Colonel Paterson was not a bad man at heart; they could not imagine that he would support the illegal overthrow and continued detention of Governor Bligh.

10

Revolutionary Justice

While the convoluted legal case involving the *Brothers* had been going on, other court cases had been instigated by John Macarthur's rebel administration, cases designed to punish members of Governor Bligh's camp who had previously crossed Macarthur.

Macarthur was particularly fixated on George Crossley, the former London attorney. Now fifty-nine, Crossley had practised as a lawyer in London for twenty-four years before being convicted of perjury – he had lied in court about a dead man's signature on a will, to benefit the widow – and was transported to New South Wales for seven years in 1796. In London, Crossley had married Anna Marie Divine, a sister of Nicholas Divine, Sydney's Superintendent of Convicts, and had paid for her to accompany him on the convict transport that brought him to New South Wales. Pardoned by Bligh's predecessor Governor King, Crossley had run a shop with his wife in Sydney for a number of years and had an 800 acre (320 hectare) property at the Hawkesbury. Because of his legal training and experience, from time to time Crossley was consulted by locals on legal matters; even, it would be said, by John Macarthur.[181]

When Richard Atkins was Judge Advocate, having no legal background whatsoever, he sometimes employed Crossley to write indictments, with the Governor's approval. It was Crossley who wrote the indictment that had brought Macarthur to trial in Sydney on 25 January. As far as Macarthur was concerned, this had made Crossley a marked man, in the same league as Chief Constable Oakes, who had attempted to arrest Macarthur; and Provost Marshal Gore, who had succeeded in arresting him. On 25 January, the day before the coup, Macarthur the backroom lawyer had been railing against Crossley being consulted by Judge Advocate Atkins in his case. Macarthur detested men who had been convicts. It offended his elevated sense of honour to deal with such people. But he had a more pragmatic motive for going after Crossley in January 1808.

Determined to trap Governor Bligh, Macarthur had used Atkins' employment of Crossley as one of his objections against Atkins sitting in the Macarthur case. In one of his legal books, Macarthur had found an English law, Act 12 George I, that made it unlawful for attorneys convicted of a crime to later practise as an attorney or agent in court in England. Using flowery language, Macarthur, in stating his 25 January objections to Atkins, had claimed that, under that law, Crossley had committed a crime in advising Atkins. This wasn't true; Crossley had merely been employed to assist Atkins, an officer of the court, with legal wording and points of law in court documents; he had not appeared in court. Furthermore, the act specifically applied to England, not to other parts of the kingdom or its dependencies. But this hadn't stopped Macarthur. Once he'd learned, from Robert Campbell's statement to a revolutionary committee, that Crossley had advised both Atkins and Governor Bligh at Government House on 25–26 January, he claimed that Bligh was also acting both unethically and illegally.

As soon as his own case was cleaned up with his acquittal on 7 February, Macarthur brought on a prosecution in the Criminal

Court against Crossley under Act 12 George I. Crossley was seized at his Hawkesbury property, dragged into Sydney and thrown into the County Jail. After a brief hearing before Acting Judge Advocate Charles Grimes and a bench made up of Captain Kemp and Lieutenants Minchin, Moore, Laycock, Lawson, and Symons, Crossley was convicted for acting as an attorney in contravention of the Act, and sentenced to seven years' transportation. He was sent in chains to the miserable Coal River mines at Newcastle.

Bligh, at Government House, was only just digesting this unpleasant news, when more tidings arrived to alert him that Macarthur's reprisals against Bligh loyalists would not stop with Crossley. Provost Marshal William Gore was next on Macarthur's list.

On 7 February, the day of Macarthur's acquittal, Acting Judge Advocate Grimes had advised dismissed Provost Marshal Gore, who continued as a prisoner in the County Jail, that the Criminal Court would sit next day to hear a case against him. The charge was of perjuring himself when he had told the Criminal Court on 26 January that Macarthur had escaped custody – the court of six officers claimed they had lawfully extended Macarthur's bail. Gore replied to Grimes that he hadn't even yet been committed for trial, a small technicality that had escaped Grimes' attention. Consequently, on 1 March, Gore was brought before a bench of magistrates for a committal hearing, where Macarthur himself appeared as Prosecutor. Captain Kemp gave evidence that Gore had illegally arrested and imprisoned Macarthur on 26 January after the court had granted Macarthur an extension of his bail. But a surprising witness now stepped forward in Gore's defence.

One of the colony's most colourful inhabitants at this time was Sir Henry Brown Hayes, an eccentric and wealthy Irish gentleman. This former Sheriff of Cork, popularly known as Sir Harry Hayes, had been transported to the colony for abducting a beautiful young heiress and forcing her to marry him. After arriving in New South Wales, Hayes had received a full pardon, and had purchased a 145-acre (54 hectare) waterfront property, Vaucluse Estate, ten kilometres east of Sydney Town, from Lieutenant Thomas Laycock's father. Sir Harry lived a very private life, rarely venturing into Sydney. On one of the occasions that he did get into a small boat to make the trip around the harbour to Sydney Cove, he had joined the court house gallery on 25 January to witness the trial of John Macarthur. And there, he'd heard a curious thing.

Sir Harry had heard Macarthur declare to the six officers sitting on the Criminal Court, after Judge Advocate Atkins had stormed out, that he declined bail and requested the officers to give him a military guard against the armed constables of the town, as he would only feel safe in the hands of the military. Dressed eccentrically and with a flowing moustache which he had vowed never to cut, Sir Harry now testified under oath as to what he had heard Macarthur say. This supported Gore's case that Macarthur had not been granted bail at the time the court ceased to lawfully sit. Sir Harry didn't stop there; as he left the court house, he told the officers of the Corps who were present that they would all hang as traitors for deposing Governor Bligh. Hayes' testimony rocked the court for a moment, before the officers on the bench composed themselves and, ignoring Hayes' statement, announced that sufficient evidence existed to prove that Macarthur had been granted bail and that Gore had perjured himself. They committed Gore to stand trial before the Criminal Court on 21 March, and returned him to the County Jail.

Several days later, Sir Harry Hayes was just sitting down to dinner in his modest stone house beside the water at Vaucluse when an armed constable walked in. Without a warrant, Sir Harry was taken away in handcuffs. Without a trial, Sir Harry was shipped up the coast to Newcastle. Without a sentence, he was kept locked up in a single-roomed hut at the Coal River penal settlement.

On the 21st, the Gore trial began in the Criminal Court, now without Sir Harry's testimony for the Defence. The Criminal Court comprised Acting Judge Advocate Grimes; Captain Abbott; Lieutenants Moore, Laycock and Draffin; and two naval officers who were cooperating with the rebels, Acting Lieutenants Kent and Ellison from HMS *Porpoise*. Moore, Laycock and Draffin had all sat on the 25–26 January case and had alleged that Gore had perjured himself, yet they were now also sitting at his trial for that alleged perjury. For a variety of reasons, the court was not legally constituted, but that did not bother the rebels, not even Captain Abbott – his misgivings about Macarthur's rule had not translated into a refusal to obey Major Johnston's orders to sit on the Criminal Court.

Provost Marshal Gore immediately objected to the hearing, in writing, on the basis that Major Johnston had no legal authority to convene courts in the capacity of Lieutenant Governor. Acting Judge Advocate Grimes cleared the courtroom, and Gore was then told the trial would continue, and was asked if he objected to any of the members of the court. Gore objected to the two naval officers, believing them to be too junior to sit in the Criminal Court. He also objected to Captain Abbott, feeling, from something that Abbott had said, that he had prejudged him. Grimes, the former Surveyor-General, was totally out of his depth. Unsure how to handle Gore's objections, he adjourned the hearing and remanded Gore back to his cell.

In the meantime, the *Brothers* dispute was coming to a head, and on 5 April, before the Criminal Court could be reconvened to hear Gore's case, Macarthur sacked Grimes from the post of Acting Judge Advocate. It wasn't until 28 May that Macarthur found a replacement for Grimes; on that day he appointed Captain Anthony Fenn Kemp to be Acting Judge Advocate. It would be said that Kemp only agreed to accept the role when no other remotely suitable candidate had put up his hand, and that he was not prepared to do the job indefinitely.[182]

Kemp's appointment, enabling the court to once more sit in criminal cases, didn't come a day too soon, according to settler George Caley. Up to this point, Caley had tried to remain neutral. He had tolerated the overthrow of the Governor, had witnessed the celebrations at Parramatta following the coup. And he had seen Chief Constable Oakes' family and other Bligh supporters at Parramatta terrorised by the rebels: 'Some of His Majesty's subjects were exposed to the grossest insults, with the danger of their lives.'[183] He had watched junta favourites Hobby, Fitz and others throw their weight around. Trying to stay on the fence, Caley had not signed either the rebel requisition to Johnston or the Fitz–Hobby address, but neither had he signed Arndell's letter of protest.

It took a crime wave to erupt in the colony in April for Caley to realise that evil flourishes when good men remain silent. He who is silent gives consent, as the ancient Romans said. This crime wave, involving 'numerous thefts and robberies which have of late been committed', was attributed by Caley to the fact there was no Judge Advocate in the colony.[184] This situation made a mockery of the junta's claim that they had acted on 26 January to safeguard law and order in the colony. In May, Caley sent an open letter to Sir Joseph Banks in England, describing the situation in rebel-run New South Wales and bewailing the administration of Johnston and Macarthur and the chaos that had ensued since their coup. Even John Macarthur was numbered among those who suffered in this crime wave. In Sydney on 16 May, a convict freed by the rebel administration helped forty others escape, and the escapees seized Macarthur's brig *Harrington*, which lay empty in the harbour after unloading a large shipment of spirits. The convicts set sail, and got clean away. The *Harrington* would be recaptured by a British frigate fifteen months later in Philippine waters.

Now that Captain Kemp was Acting Judge Advocate, the Criminal Court once again sat. No one seemed to notice that for the past two months the junta had acknowledged that the Criminal Court could not legally sit without a Judge Advocate, yet it had endorsed and acted upon the declarations of the six officers of the Criminal Court of 25–26 January who had continued to sit without Judge Advocate Atkins. On 30 May, the case against Governor Bligh's chief enforcer was reconvened in the Orphan School courtroom, with Kemp now in the Judge Advocate's chair, despite the fact that he had been chief witness for the prosecution in the committal hearing for this same case two months before. To complete the farce, four of the officers on the bench – Moore, Laycock, Lawson and Draffin, had been involved in the complaint against Gore. And, despite Gore's objection, Captain Abbott was back as senior officer on the bench.

The gallery was filled to overflowing. Provost Marshal Gore, not a popular figure with rowdy soldiers and larcenous ex-convicts, had attracted a crowd eager to see him humbled by the rebel court. Nor was he popular with the elite. Garnham Blaxcell in particular would enjoy seeing Gore on the receiving end of colonial justice, rebel-style. During the tenure of Governor King, Blaxcell had himself served as the colony's Provost Marshal, and he'd wanted to stay on in the role once King returned to England. King had recommended that Blaxcell retain his job under Governor Bligh, but London had appointed Gore instead.

From the Judge Advocate's table, the harsh-voiced Captain Kemp called for silence. Known for his quick temper, Kemp was not popular with his fellow officers; it would even be noted in the official regimental record that he had a 'cruel' nature.[185] Once the crowd had hushed, Kemp read the indictment. Then he asked Gore for his plea. Standing in the dock, tall, thin and pale, Gore felt inside his hat, where he'd hidden prepared notes so they couldn't be taken from him by his guards. 'I have a few observations to make. I believe I have them in my hat.'

'We do not wish you to say anything,' Kemp retorted impatiently. 'We do not wish you to speak. Are you guilty, or not guilty?'

'I deny your jurisdiction,' Gore then firmly declared.

'We are not to be harangued by you, Mr Gore!' raged Kemp. 'We are not come here for you to harangue us!'

Gore folded his arms. 'I will not plead. I deny your jurisdiction.'

'It is not for you to deny our jurisdiction. I will pass sentence on you if you will not plead.'

'You are an unlawful assembly, and illegally constituted.' Gore looked along the line of red-coated officers on the bench. 'The most disgraceful, the most rigorous sentence you can pronounce on me I shall receive as the greatest honour you can confer on me. I shall not acknowledge your authority. I deny your jurisdiction.'

Now Captain Abbott, senior officer on the bench, interjected. Sounding unnerved by Gore's declaration, which Abbott knew was fully justified, he told Gore that he could challenge the right of any member of the court to sit in judgment on him, as if that might somehow legitimise this kangaroo court.

'No!' Gore returned. 'Possessing my fealty and my allegiance to my King, I deny your jurisdiction. I will not plead! For you are an unlawful assembly!'

The gallery erupted in uproar.

'Clear the court!' bellowed Anthony Fenn Kemp. 'Clear the court!'

The courtroom was cleared, Gore was removed, and the members of the court went into a huddle. Twenty minutes later, the case resumed. The audience trooped back in, and Gore was once more installed in the dock. Kemp now announced that the court had recorded that Gore refused to plead.

'I have,' said Gore with satisfaction. 'I do.'

'And,' said Kemp, 'we have sentenced you to be transported for seven years.'

Gore looked at Kemp, and nodded. 'You have conferred on me the greatest honour you are capable of conferring, the only honour I could receive from such men.' Gore sounded proud to accept the sentence. 'Loyalty and treason could not unite. Treason and loyalty could not associate, could not agree . . .'

'Take him away!' yelled Kemp, cutting Gore short. 'Take him off!' His voice was rising, making him sound almost demented. 'Take him away! Take him away!'[186]

Five days later, William Gore was removed from the County Jail cell where he'd spent the past four months and, in chains, was put aboard a ship heading north for the Coal River penal settlement.

When Governor Bligh heard of Gore's sentence, he was to lament, 'Thus they have treated a loyal officer of the Crown who had always done his duty with attention and great humanity.'[187] This assessment was at odds with the picture that the rebels and their sympathisers strove to paint of Gore, then and later – that of an odious, devious, sinister character. Yet never once were the rebels able to prove that Gore had acted illegally, cruelly, vindictively or corruptly during Bligh's governorship. But the kangaroo court convictions of Gore and Crossley and the harsh sentences handed down against them, while wholly illegal, helped contribute to the impression Macarthur was trying to create about Bligh: that the Governor had surrounded himself with a bunch of crooks.

Before long, Gore would be joined in the coal mines by a creative critic of the junta. Lawrence Davoren was accused of writing a scurrilous but witty song that lampooned the entire rebel hierarchy. The 'Song on the New South Wales Rebellion' was written anonymously, but it was traced to Davoren, an ex-convict handy with a pen who had originally been transported for forgery. Davoren was hauled into the rebel court, convicted, given 100 lashes, then sent to the Coal River for seven years. Other critics of the junta and supporters of Governor Bligh would suffer equally rough justice in the coming months. The pages of the *Sydney Gazette*, which Macarthur was now publishing regularly with his name in the banner as authoriser, became a catalogue of court sentences that were 'extremely severe'.[188]

Meanwhile, if someone within the rebel ranks wavered, Macarthur had ways of bringing them back into line. He must have heard that Robert Fitz, the Deputy Commissary at the Hawkesbury, was becoming close to Bligh supporter Dr Martin Mason, for Fitz suddenly found his books and himself being 'examined' by agents of the Secretary to the Colony. This was enough to bring Fitz back into the fold. He would go on to become a rebel stalwart, and receive his due rewards.

As the winter of 1808 loomed, Bligh, meanwhile, was fretting away empty, ineffectual days as a prisoner at Government House. The disputes between the members of the rebel junta had resulted in several of them being ejected from the colony, but Macarthur was still in firm control of New South Wales. Bligh knew that his own account of the coup, smuggled out of the colony by Captain Brooks in May, would generate action by the Secretary of State in London, but he also knew that it would take as long as eighteen months for that report to reach His Lordship at Whitehall and before a military expedition could be subsequently mounted and transported from the British Isles to remove the rebel regime in New South Wales. He was not prepared to wait that long. If Bligh was to be reinstated sooner rather than later, it would have to be through his own actions, and with the help of the military and/or civilians in the colony. All his thoughts were now focused on this course.

11

The Foveaux Factor

May was almost over, and Lieutenant-Colonel Paterson had not come up from Van Diemen's Land, despite his declaration in March that he planned to do so without delay. Lieutenant Kent had arrived back in Sydney with HMS *Porpoise* to say that Colonel Paterson declined to leave the Tamar after all. It seems that Macarthur's friend Walter Davidson had succeeded in dissuading Paterson from making the trip. Later, it would emerge that Paterson had been told that Governor Bligh had conspired with his supporters in Sydney to kidnap Paterson the moment he stepped ashore at Sydney Cove.[189] That certainly had the desired effect; jelly-legged Colonel Paterson no longer had any intention of leaving Van Diemen's Land.

This was both a blessing and a curse for Macarthur. He could do without Paterson's presence, but another potential replacement for Major Johnston as Lieutenant Governor was looming nearer with each passing day. Joseph Foveaux had originally come out to New South Wales in 1791 as a captain in the New South Wales Corps. Promoted to Major, he had spent most of his posting as commandant of Norfolk Island. In 1804 he had returned to England because of severe asthma and to attend to family business. In late 1807, the Secretary of State in London had sent a dispatch to Governor Bligh informing him that Foveaux, newly promoted to Lieutenant-Colonel, would set sail in the new year for a return to New South Wales.

Foveaux's orders from London, drafted prior to the coup, were to report to Governor Bligh at Sydney and then take command once more at Norfolk Island, if settlers remained there, replacing Captain Piper. If the island had been fully abandoned, as London hoped, Foveaux was ordered to become military commandant at Sydney. At this time some settlers were still on Norfolk Island, despite the government's attempts to convince them all to move to Van Diemen's Land because of the difficulties in supplying the island. It would not be completely abandoned until February 1814. Later, in an episode with an ironic Bligh connection, descendants of *Bounty* mutineers would be relocated to Norfolk Island from Pitcairn Island.

If Foveaux obeyed his orders from London, he would continue on to Norfolk Island after making a stopover at Sydney. But Macarthur knew Foveaux well. Foveaux had a head for business, and did not let rules and regulations hinder him. On Norfolk Island, Foveaux had sold female convicts to settlers, which was quite illegal, and had hanged riotous convicts without bothering to give them a trial.[190] Foveaux had also quickly developed several land grants on the mainland. So much so that his flocks of sheep had been the largest in New South Wales. On his 1804 return to England, he'd sold Macarthur his land and his sheep. Macarthur now had good reason to suspect that the opportunistic Foveaux would ignore his orders to go to Norfolk Island and find an excuse to take the command at Sydney from Johnston, his military subordinate.

Macarthur was by this time deeply depressed, as a letter to his friend Captain Piper of 24 May reveals. He had survived the multiple attempts to unseat him by his former allies, but he had lost the *Harrington*. His daughter Elizabeth was once more seriously ill, seemingly 'with little or no chance of recovery'.[191] His wife Elizabeth, aged forty-one, was in the last stages of a difficult pregnancy and was not at all well. And now Macarthur had to look forward to the arrival of Foveaux, a man he could not control. 'If Foveaux arrives safe there will be a pretty scenery here,' Macarthur told Piper. 'One Governor in arrest, and two rival lieutenant governors laying claim to the command.'[192]

Governor Bligh had also calculated that Foveaux must soon arrive, and he had high hopes that the Lieutenant-Colonel would restore him to office and arrest the leading rebels. Bligh was unaware that Foveaux, a man he had never met, was his enemy, just as Foveaux, who had been at sea since February, had no idea that Bligh had been overthrown by a coup. Unbeknownst to Bligh, in England the previous year Foveaux had joined attempts to have Bligh recalled and a new governor appointed by the Secretary of State. There had in fact been a major campaign waged against Bligh in England in late 1807, after he had been in the colony for little more than a year.

The catalyst for that campaign had been the court martial of Captain Joseph Short, originally the commander of HMS *Porpoise* when it escorted Governor Bligh's convoy to Australia in 1806. On the way out to Australia, where he'd intended to settle, the ill-tempered Captain Short had behaved extremely rudely to Bligh, and had long-running disputes with two subordinate officers, Lieutenant J. S. Tetley and the Master of the *Porpoise*, Daniel Lyle. Those two officers took Short before a Court of Enquiry in Sydney, which found against Short. Short had then laid counter charges against Tetley and Lyle, and again lost. Bligh then ordered Short home to face a court martial, and sent Tetley and Lyle to England to testify against him. Adding to Short's burgeoning hate of Bligh was the fact that on the voyage home, Short's wife and child both died. The Short Court Martial had become the focus for the

1807 campaign against Bligh, as Bligh was about to learn.

The ship bringing Lieutenant-Colonel Foveaux to Australia was also bringing Bligh a letter from his devoted wife Betsy, written in February, just before the ship sailed. In an earlier letter, sent to Bligh via the transport *Lady Madeleine Sinclair* the previous year, Betsy had told her husband that she was hearing worrying reports about the upcoming Short trial. 'You will now see my love,' Mrs Bligh wrote in the latest letter, 'that the alarm I felt when I wrote to you by the *Sinclair* was not without foundation. For thank God your enemies have not gained their ends. Their only wish was to have you recalled.'[193]

Mrs Bligh went on to recount how a conspiracy had taken place between Captain Short; former governor of New South Wales, Admiral John Hunter; Philip Gidley King, Bligh's immediate predecessor as governor; and Royal Navy officer Captain William Kent. Kent, who was the nephew of Admiral Hunter, had served in New South Wales for a number of years. He still had land and stock in the colony, managed by his agent, who happened to be Surgeon John Harris, but had sold much of his livestock and his grand mansion in Sydney to the government before he returned to England. Ironically, at the urging of Colonel Paterson's wife Elizabeth, Kent's mansion had become the government Orphan School, whose assembly hall had since been doubling as the Sydney court house, centre of the Bligh–Macarthur overthrow drama and scene of rebel kangaroo courts in the period since.

'Kent went down to Portsmouth in the same chaise as King,' Betsy Bligh wrote to her husband, 'and at Hunter's lodgings with Short planned the business – Foveaux was very active against you.' She also reported that the president of the Short Court Martial, Admiral Sir Isaac Coffin, 'went the greatest lengths against you'.[194]

It turned out that Admiral Coffin was pushing for his friend Captain Kent to replace Bligh as Governor of New South Wales.

Captain Kent had previously applied for the post of Norfolk Island commandant and then sought appointment as deputy to Governor Bligh; the Colonial Office had not been impressed with Kent, and both applications had been turned down. Kent was not the only man with his eyes on Bligh's job. At the same time, unaware of his nephew's covert ambitions for the job, elderly ex-governor Hunter was urging his friends to push Secretary of State Lord Castlereagh to reappoint him as Governor of New South Wales.[195]

There were two other contenders in this undeclared race. In an approach to the Duke of Clarence, son of King George III, ex-governor King agitated for his own reappointment, at a fifty per cent increase on Bligh's salary.[196] King chose the wrong man to lobby – the Duke, it would later transpire, was a supporter of Bligh. To stir the pot even more, General Francis Grose, former commanding officer of the New South Wales Corps, also put up his hand for Bligh's job.[197] Another report had it that ex-governor King was trying to have Bligh replaced by a civilian.[198] As the astute Mrs Bligh had warned her husband, the vultures had been circling.

Just the same, even though Captain Short had won his court martial, with a recommendation for compensation (which did not eventuate) from court president Admiral Coffin, Captain Kent's friend, all the clamour in England for Bligh's replacement had fallen on deaf ears. The people at the top were well-pleased with the job that Bligh was doing. So much so that the ship bringing Foveaux to the colony was also bringing a dispatch for Bligh from Lord Castlereagh, in which His Lordship said, 'I am to express His Majesty's approbation [approval] of the determination you have adopted to put an end to the barter of spirits, which appears to have been abused, to the great injury and morals of the colony.'[199] This was accompanied by a second dispatch, from the Downing Street office of Castlereagh's deputy minister, Under Secretary of State Edward Cooke, in which the

William Bligh, c.1814, six years after his Sydney overthrow, and by this time an admiral. (Artist unknown; Mitchell Library, State Library of New South Wales)

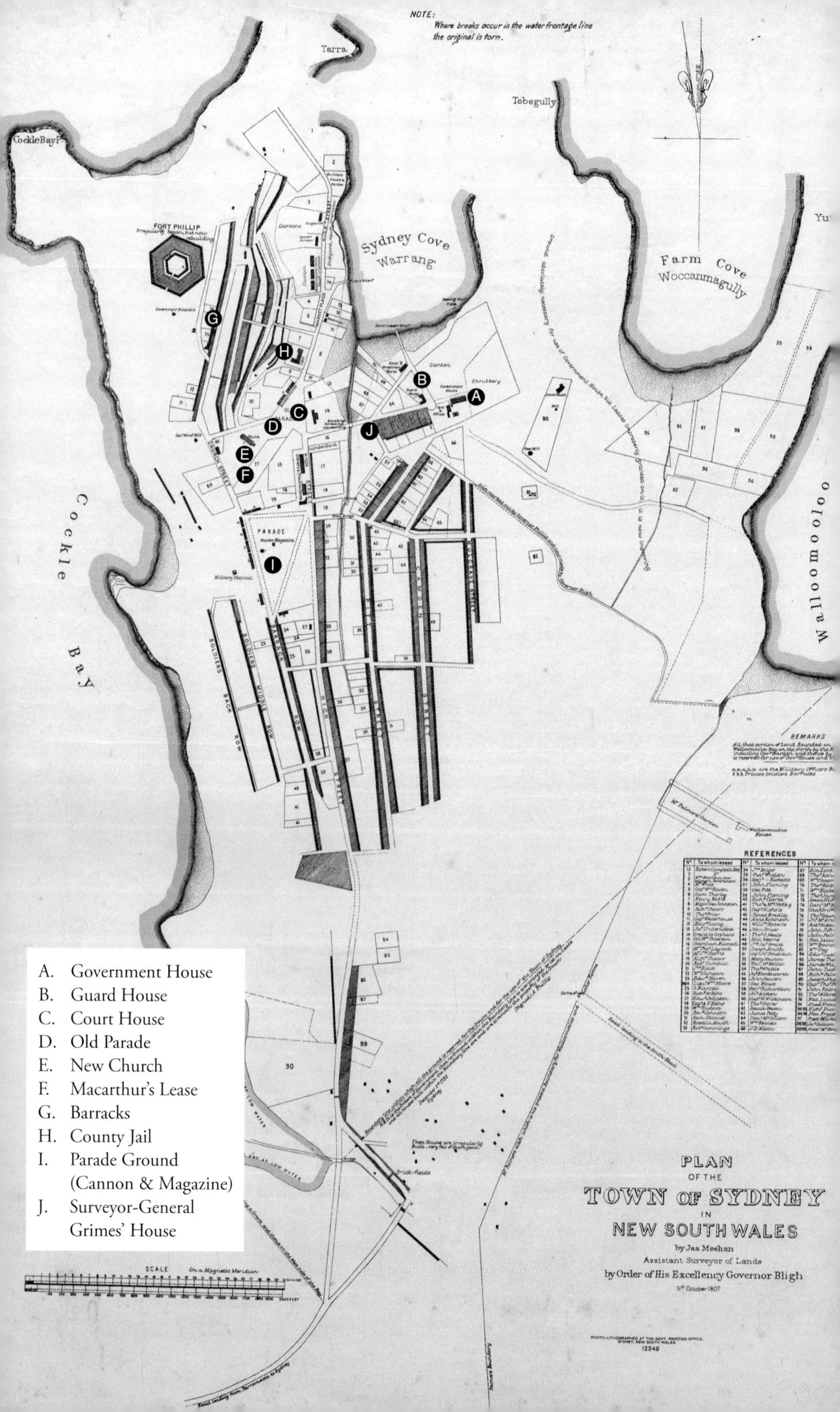

NOTE:
Where breaks occur in the water frontage line the original is torn.
Tarra
Tobegully
Cockle Bay
FORT PHILLIP
Sydney Cove
Warrang
Farm Cove
Woccanmagully
Walloomooloo
Cockle Bay
PARADE
SOLDIERS BACK ROW
SOLDIERS MIDDLE ROW
BARRACK ROW
HIGH STREET
CHURCH STREET
MARKET PLACE
REMARKS
REFERENCES
A. Government House
B. Guard House
C. Court House
D. Old Parade
E. New Church
F. Macarthur's Lease
G. Barracks
H. County Jail
I. Parade Ground (Cannon & Magazine)
J. Surveyor-General Grimes' House
SCALE
PLAN
OF THE
TOWN OF SYDNEY
IN
NEW SOUTH WALES
by Jas. Meehan
Assistant Surveyor of Lands
by Order of His Excellency Governor Bligh
31st October 1807

Mary Putland, Bligh's feisty widowed daughter, who served as his 'first lady' in Australia and shared his imprisonment by the rebels. (Artist unknown; Mitchell Library, State Library of New South Wales)

Facing Page: Map of Sydney in 1808, drawn up by James Meehan for Governor Bligh, and used at the Johnston Court Martial in London. (National Library of Australia, MAP F 105A)

John Macarthur, former New South Wales Corps officer, ambitious colonist, and Bligh's arch foe. (Artist unknown; Dixson Galleries, State Library of New South Wales)

Elizabeth Macarthur, John Macarthur's wife, who very capably managed his interests during Macarthur's extended periods of exile. (Artist unknown; Dixson Galleries, State Library of New South Wales)

The one surviving contemporary illustration of the capture of Governor Bligh during the military coup of 26 January 1808. It depicts the version told by Corporal Michael Marlborough, in which he claimed to have dragged the Governor from beneath a bed – a claim later proved to have been untrue. (Artist unknown; Mitchell Library, State Library of New South Wales)

Government House, Sydney, 1808–1809, by George William Evans. Painted at the time Bligh and his daughter were prisoners inside, it shows armed guards stationed outside and civilian visitors waiting on the veranda for rebel permission to see Bligh. (Mitchell Library, State Library of New South Wales)

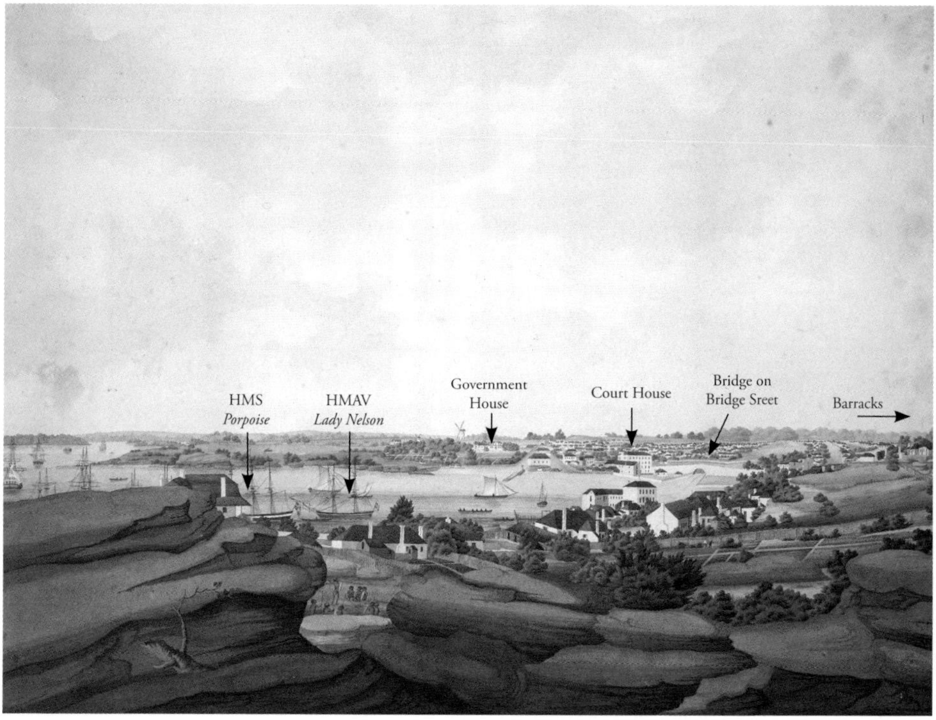

Sydney, 1807, when Bligh was in his second year as Governor, looking east from the Rocks. The larger of the two warships in port is the frigate HMS *Porpoise*, which was instrumental in Bligh's plans to counter the rebels. (Painting attributed to John Eyre; Dixson Library, State Library of New South Wales)

The New Church, Sydney, later the first St Phillips (ie St Philips), used for public meetings during and after the rebel administration between 1808 and 1810. (Painting by J. W. Lewin; Mitchell Library, State Library of New South Wales)

Major, later Lieutenant-Colonel, George Johnston, Sydney commandant of the New South Wales Corps and figurehead of the military coup and subsequent rebel rule. (Painting by Henry Robinson Smith; Mitchell Library, State Library of New South Wales)

Government House, Parramatta, where the junta leaders installed New South Wales Corps commander Lieutenant-Colonel William Paterson in 1809 as the new figurehead of the rebel regime. (Painting by George William Evans; Mitchell Library, State Library of New South Wales)

Lieutenant-Colonel Lachlan Macquarie, sent to New South Wales by the British Government with the 73rd Regiment to terminate the rebellion, arrest the ringleaders, and reinstate Bligh. (Painting by R. Read Senior; Mitchell Library, State Library of New South Wales)

Under Secretary also praised Bligh for regulating the liquor trade, and noted, 'His Lordship hopes there is no officer, or gentleman, or planter in the colony, who will not give you the most cordial assistance.'[200]

At the time of their writing, neither Castlereagh, nor Cooke nor Mrs Bligh were aware that John Macarthur and the New South Wales Corps had achieved with force of arms what Bligh's enemies in England had failed to achieve with force of argument. 'You must be much on your guard,' Betsy Bligh warned her husband in the letter he had yet to receive. Very much awake to the threat that the New South Wales Corps posed to him, she wrote, 'I wish the troops could be changed.' And then she mentioned Lieutenant-Colonel Foveaux again. 'Foveaux is very ill-disposed to you and I hope you will send him to Norfolk Island.'[201]

Lieutenant-Colonel Foveaux arrived at Sydney in the transport *Lady Madeleine Sinclair* on the morning of 28 July 1808. Governor Bligh had seen the flags flying from the signal mast on the rise behind Government House indicating that the ship had passed through Sydney heads, and saw her coming up the harbour. As soon as the *Sinclair* dropped anchor in Sydney Cove, Bligh sent three emissaries out to her to extend his compliments to Lieutenant-Colonel Foveaux and to request that he come to Government House to meet with him at once in private.

The Governor's envoys, Commissary Palmer and Chaplain Fulton, both of whom Foveaux had known previously in the colony, and the Governor's secretary Edmund Griffin, reached the ship only to find that John Macarthur, Major Johnston and Nicholas Bayly had boarded ahead of them. Palmer, Fulton and Griffin were denied permission to board the *Sinclair*, even though they announced that they had come from the Governor. A verbal message was passed on to them that Foveaux was feeling unwell after the long voyage out from England but would meet with Governor Bligh as soon as possible.

Macarthur, Johnston, and Bayly stayed on the ship with Foveaux all day. Bligh, watching from Government House, could only guess that a great deal of discussion, and perhaps argument, was going on between the four men. The journal of Foveaux's secretary, Lieutenant Finucane, indicates that the rebel trio set out to convince Foveaux that they had deposed Bligh for good reasons. Presenting him with a copy of Johnston's April dispatch to London, Macarthur's requisition from the colonists to arrest Bligh, and the address of thanks from settlers, they went through their reasons for leading a military coup, with Macarthur no doubt going into great detail about his trial in the Criminal Court.

Finally, late in the day, the Johnston party came down the side of the ship, clambered into their waiting boat, and came ashore. Foveaux remained on board the *Sinclair* for the night. That evening, there was a flurry of activity in the rebel camp in Sydney, in dread and expectation that Foveaux would choose to take charge and not sail on to Norfolk Island as ordered. Among the last-minute pieces of documentation signed that night by Major Johnston was a land grant of 2000 acres (810 hectares) to George Julian, his eldest son by Esther Julian.

Next morning, Lieutenant-Colonel Foveaux came ashore with his secretary, thirty-three-year-old Irishman Lieutenant James Finucane, and walked up the slope to Government House for the requested meeting with Governor Bligh. Forty-two-year-old Foveaux waddled rather than walked – he was an immensely fat man who ate and drank very well. He paid the penalty for his appetite; he suffered so badly from gout that he had to wear oversized shoes on his swollen feet. Yet, despite his great girth, he was a good-looking man, and would have been considered quite handsome if he were slimmer. At home in Ireland, Foveaux's father was chief steward to the Earl of Upper Ossary, which inspired Lawrence Davoren the lampoon-writer to call Foveaux a 'cub of a cook'.[202] Lieutenant Finucane was to say of his chief, 'The colonel has not the brilliant accomplishments of a statesman nor the highly polished manners of a courtier, but he possesses a plentiful stack of understanding, integrity and humanity.'[203] It would remain to be seen if Foveaux displayed the characteristics with which his loyal secretary credited him.

Inside Government House, Governor Bligh gave the pair a cordial welcome, and the blunt, businesslike Foveaux handed over the dispatches from London addressed to the Governor, and the personal letters the *Sinclair* had brought out for Bligh including the one from his wife warning the Governor against Foveaux. In return, Bligh gave Foveaux a letter in which he formalised a request for the Colonel to 'put himself at the head of the New South Wales Corps' and reinstate Bligh as Governor.[204] Bligh then asked the officers to wait while he read his dispatches and mail. When Bligh resumed the interview, he was armed with Betsy's warning about Foveaux. Hence Bligh changed his tactics. Now he said not a word about his request for Foveaux to reinstate him as Governor. Lieutenant Finucane said of the meeting with the Governor, 'In the long interview we had he did not appear to me to expect that the Colonel would replace the command in his hands, nor did he at all press it.'[205]

Bligh casually pointed out that he had orders from London that Foveaux should resume the command at Norfolk Island, and Foveaux acknowledged that he had the same orders. But Bligh did not let on that he now suspected, as a result of Betsy's letter and from what he now knew of Foveaux, that the Colonel would take control at Sydney. As for Bligh's own plans, Lieutenant Finucane would note, 'He professes an intention of proceeding to England in his own ship the *Porpoise*, as soon as she can be got ready for him.'[206]

Matter-of-factly, Bligh told Foveaux that he would be grateful if the Colonel would ask Lieutenant Kent of the *Porpoise* to meet with him at Government House to discuss those plans. Foveaux, who was anxious to remove Bligh from the colony as soon as possible, and not realising that Macarthur had cut off all contact between Bligh and the officers of the *Porpoise*, with good reason, told Bligh that his request would be met. The meeting ended as amicably as it had begun. There had been no raised voices, and not a single swear word had been uttered.

With his parting words, Foveaux regretted that the Governor's house arrest would have to be continued for the moment, until the situation became clearer to him. Said Lieutenant Finucane of his superior, 'The strange events that have occurred here render it necessary for him to enquire minutely and reflect seriously before he ventures to act.' Lieutenant Finucane left Government House with the impression that the Governor was relieved that Foveaux was not going to order him more closely confined.[207]

Foveaux and Finucane returned to the *Sinclair*, believing they had Governor Bligh's measure. During the afternoon, Foveaux sent a letter ashore to Bligh, telling him that as he had only just arrived in the colony and had yet to fully acquaint himself with the situation that he had found there, he did not feel able to comply with the requests contained in the Governor's letter to him. That night, in darkness, Foveaux and Finucane again came ashore, and went directly to the barracks of the New South Wales Corps. It would seem that the Colonel had completed his 'minute inquiries' and 'serious reflection' in the few hours since he had seen the Governor, for Foveaux now announced that he was assuming command from Major Johnston, and assuming Johnston's title of Lieutenant Governor of New South Wales. Further, the arrest of Governor Bligh would be continued. Foveaux also declared that John Macarthur's position of Secretary to the Colony was no longer necessary and was abolished forthwith. The responsibilities entailed in the post, he said, would now be handled by his secretary, Lieutenant Finucane.

In one fell swoop, Foveaux had superseded Johnston and toppled John Macarthur to become both president and prime minister of this Antipodean 'republican government', as Sir Harry Hayes was to describe the rebel regime from his Coal River incarceration.[208] The printing press at Government House would go into action on 31 July, pumping out a brief edition of the *Sydney Gazette* containing the details of the latest change of government. Foveaux's first General Order, published in the *Gazette*, provided ten gallons of spirits to all licensed liquor sellers, in celebration of his taking power.

Writing in his journal on the night of the 31st, Lieutenant Finucane excused Foveaux's assumption of the governorship, using both the words and spirit of the Johnston dispatch written by Macarthur for London's benefit in April. After just four days in the colony, and based solely on the word of Macarthur and Johnston, Finucane accused Bligh of having 'acted upon a settled plan of enriching himself and his confederates', of 'deterring or influencing the Courts of Justice from pronouncing any judgment in opposition to his views or wishes', and of 'wasteful expenditure of the public stores, a shameful appropriation of the Government stock to his own immediate uses, and the most unjustifiable and often wanton invasion of private property and personal liberty'.[209] It all sounded uncannily like a description of the Johnston–Macarthur regime.

In summing up Governor Bligh's time in the colony, Finucane said it was plain 'that the rapid accumulation of wealth by the plunder, oppression and ruin of the colony was the object of his unceasing exertions'.[210] Macarthur had indeed been persuasive. Finucane was naïve and gullible, as would later become even more apparent, but before long even he began to doubt the Johnston–Macarthur tale about Bligh's plunder of the colony. Some time later, on an inspection of the inland districts with Foveaux, Finucane visited Bligh's property on the Hawkesbury River, Blighton, one of the three land grants Bligh held in the colony in the same way that the previous governors had government land granted to them.

Finucane would say of Bligh and his farm, 'He is charged by Colonel Johnston with having lavished vast sums of the public money' on this property. 'It appeared to me, however, that very little money of any kind had been expended.' Johnston had accused Bligh of using government money to build 'farmhouses, exterior offices etc' on the property. All Finucane could find were a barn, a sheep shed, and a hog sty, all of them in need of repair.[211]

By the time that Finucane and Foveaux had, with their own eyes, seen the claims of Johnston and Macarthur exposed as fabrications, Foveaux was in too deep. He had embraced the rebellion based on these claims, and to publicly admit that Bligh had no case to answer for corruption would have been to destroy one of the bases for Foveaux's assumption of power. As the true picture of the New South Wales Corps' insurrection emerged, Lieutenant Finucane came to realise, to his horror, that he would be considered 'an accessory after the fact' and might well be ordered home to face charges.[212] But in his first weeks in the colony, Finucane genuinely believed that Bligh fitted the picture of a wicked, plundering tyrant that the rebels had painted of him.

Macarthur may well have been able to persuade the young lieutenant to his way of thinking, but Joseph Foveaux was neither naïve nor easily led. Macarthur's attempts to persuade Foveaux to retain him in his position of power failed. Nothing Macarthur could say could change Foveaux's determination to rule the colony alone. Yet Macarthur had several reasons to be happy at this time. In early June, his wife Elizabeth had given birth to their ninth and last child, Emmeline Emily, and both mother and daughter were doing well. Meanwhile, the health of their teenage daughter Elizabeth had improved markedly. None of this good news could compensate for his loss of power now that Macarthur had been deposed as the colony's ruler. He had tried to persuade Foveaux that they could share power, but the new arrival was not interested. According to

Foveaux's secretary Finucane, writing some time later, after he had woken up to him, Macarthur was 'piqued at not being the director of the affairs of the colony, as he was under the nominal government of Johnston'.[213] That Macarthur was piqued was an understatement.

At first, Foveaux attempted to placate Macarthur. Foveaux, who had no authority from London to do so, would prove liberal in the granting of government land to rebels, and five days after assuming power he announced that he was granting a valuable block in Sydney to Macarthur. Foveaux would attempt to excuse this to London by saying that he was swapping the Sydney block for a piece of riverside land of similar size owned by Macarthur at Parramatta, which was 'suitable for a government store'.[214] Macarthur would accept the block of land, but he wanted far more than that. Major Johnston could no longer help him, as he was outranked by Foveaux. Paterson, still in Van Diemen's Land, outranked Foveaux, but Macarthur had convinced Paterson that it would not be a good idea to come to Sydney; that ploy had certainly backfired. Now Macarthur set his mind to convincing Paterson to come up to Sydney after all. His envoy, Walter Davidson, would soon set off back to the Tamar River to work on the colonel.

Lieutenant-Colonel Foveaux, in the meantime, had slipped his bulky rump into the dictator's chair with ease. While he kept a tight rein on public expenditure – something he prided himself on – he didn't end any of the previous rebel practices. The junta still monopolised imports. Wine and spirits were still purchased exclusively by the officers and their friends and were the primary means of payment in the colony. Friends of the regime received convict labour and grants of land. The rebel firm might be under new management but it was business as usual. At the same time, the military dictatorship ruthlessly stamped out opposition to the regime.

It seemed that the only way Macarthur would rid himself

of Foveaux was by shooting him. Back at Elizabeth Farm at Parramatta, and a private citizen once more, Macarthur may well have taken out his duelling pistols and begun to clean them. He would have need of them before long.

12

Prostitutes and Mistresses

As August arrived, William Bligh was seething. Not only had Lieutenant-Colonel Foveaux disobeyed his orders from London – which required him to go on to Norfolk Island and resume command there – he had also ignored Governor Bligh's illegal overthrow and had become implicit in it by taking charge at Sydney as Lieutenant Governor and continuing Bligh's house arrest, which was now into its seventh month. It must have been incomprehensible to Bligh that Foveaux, Macarthur, Johnston and the other officers imagined they would ultimately get away with their treasonous acts.

At first, Foveaux made a concession to Bligh. On 29 July he had agreed to allow Acting Lieutenant Kent, now commanding HMS *Porpoise* at rebel behest, to meet with the Governor at Government House. And he kept his word. At this time Lieutenant Kent was based ashore, as the *Porpoise* was undergoing a refit. Her guns had been lifted out of her,[215] and she had been hauled out of the water and dry-docked on a slip. This was probably at Isaac Nicholls' shipyard at the Rocks; Robert Campbell's shipyard at Kirribilli Point on Sydney harbour's northern shore was Sydney's first and largest shipyard, but being a Bligh supporter, it's unlikely he would have been given any government business.

On the surface, it seems incautious of Foveaux to permit the commander of the *Porpoise* to meet with Bligh. Macarthur had prevented all Royal Navy officers in the colony from having the slightest contact with Bligh, fearing that he would try to convince them to follow his orders rather than those of Major Johnston. And this is just what occurred when Lieutenant Kent went to Government House with Foveaux's approval. The Scottish-born Kent was only twenty years of age. But he had plenty of experience in the colony, having served in Australian waters for the past six years, initially as a fourteen-year-old midshipman. He had sat as a magistrate from time to time during Bligh's governorship, and had dined at Bligh's table.

Young Kent was to say that when he went to Government House on 30 July, on Foveaux's orders, Bligh took him into a room and locked the door. The two versions of the meeting that followed differ greatly. Kent would later say that Bligh abused him for not reinstating him as Governor, was extremely objectionable in his manner, and 'proposed' that the lieutenant should start battering down Sydney with the *Porpoise*'s guns until the rebels surrendered the government to Bligh. Lieutenant Kent would say that he refused to do this, at which Bligh flew into a violent rage and threatened to make him pay for his disobedience.[216] In Kent's version, told three years later, Bligh then merely unlocked the door and let him leave.

Bligh's version of events was that he ordered young Kent not to obey the orders of Major Johnston and to obey him exclusively, and to fly Bligh's broad pennant from the *Porpoise* as a symbol of his command. Bligh did have a hot temper and he could swear like a trooper. He had been reprimanded by a court martial in 1805 for his bad language,[217] and his temper was well known to family and friends. When his wife Betsy had written to him in

February, she had remarked that the Bligh family lawyer, Robert Gatty, of Angel Chambers in London's Throgmorton Street, had 'made a little free with Your Excellency in lecturing you about keeping your temper, but he appears our friend'.[218] Another friend of Bligh, Captain George Tobin, who had sailed as a lieutenant under him when Bligh commanded HMS *Providence* on its completion of the *Bounty*'s breadfruit mission, was to say of him, 'It was in those violent tornadoes of temper when he lost himself.' And, 'Once or twice I felt the unbridled licence of his power of speech, yet never without soon receiving something like an emollient plaister [plaster] to heal the wound.'[219] Bligh himself acknowledged his own 'warmth of temper, which I may at intervals have discovered'.[220]

Clearly then, Bligh could quickly fly off the handle and let go with a torrent of invective until, like a lashing tropical storm, the temper quickly passed. That temper had contributed to Bligh's falling out with his protégé Fletcher Christian aboard the *Bounty*, yet many of those who served under Bligh, like George Tobin, became accustomed to his flare-ups and forgave him for it. When all was going right, said Tobin, never 'could a man be more placid and interesting' than Bligh.[221] Others took exception to his temper and his language, and some took it to heart when he called them 'wretches' and buggers'.[222] Bligh had every reason to fly off the handle as a deposed Governor and prisoner at Sydney. But did he really tell Lieutenant Kent to batter down Sydney until the rebels submitted to him? Later evidence would suggest otherwise.

Once the lieutenant left Government House, Bligh was under the impression that the meeting had gone well, and that Kent would from that point refuse to accept any orders coming from Johnston, allowing Bligh to convince the rebels to permit him to board the *Porpoise* to go home to England, as he had told Foveaux he wished to do. Apart from later evidence in support of Bligh's interpretation of the meeting, there is another reason to suspect the reliability of Lieutenant Kent's account. Bligh had by that point read the letter from his wife in which she had warned him that one of the key players in the conspiracy against him in England, a man who had been trying to win Bligh's job for himself, was Captain William Kent. As Bligh knew, Captain Kent was the uncle of young Lieutenant William Kent.

It is likely that Lieutenant Kent was influenced by his relationship with his uncle, having served under him in the colony and regularly been at his Sydney mansion. Almost certainly, Captain Kent would have written to his nephew in 1807, telling him about the moves in England to unseat Bligh. Conceivably, Captain Kent had also urged Lieutenant Kent to be as uncooperative with the Governor as possible, and to supply unflattering information about Bligh's activities to help the campaign against the Governor in England. During the course of that campaign, Bligh had been accused of using stores from a ship that had come into Sydney from India for his own benefit, a claim that soon dissolved for lack of evidence. It was later assumed that the information on which this claim was based came from ex-governor King. In fact, it is more than likely to have reached Captain Kent from young Lieutenant Kent who, unlike King, was in the colony at the time and was involved in maritime affairs – commanding the *Lady Nelson*.

Despite all this, Bligh gave Lieutenant Kent the benefit of the doubt. Kent was a Royal Navy officer and Bligh's subordinate, and should have obeyed his orders. But the Governor's hopes in him were soon dashed. Bligh's pennant was not hoisted up the *Porpoise*'s mainmast, and young Kent continued to take orders from the rebels. Perhaps Lieutenant-Colonel Foveaux's decision to allow Kent to have an interview with Bligh was not so naïve after all. Foveaux was a clever man, and showed no signs of naïvete in other areas. For one thing, with the *Porpoise* out of the water, even if the young officer had left the meeting with Bligh determined to use the warship to the Governor's benefit, he couldn't; not at once, anyway. But, quite probably, Foveaux knew exactly what Kent's reaction would be to Bligh's overtures to resist rebel orders, because the young man was firmly in the rebel camp, and always had been. In sending Kent to Bligh, Foveaux had been humouring the Governor; toying with him even.

When a week had passed after the Government House meeting with Lieutenant Kent and it had become patently obvious that the young commander of HMS *Porpoise* was not going to obey his orders, Bligh wrote to Lieutenant-Colonel Paterson in Van Diemen's Land, acquainting him of his situation and the fact that Foveaux had not seen fit to release him. He also asked Paterson to intervene and use his seniority as commanding officer of the Corps to reinstate him. Six weeks later, Paterson would reply, telling Bligh that he was unable to act as he had requested and suggesting that the Governor leave the colony as soon as possible and take up the matter with Their Lordships in London.

Those colonists who had hopes that Colonel Foveaux would restore the Governor and deal with the rebels were also sorely disappointed. In August, at Baulkham Hills and Portland Head, settlers came together to discuss what they could do about Foveaux's continuation of rebel rule. They decided to send two delegates to London who would tell the authorities about the true state of affairs in the colony, to describe 'the sufferings and general abuses' under the rebels, and to stress that the settlers had no prior knowledge of the January coup and had only subsequently cooperated with the rebels through 'fear and terror, after the act had been committed'.[223] It was agreed that the delegates were also to urge the home government to send out a large military force to reinstate Bligh as Governor and to arrest and bring to justice those who had overthrown him. The delegates they chose to send to England were Baulkham Hills settler George Suttor and Green Hills surgeon Dr Martin Mason.

Dr Mason prepared to sail on the next ship to London, a sailing which could yet be several months away, and placed an advertisement in the *Sydney Gazette* calling on all creditors to submit their claims to him for payment and for all debtors to pay him what they owed him. In one respect this was a necessary move, for legally he could be prevented from leaving the colony if he had outstanding debts. But the rebels, who had already marked him as an opponent to their regime, were now alerted to his intention to leave the colony.

Governor Bligh learned from settler George Caley, who was now in regular secret contact with him, that the two settler delegates were planning to go to London. So, on 31 August, Bligh sat down to write a letter to Lord Castlereagh for the delegates to carry with them. This letter would inform the Secretary of State of how Lieutenant-Colonel Foveaux had gone over to the rebels. At the same time, Bligh wrote to the Earl of Minto, Governor-General of India, telling him about his predicament and of Lieutenant-Colonel Foveaux's betrayal.

John Macarthur, in the meantime, had not given up on convincing Colonel Paterson to come up from Van Diemen's Land to supersede Foveaux. On Wednesday 17 August, the schooner *Estramina* sailed from Sydney bound for Port Dalrymple. She carried dispatches for Colonel Paterson from Colonel Foveaux, and a passenger, Walter Davidson, who would renew efforts to convince Paterson to come up to Sydney. It seems that Foveaux did not oppose Paterson coming up. He knew how weak the man was, having served under him for years, and believed that he could dominate him and continue to have his own way if they were both in the same location.

Foveaux had quickly settled into the commandant's quarters at Sydney. Major Johnston had gladly vacated the barrack and withdrawn to his homestead at Annandale. Johnston would not learn until later in the year that on 25 April the authorities in London, as yet blithely unaware that he had led a mutiny in New South Wales, had promoted him to Lieutenant-Colonel. From his new quarters, Foveaux finally wrote to Lord Castlereagh in

London, six weeks after illegally taking control of the colony, to tell him what he had done. On 4 September, he put pen to paper to explain to the Secretary of State why he had taken charge at Sydney in contravention of his orders and his legal powers, and why he had kept Bligh under arrest. Since he'd taken the command, he said, he had used every opportunity to determine the truth of just a few of the many accusations that were being made to him against Governor Bligh. To investigate them all, he said, would take years, but, 'I do not hesitate to declare that he has appeared to me, throughout his administration, to have acted upon a settled system of enriching himself, and a few of his necessary agents, at the expense of the interests of His Majesty's Government.'[224]

Commissary Palmer and Robert Campbell would be named by Foveaux as among those 'necessary agents'. Foveaux accused them of profiting from the liquor trade under Governor Bligh. Bligh himself, said Foveaux, 'has been guilty of the most oppressive, and often most wanton attacks on the private property and personal liberty, as well as the most flagrant waste and shameful misapplications of the public stores and revenues of the colony'.[225]

Foveaux didn't stop there. In another letter to the Colonial Office just six days later, he would claim that Governor Bligh had used many convict labourers 'in erecting and ornamenting a residence for one of the several prostitutes whom – notwithstanding his constant profession of religion and morality – he was in the habit of maintaining'.[226] No proof was offered by Foveaux of any of these astonishing accusations. At least Macarthur had gone to the trouble of trying to force statements out of Bligh loyalists to support his claims. Just six weeks into his regime, Foveaux had ventured into a level of muck-raking and wild, unsupportable accusation that not even Macarthur had stooped to.

This extraordinary accusation by Foveaux – that Bligh kept prostitutes – may have had a very personal motivation. It's likely that Governor Bligh had made a cutting remark about the false morality of the senior officers of the New South Wales Corps, who not only took part in military coups against their king but kept mistresses and fathered bastards by them. He would have been referring to Major Johnston. In 1787, while sailing to Australia in the First Fleet aboard the transport *Lady Penrith*, Johnston had spotted a raven-haired, almond-eyed beauty among the female convicts aboard – Esther Abrahams, a twenty-year-old Jewish girl. After the troops and convicts had landed at Sydney Cove on 26 January 1788, Johnston had moved Esther into his quarters, and his bed, and she had been with him ever since. Esther had fallen pregnant while in Newgate Prison prior to the fleet's sailing, and after the child, Rosanna, was born, Johnston raised her in Sydney as his own. He had since fathered six illegitimate children by Esther who, in 1800, changed her last name to Julian, probably because it sounded like Johnston.

Bligh may have made his remark about mistresses and bastards on or about 5 September, probably to Foveaux's secretary Lieutenant Finucane, who reported it to his chief. Since 1793, Foveaux had also kept a mistress, Ann Sherwin. He had taken her from her husband, a sergeant in the New South Wales Corps. Ann was now sharing the commandant's quarters in Sydney with Foveaux, along with their illegitimate seven-year-old daughter, also Ann. In all likelihood, Foveaux had taken Bligh's remark about mistresses and bastards personally. This would explain why he wrote his second venomous dispatch to London just six days after his first, to include the smutty accusation about Bligh and prostitutes. That ludicrous accusation would never again be levelled against Bligh, by Foveaux or anyone else, which also suggests that the reference in the letter of 10 September was merely a knee-jerk reaction on the part of Foveaux. Just the same, Foveaux would leave no stone unturned in his quest for ammunition against the Governor.

Foveaux also turned the screws on Bligh's key supporters. Robert Campbell, Bligh's treasurer, had been in rebel sights from the beginning of the rebellion. For months, during Macarthur's reign as Secretary to the Colony, Macarthur had tried to pin something on Campbell, without success. Then he'd tried to compromise him by instructing him to fill the post of government coroner at Sydney. Campbell had refused to even consider an appointment under the rebel administration. For his defiance, Campbell had been dragged into court by Macarthur and charged with disobeying a lawful order. Like other Bligh loyalists before him, when Campbell came to face his accusers he denied the competency of the rebel court and refused to plead. He was found guilty, and fined £50. The biggest surprise in this episode was that Campbell was not jailed. In late August, Joseph Foveaux also came into conflict with Campbell.

Foveaux was planning to send his first dispatches to London, and when he learned that Campbell's ship, the *Rose*, would again be sailing for Cape Town in early September after returning from her last trip, he advised Campbell that he would be sending a courier aboard, carrying his dispatches. The rebels were still ignorant of the fact that, after the *Rose*'s last trip to Cape Town, John Blaxland had been arrested and Governor Bligh's secret dispatch passed on to London – it had already arrived on the Secretary of State's desk by this time. The master of the *Rose*, Captain Brooks, had not only remained loyal to Governor Bligh, he had come back to Sydney and kept the secret, so that only Bligh and his closest allies, Campbell, Palmer and Griffin, knew that Blaxland was now chained in the brig of a British man o' war, on the way to an English prison. Now, Campbell flatly refused to accept either a rebel courier or rebel dispatches on board the *Rose* for its next sailing to Cape Town.

Foveaux reacted quickly, and characteristically. On 2 September, he announced that he was launching an inquiry into 'suspicious circumstances' surrounding the operation of the *Rose* in waters east of the Cape of Good Hope. Under a British act of parliament, the East India Company had a monopoly on the carriage of goods from India across the Indian Ocean, and Foveaux was implying that on her last voyage the *Rose* had somehow infringed that law. It was a nonsense comparable with John Macarthur's most inventive legal concoctions, but it was excuse enough for Foveaux that same day to send constables aboard the *Rose* to seize her, saying that she was forfeited to the Crown as an illicit trader. The message was clear – Campbell and his co-owners, William Wilson and Captain Brooks, had either to back down or lose the ship.

This piece of blatant blackmail made even Foveaux's secretary James Finucane uneasy. The next day, Finucane noted, with some relief, 'I am glad to find that the difficulties with respect to the *Rose* are arranged, and she is to proceed immediately to England.'[227] Campbell was forced to lodge a bond to gain the ship's release. Foveaux was sending as his courier on the *Rose* young Lieutenant Symons, who had been relieved of the command of the *Porpoise* by Macarthur back in April. The understanding was that, while Captain Brooks would still be her master, the *Rose* would be sailing under the care of Lieutenant Symons. In effect, Foveaux was commandeering the ship for the duration of the voyage. But Campbell would have the last laugh – as the ship sailed out of Sydney heads, Captain Brooks was carrying another secret letter to British authorities from Governor Bligh, requesting the arrest of Lieutenant Symons for leaving the colony without his permission. Like John Blaxland, Symons would also find himself a prisoner the next time he stepped ashore on British soil.

Even though he believed he had won the *Rose* battle, Foveaux was determined to make Campbell pay for his defiance. First, he held the *Rose* back until he had written his dispatches. Her cargo and her crew were made to wait until she finally got away in the second week of September. Subsequently, the vindictive Foveaux looked for ways to cause Campbell financial pain.

He soon found one. After Lieutenant Governor David Collins at Hobart Town signed a contract with Campbell for the supply of Bengal cattle to the Derwent settlers, Foveaux cancelled it. Van Diemen's Land settlers might starve, but Foveaux had the satisfaction of punishing Campbell.

Commissary Palmer was also in the rebel spotlight. Prior to Foveaux's arrival, Macarthur had ordered a stocktaking of all government storehouses, in the hope of finding evidence of graft by Little Jack Palmer and Governor Bligh that could be used against them in London. Palmer was given the opportunity to be present while the stocktaking took place, but he didn't bother turning up for the inspections, realising the rebels could alter records to suit themselves whether or not he was present. Yet, for all their claims that Palmer was a crook, the rebels were wasting their time. They must have known that he had a shining reputation for honesty in the colony that went back years. In 1806, following severe flooding of the Hawkesbury River that had wiped out the wheat harvest, instead of capitalising on the colonists' plight as the huckster officers would have done, Palmer had sold grain from his warehouses for less than the going price.

Among Little Jack Palmer's admirers was none other than noted explorer, Captain Matthew Flinders, the man who gave Australia its name. Flinders had known Palmer while serving in New South Wales waters, and considered him 'one of the honester, best little good-natured fellows breathing'.[228] Palmer, meanwhile, was preparing to turn the tables on the rebels. Through loyal contacts inside the Commissary department, he was keeping track of rebel misuse of government stores. He would put together three separate secret reports of greedy 'peculation' by Macarthur and Foveaux, in expectation of the rebel leaders finally being brought to account.

On 8 September, Colonel Foveaux charged the man Macarthur had appointed to replace Palmer as Commissary,

James Williamson, with graft. Just four days after Foveaux ordered an inquiry into Williamson's records, he had him tried before a general court martial of the New South Wales Corps, appointing his secretary, Lieutenant James Finucane, to preside as Deputy Judge Advocate of the Corps. The court martial shortly after sacked Williamson from his post and ordered him to pay the treasury for the losses resulting from his graft 'as far as they could be ascertained'.[229] Those losses were apparently never ascertained, if they ever existed; the matter was not raised again in Foveaux's time. It is possible that Williamson had secretly been providing Palmer, his former boss, with information for his secret reports on rebel storekeeping, and Foveaux came to hear of it through informants. To replace Williamson as Commissary, Foveaux appointed Robert Fitz. To cement Fitz's loyalty, Foveaux gave him a land grant of 1700 acres (680 hectares).

Foveaux was also soon issuing full pardons to convicts in the colony, many of them fellow Irishmen, and often on the recommendation of his Irish secretary, Finucane. One, Irishman William Alcock, a Wolfe Tone rebel, was immediately made the colony's Assistant Engineer. Lieutenant Finucane was to acknowledge that he personally now occupied a very powerful position. He could, for example have secured the release of another Irishman, Sir Harry Hayes. Prior to leaving Britain, Finucane had been asked by friends of Sir Harry to look into improving his welfare once he reached the colony. But Finucane was soon advised by stalwarts of the previous rebel administration such as Captain Kemp and Lieutenant Lawson that Sir Harry supported Governor Bligh and had defied the rebel leadership, and so had been exiled to the Coal River for his trouble. Once in possession of that information, Finucane made no attempt to help the hapless knight. According to Finucane, Sir Harry had been 'uniformly imprudent and indecorous'.[230] Sir Harry stayed where he was, illegally imprisoned at the coal mines.

Two clerks in Secretary Finucane's own office received more fortunate treatment. Matthew Sutton and Walter Mosley were pardoned within seven weeks of the commencement of the Foveaux administration. One soon returned to Ireland, the other to England. As the self-appointed Lieutenant Governor of the colony, Foveaux had no legal authority to issue pardons. Ordinarily, a convict whose sentence expired or who received a conditional pardon, a so-called ticket of leave, was not permitted to return to Britain or Ireland. As Charles Dickens' novel *Great Expectations* so graphically illustrated, if caught on home soil, ticket of leave men were liable to be hanged. The men who were pardoned by Foveaux and returned home did so with worthless pieces of paper, unwittingly running the risk of meeting the hangman if discovered.

Now that he had assumed the role of Lieutenant Governor, Foveaux had no compunction about signing death warrants for men convicted of robbery in the colony. In one day, four robbers were hanged at Sydney on his authority. Again, that authority was non-existent; the trials, convictions and executions of these men by the rebel administration were all illegal. Such is the nature of a dictatorship. Foveaux, the hard man, was showing that he was in charge.

13

Squashing the Resistance

Bligh supporter Dr Martin Mason had made a serious mistake. The August meetings of settlers who had chosen Mason and George Suttor as their delegates to go to England had been held in the strictest secrecy. Had Mason not placed an advertisement in the *Sydney Gazette* calling in his debts, Colonel Foveaux might never have known that Mason, a known Bligh loyalist, was planning to leave the colony, and would not have put two and two together.

Dr Mason lived in the main street at Green Hills, today's Windsor. In the front of his premises he kept a shop which he and his family operated as a dispensing pharmacy, while he lived in the back with his wife, son, and four daughters. On Saturday, 1 October, while Dr Mason was out attending a patient, Sergeant Lowther, the military commandant at Green Hills, entered the shop from the front with a party of armed soldiers. At the same time, Senior Constable Fitzgerald and a group of convicts crashed into the house from the rear. Sergeant Lowther showed Mrs Mason, who was tending the shop, a search warrant, then he and his men turned the entire place upside down. In the kitchen, they found a 10-gallon (38-litre) still, home-made from a kettle, which Dr Mason had operated for years to produce various medicinal preparations that he used in his practice. Declaring the still contrary to revenue regulations, which banned the production and sale of liquor without a licence, the invaders carried it away, along with several gallons of spirits in various stages of distillation.

The search party then went from room to room. They ransacked Dr Mason's writing desk and examined all his books. In the bedroom they opened Mrs Mason's trunks and jewellery boxes, and even searched the bed. What they were looking for they refused to tell Mrs Mason or her terrified daughters, but it seems they were searching for a document – probably the settlers' petition to the authorities in London which detailed grievances against the rebel government of the colony and which Mason and Suttor had secretly drawn up.

Dr Mason, who returned home after the search party had left, to find his premises in chaos and his frightened wife and daughters in tears, applied to the local magistrates to find out why they had issued the search warrant and what he was accused of. Two weeks later, he was heard by the local bench, made up of Robert Fitz, Ensign Bell, and Assistant Surgeon Mileham. Not only had he not made and sold spirits illegally, he said, 'I had actually about this time paid three guineas out of my own pocket to buy wine and spirits for poor invalid people.'[231] Dr Mason asked the magistrates to recommend to Colonel Foveaux that his still be returned, as Mason needed it to be able to practise his profession. Appearing to be sympathetic to his request, the magistrates adjourned the hearing.

The next day, 16 October, Dr Mason read to his horror, in the latest edition of the *Sydney Gazette*, a General Order issued in the name of Colonel Foveaux declaring that Mason had been previously dismissed from his post as Assistant Surgeon for misconduct. This was not the case; Mason had declined reappointment. Foveaux's General Order went on to state that Mason was now guilty of illegally using a still at his premises. The General Order was dated 13 October, two days before the magistrates had even sat to hear his case. The *Gazette* said that Lieutenant Governor Foveaux had seen fit to be lenient with Mason because he had a large family, and so no further penalty would be imposed other than the confiscation of his still. The *Gazette* also noted that Charles Thorpe, a convict serving a fourteen-year sentence, had been pardoned by Foveaux and paid a reward of £10 for informing the authorities that Mason was operating a still.[232]

Furious, Dr Mason wrote to Foveaux on the 18th, spelling out the circumstance of his leaving government service and demanding a retraction of the libel. 'I left government employment with clean hands and empty pockets,' he told Foveaux. He also called on the informer Thorpe to accuse him in court. He declared, 'If unshaken loyalty to His Majesty's Governor [Bligh] be a crime, if that be misconduct, I plead guilty in an eminent degree.'[233] At the same time, Mason applied to the magistrates for another opportunity to appear before them and have his case cleared up. He heard nothing back from either the magistrates or Foveaux.

Colonel Foveaux had suddenly become distracted. On the 13th, the schooner *Estramina* had arrived back at Sydney. She had been sent to collect Colonel Paterson from Van Diemen's Land, but returned without him. 'He says his ill state of health would not allow him to venture in so small a vessel,' noted an exasperated Lieutenant Finucane. Now, Paterson was demanding another ship 'of more ample size and suitable accommodation'.[234] It was obvious that Paterson was coming up with lame excuses for staying down where he was, and this seemed to throw Colonel Foveaux. Up till now, Foveaux had expected Paterson to arrive any day to give his rule legitimacy. Now he was left exposed at the top of the rebel tree, and he seems to have panicked.

'Colonel Foveaux has very suddenly and unexpectedly formed a resolution of returning to England,' said a bamboozled Lieutenant Finucane on the 18th. 'I am entirely unacquainted with the motive for what appears to me to be so strange a measure.'[235] Finucane was instructed to write to the captain of the whaler *Albion*, which was due to sail for England in November, asking how much he would charge to carry Foveaux, his family and staff as passengers.

The next day, Foveaux instructed Finucane to bring the exiled Sir Harry Hayes down from Newcastle and return him to his home at Vaucluse, where he was to be kept under house arrest; it was as if he was trying to soften his image prior to departing the colony. Two days later, on the 21st, the captain of the *Albion* wrote back to Finucane to say that he was unable to accommodate Colonel Foveaux in his vessel. As it happened, the *Albion* was another vessel part-owned by Robert Campbell. And Campbell knew that Governor Bligh wanted to keep the chief rebels, of whom Foveaux was now one, in the colony so they could be tried there once he was reinstated, as he was sure he soon would be. Once more, with the help of the skipper of the *Albion*, Campbell stubbornly resisted the rebel leadership.

Lieutenant Finucane had resolved to go home to England with Foveaux when the next available ship sailed. The prospect of going home thrilled Finucane. As his journal reveals, he was dreadfully homesick and detested the insular people and unfamiliar flora and fauna of New South Wales. But that day, 21 October, he confided to his journal, 'I fear something may occur to alter a determination so suddenly adopted.'[236] Finucane seems to have been aware that moves were afoot locally to convince Foveaux to stay, perhaps by John Macarthur's rivals within the junta, who would prefer Foveaux over Macarthur any day. Either that, or Finucane had become accustomed to Foveaux suddenly changing his mind, and fully expected his erratic commander to do so again.

And so it proved to be. Again Foveaux changed his mind. Within days, he once more took a firm grip on the reins of power, almost certainly with an assurance of the solid support of key junta members. Two New South Wales Corps officers in particular would have helped sway him – Major Abbott (newly promoted, like Johnston) and the recently rebel-reinstated assistant surgeon D'Arcy Wentworth, both of them old friends of Foveaux from his earlier days in the colony. What's more, Surgeon Harris and leading civilian rebels including Bayly, Lord, Kable, Blaxcell, and Gregory Blaxland would have all backed Foveaux in preference to Macarthur.

With that storm having passed, the muzzling of Dr Mason now reoccupied the Colonel's attention. On 22 October, Mason was called before the local magistrates to satisfy his ongoing demands for a hearing on the still affair. When he appeared, Mason demanded a copy of the accusations made against him by the informant Thorpe, but Ensign Bell steadfastly refused his request. Again the case was adjourned. The following day, the libellous General Order of 13 October was reprinted in the *Sydney Gazette.* It was repeated a second time on 30 October and, to rub it in, again on 6 November. Dr Mason never received a reply to his letter to Lieutenant-Colonel Foveaux. The case never again came up in court, but Mason's still was never returned. Yet, officially, because the General Order said it was so, Mason was now technically a convicted felon. And convicted felons were not allowed to leave the colony.

With Dr Mason's planned journey to represent the interests of the colony's settlers to the home government cancelled because of this manoeuvre, on 4 November his fellow settlers reacted by sending a petition to Colonel Foveaux. 'Many of the inhabitants have just reason to complain of a partial administration of the law,' they wrote. They said that the overthrow of Governor Bligh was having a disastrous effect on the colony. And, they complained, because the colony's officers were using much of the convict labour, 2000 fewer acres (810 hectares) had been sown with wheat this year than the last, which would result in many people going hungry. The first signature on this petition was that of George Suttor.[237]

Foveaux didn't respond to the petition. Instead, he went after Suttor and other disaffected settlers. First, Suttor found his convict labourers withdrawn by the regime, just as the latest wheat harvest was approaching. Then, in late November, Foveaux issued an order for all persons in the colony, free and convict, to attend musters in their areas. Suttor and four other farmers refused to attend, as a protest against the unlawful rebel administration. 'I had therefore decided to follow the dictates of my own conscience,' Suttor was to write, 'knowing that His Majesty's Governor was a close prisoner within the territory, and forcibly and unjustly held from the exercise of his lawful authority.'[238] Next day, a constable came to Suttor's house and informed him that if he failed to attend the next muster he would be brought before the magistrates in Sydney. But Foveaux suddenly decided to act, and the next thing Suttor knew, he was being summonsed to appear before the Sydney bench.

Writing to Acting Judge Advocate Kemp, Mason asked for an adjournment until after the upcoming harvest, but his request was denied. Another muster was called for Suttor's district shortly after. Sending his employees to attend the muster at Parramatta, Suttor himself rode into the capital to deliver a letter to Lieutenant-Colonel Foveaux, 'addressed to his humanity and good sense'.[239] While Suttor was away from the farm, convicts came and drove away a portion of his cattle.

Foveaux took exception to Suttor's letter, in which the settler complained of unfair treatment, and handed it to the magistrates. Suttor was committed for trial for libel, but given bail. Before Suttor came to trial in the Criminal Court in the second half of December, Foveaux made a key personnel change. Unhappy with the job that Captain Kemp had been doing as

Acting Judge Advocate General, in early December Foveaux removed him from the post and sent him out to Parramatta to take over as commandant there, at the same time transferring Major Abbott in to Sydney.

In seeking a replacement for Kemp as Judge Advocate, Foveaux claimed to have offered the post to several people, all of whom declined it. In desperation, on 13 December, he reappointed Richard Atkins, the rightful holder of the position. Foveaux didn't have the same history with Atkins that Macarthur had; that pair had been bitter enemies for years. Since 26 January, Atkins had been without a job and without an income. Almost constantly in debt throughout his life, Atkins succumbed to Foveaux's invitation to once again take a salary and take his seat in court and wield judicial power. The deal was greased with a little graft – Foveaux granted Atkins 500 acres (200 hectares) near Minto. Another former government employee also joined rebel ranks around this time. With Robert Fitz now Commissary, John Jamieson accepted his old job as Superintendent of Stock when Foveaux offered it, now that Macarthur was no longer involved in the administration. Atkins and Williamson were the only two members of the Bligh administration who subsequently crawled into bed with the rebels after initially being removed from their posts.

In late December, the Criminal Court sat in the Orphan School courtroom, with Judge Advocate Atkins back at his table. On the previous 26 January, the six officers of the then Criminal Court had told the constable sent back for Atkins' papers that he could have the Judge Advocate's table, but not the papers that lay on it. Back then, eleven months before, Atkins had wanted Governor Bligh to charge six officers of the New South Wales Corps with High Treason. Now he was sitting in the same court with several of them, as if nothing had ever happened. The most senior member of this panel of six military officers on the current bench was none other than newly promoted Lieutenant-Colonel Johnston, the superseded lieutenant governor.

From his Judge Advocate's table, Atkins, sixty-three years old, tall, and rosy-cheeked, looked across the courtroom to the Accused. Atkins was mustering all the dignity he could, trying to put events of the recent past behind him and to reflect the fact that he was the son of a baronet and the brother of three knights of the realm. In the dock, thirty-one-year-old George Suttor, handsome, with a chisel chin and thick, swept back hair and equally thick sideboards, returned Atkins' gaze without a flinch. Suttor knew what to expect from this rebel court, and had prepared himself and his wife Sarah and young family back at home for what was to come. Atkins' eyes dropped to the charge sheet in front of him, and in a cultivated accent, this native of Dublin read the indictment aloud. Suttor was being charged for the disrespectful comments in his letter to Lieutenant-Colonel Foveaux and for failing to obey the order to attend the muster in his district. Once he had read the charges, Atkins called on Suttor to plead.

'Gentlemen,' said Suttor, 'I deny the legality of this court. You can do with myself as you please. My unfortunate wife and family I leave to the mercy of God, until peace shall be restored in the colony. I have nothing more to say.'

Atkins told him he must plead, and again asked if he was guilty, or not guilty.

'Sir,' Suttor responded, 'all I have to say I have already said. I deny the legality of this court. My allegiance is due to Governor Bligh, and Governor Bligh alone, and every drop of blood within my veins prevents me from ever acknowledging the legality of this court. You may do with me as you think proper.'

Atkins, becoming frustrated, informed Suttor that under then British law a man who refused to plead was to be treated as if he had pleaded guilty. Again he asked Suttor to plead. Once more, Suttor refused. Atkins cleared the court.

Twenty minutes later, the court resumed, and the Judge Advocate addressed the Accused. 'Prisoner at the bar, in consequence of your refusal to plead to your indictment, the Court, in conformity to Act of Parliament, have found you guilty, and sentence you to be imprisoned six calendar months, and to pay a fine of one shilling.'[240]

Suttor was led off to the County Jail. In quick succession, the four other settlers who had refused to attend musters were hauled into court and each sentenced to a month in jail. The signal from Colonel Foveaux to all in the colony was now very clear – defy him, and you would pay for your defiance.

14

Pistols at Dawn

New Year's Day, 1809. It hardly seemed possible that close to a year had passed since the coup that had turned New South Wales into a military dictatorship. To Governor Bligh, confined at Government House with little to do but write letters to friend and foe, it must have seemed like a decade. His hopes of salvation had plummeted after Lieutenant-Colonel Foveaux took charge and Bligh came to hear of the oppressive treatment of loyalists under this latest incarnation of the rebel regime. Gazing out over the harbour this hot summer's day, Bligh had just one hope. The previous 17 November, the 600-ton transport *Speke* had arrived in Sydney from England. She had disgorged a shipment of convicts, a draft of reinforcements for the Corps, and two naval officers. One of those officers potentially offered Bligh the chance to finally gain control of HMS *Porpoise.*

Captain John Porteous had been sent out by the Admiralty as replacement for Captain Short as commander of HMS *Porpoise.* With him came Lieutenant John Oxley, to add to the *Porpoise*'s depleted complement of junior officers. Porteous was new to the colony, but twenty-two-year-old Oxley had previously served as a midshipman in New South Wales.

Colonel Foveaux instructed Oxley to take command of the schooner *Estramina*, and he readily accepted the appointment. To keep all the naval officers onside, land grants in the colony were hurriedly approved by Colonel Foveaux for Captain Porteous and his senior officers – Lieutenants Kent, Ellison, and Oxley. Each of them was awarded 1000 acres (400 hectares), their grants being surveyed and formalised by February.

Captain Porteous was not as easily suborned as young John Oxley. Porteous had written orders from the Admiralty to take over the command of HMS *Porpoise*, and that was what he meant to do. So, he'd been sitting stubbornly in his quarters in Sydney since 17 November waiting for the *Porpoise* to return from Van Diemen's Land. Bligh had hopes that, as Porteous was principled enough to follow the Admiralty's orders, there was a chance that once he took command of the *Porpoise* he might also follow the orders of his Royal Navy superior – Commodore Bligh.

The *Porpoise* was not far away. Neither was the most senior army officer in the colony. Unbeknownst to Bligh, that New Year's morning, Lieutenant-Colonel William Paterson, Commanding Officer of the New South Wales Corps, had stepped ashore east of Sydney. Somehow, the regime's envoy had this time done the trick and convinced Paterson to come to the capital. It hadn't been easy. After Paterson had sent the *Estramina* away as being too small for him, in November Lieutenant Kent had been sent south to fetch him in the much larger *Porpoise*. When, by 19 December, HMS *Porpoise* had failed to return after seven weeks – the round trip should have only taken three weeks – there were concerns at Sydney that the *Porpoise* had been wrecked, and Lieutenant Oxley had been sent south in the *Estramina* to look for her.

The *Porpoise* hadn't been wrecked. She had sat off Yorktown on the Tamar for weeks on end while the junta's envoy tried to persuade Colonel Paterson to leave his little bush idyll, go aboard the warship, and make the trip to Sydney. That envoy had obviously been ordered not to return without the Colonel. Eventually, in the second half of December, Paterson had given in. What promises were made, deals done, or threats of complaints to London about his failure to assume command were suggested to achieve this we don't know. To allay Paterson's previous fears that Governor Bligh had arranged for the Colonel to be kidnapped if he set foot in Sydney, Paterson had since been told that Bligh would only attempt to arrest him and make him a prisoner aboard the *Porpoise* – by what means, is anybody's guess.

So, to a preconcerted plan, before dawn on 1 January, Lieutenant Finucane had embarked from Sydney's Government Wharf in a small boat. This took him down the harbour to the *Porpoise*, which lay off Watson's Bay, just inside the heads. By 8.00 am, Finucane was climbing up the side of the warship. On deck, he was greeted by fifty-three-year-old Colonel Paterson, a long-faced, bleary-eyed Scotsman. The officers of the New South Wales Corps had a nickname for their affable but weak-kneed colonel: 'Poor Pat'. Finucane brought Poor Pat, Mrs Paterson, and the Colonel's secretary Alexander Riley ashore at Watson's Bay in one of the *Porpoise*'s boats. There, a carriage and an escort of mounted dragoons awaited. Because Paterson could barely walk as a result of severe gout, it's likely Finucane and Riley had to help the Colonel to the carriage.

Officially, the wind was blowing too strongly against the *Porpoise* that day for her to come up the harbour, but this little charade of the Colonel's covert disembarkation was designed to curb Paterson's fear of kidnap. Lieutenant Finucane had not been let into this part of the intrigue. He was told that the warship was being kept out of port to prevent Captain Porteous from boarding her and taking over the command on Governor Bligh's behalf.[241] But the *Porpoise* would be in port soon enough.

Once the Paterson party was in the carriage with Finucane, the little column trotted through the thickly forested region east of the capital, today the affluent and leafy eastern suburbs of Sydney, and slipped into the town with hardly a soul aware that the Colonel had arrived. There followed eight days of official silence. From his prolonged reluctance to come to Sydney, it's clear that Paterson didn't want the responsibility of command in the capital. Foveaux, meanwhile, wanted him there to legitimise his de facto rule. Macarthur now also wanted him there, feeling he could control Paterson and, hopefully, sideline Foveaux.

Days of countless meetings, of interminable haggling went by. Foveaux had officially stepped down as Lieutenant Governor the moment Paterson arrived; the days passed without anyone taking charge. On 5 January, with the discussions not going the way he wanted, Foveaux declared, for the second time in several months, that he would leave the colony at once, and sought and received Paterson's permission to return to England at the first opportunity. He said he had ambitions to replace Lieutenant-Colonel David Collins as Lieutenant Governor in Hobart Town, and would pursue that appointment once he was back in London. Lieutenant Finucane was told that the Foveaux party would be going home in the merchantman *Admiral Gambier* when she sailed later in the month, and he happily began to pack his belongings.

This caused Abbott, Wentworth and the anti-Macarthur members of the junta to rally their forces in support of Foveaux remaining in the colony. Shortly after, Colonel Foveaux unexpectedly re-entered the negotiations. While officially he was still going home, he held out for a role in any new administration. Johnston announced that he had no further interest in the colony's affairs and was also planning to return to England, taking Macarthur and other witnesses with him, to present himself before the home government. Johnston said he would explain the coup of the previous 26 January, would absolve himself and them from blame, and would lay charges against Governor Bligh.

On 9 January, the *Sydney Gazette* finally announced that Lieutenant-Colonel Paterson had arrived in Sydney and had taken control of the colony from Lieutenant-Colonel Foveaux. He was assuming his legitimate title of Lieutenant Governor, although without legitimate cause. The arrangement that had been agreed between the rebel players was that Paterson and his wife Elizabeth would take up residence at Parramatta, where the Lieutenant Governor would sign whatever proclamations were put in front of him. This left Foveaux in charge at Sydney for the time being as commandant of the Corps at headquarters although, officially, he was still going home to England.

New South Wales was well-endowed with gubernatorial residences at the time. In addition to Government House in Sydney, there was a cottage for the use of the Governor at Green Hills when he was there, and a two-storey Georgian mansion serving as a second Government House at Rose Hill in Parramatta. This Parramatta Government House which, according to Lieutenant Finucane, 'would not be unsuitable for a country gentleman of fortune in England'[242], had been the favourite residence of the colony's first governor, Captain Arthur Phillip.

At Parramatta, Paterson could enjoy the extensive gardens, even though they had been leased out to friends of the regime by the rebels, could sign documents, and could drink as much as he liked in solitude. Meanwhile, Major Abbott's wife Louisa had been delegated to be Mrs Paterson's companion. Foveaux, in Sydney, would run the colony day-to-day. With Paterson at Parramatta, Macarthur could pay a daily visit to him from his nearby Elizabeth Farm estate and attempt to coerce him into authorising whatever Macarthur wanted. The contentious third rebel administration was now in session.

With the likelihood that Macarthur would soon be leaving the colony, Foveaux, the self-styled master bookkeeper, now announced that he had discovered a discrepancy in the account books that Macarthur had kept when Secretary to the Colony. Items to the value of £500 had been appropriated by Macarthur for his own use, and Foveaux now demanded that Macarthur pay £500 to the colonial treasury in compensation.

Macarthur had become heartily fed up with Foveaux, who had treated him with disdain once he had eased his bulk onto the colony's unsteady throne. Foveaux hadn't even confirmed the promised Sydney land grant to Macarthur announced just days after taking office. This accusation of fraud, even though the £500 discrepancy would prove to be genuine, was too much for the proud squire of Elizabeth Farm. Old habits die hard. Exploding with indignation, he demanded satisfaction – Macarthur challenged Foveaux to a duel. Duelling was discouraged by the authorities in England but, while contests were discreet, and unless a man was killed or seriously wounded in a duel, a blind eye was generally turned to individual examples of gentlemanly combat.

On the morning of Thursday, 19 January, both duellists arrived with their seconds. Lieutenant Finucane came for Foveaux and Lieutenant-Colonel Johnston, Macarthur's last friend in the rebel clique, for the challenger. The rules of duelling allowed the man who had received the challenge to choose the location for the duel, and the weapons. Five decades later, in the United States of America, future American president Abraham Lincoln would succeed in avoiding a duel with James Shields by choosing to fight with cavalry broadswords in a hole in the ground three metres across and four deep – Shields, a short man, called it off after Lincoln sliced off a tree branch with a practice stroke that demonstrated his far superior reach.[243]

On this occasion, Joseph Foveaux chose pistols; duelling with swords was by this time rare. When Macarthur fought his duel with Colonel Paterson, he had provided the duelling pistols. In fact, he had raised some eyebrows among his fellow officers by personally loading both pistols, something that was considered inappropriate at best and ungentlemanly at worst, for a gentleman was keen to avoid the suggestion that he had tampered with his opponent's weapon. It seems that Foveaux, like Paterson, had never felt the need to own a brace of duelling pistols. If Macarthur again provided the pistols for this duel, he let the seconds load them.

Because there was no referee present, Lieutenant Finucane, as the challenged man's second, proposed that the two combatants take ten paces then toss a coin. The winner of the coin toss would be permitted to shoot first, after which the other, if he was still on his feet, could return fire. It was likely that this unorthodox idea, a form of Russian roulette, was devised by Foveaux for much the same reason that Abraham Lincoln suggested his swords-in-a-hole duel – to cause his opponent to back down. If that was the case, Foveaux had misjudged John Macarthur, who never backed down, often to his own detriment. Macarthur unhesitatingly accepted the conditions.

The two men were handed their loaded, single-shot, flintlock pistols by their seconds, and stood back to back. On the word of Lieutenant Finucane, each took ten paces while holding their pistols vertically, then turned to face each other, separated by a distance of no more than twenty metres. Observed closely by Lieutenant-Colonel Johnston, Finucane now tossed a coin. Macarthur called, and won the toss. He would shoot first, while Foveaux would have to stand and await his fate. According to Lieutenant Finucane, Macarthur 'took very deliberate aim' at Foveaux 'and was perfectly cool'.[244]

Some duellists purposely failed to aim directly at their opponents. It was enough for them to show their courage by taking the field of combat. Others set out to kill their adversaries. In both his previous duels, Macarthur had apparently aimed to kill. He had hit Paterson in the right shoulder, but had probably been aiming for the heart; flintlock pistols were notoriously inaccurate. He left Paterson so seriously wounded that the doctors had thought the Colonel would die. Paterson had taken many weeks to recover. In the case of Captain Gilbert in the 1790 duel on the Gun Wharf at Portsmouth, the ball from Macarthur's pistol had pierced Gilbert's sleeve, suggesting that Macarthur was similarly aiming at his opponent's chest.

Looking down the barrel of his pistol at the oversized figure of Foveaux, who did not flinch, Macarthur pulled the trigger. The weapon boomed. 'Yet,' Lieutenant Finucane was to observe, Macarthur 'missed his object, which was of no small magnitude.'[245] The ball went whizzing past Foveaux. Shaking his head, Foveaux then lowered his pistol, not even bothering to fire. In the etiquette of duelling, this refusal to fire was called 'deloping'. It signified that the duellist did not consider his opponent worth shooting at. To be treated in such a disdainful manner could be humiliating.

Foveaux now said: 'I came to the ground [of combat] without having been given any reason whatever to justify my being called out, or without any resentment against Mr Macarthur.' But, he added, handing his pistol back to his second, he thought himself hard done by in being called to account for any opinion he felt it his duty to express with respect to the service of the government while he commanded in the colony.[246]

Colonel Johnston now suggested that the pair shake hands, and Lieutenant Finucane agreed. Foveaux walked to Macarthur with his hand outstretched, and Macarthur briefly shook it. While, technically, satisfaction had been obtained, for once Macarthur had met his match. The duel achieved nothing and, to give substance to his claim that he had not personally profited from his time as the colony's ruler, Macarthur had to pay back the £500. Following the duel, Macarthur would not talk to Foveaux or even sign a letter to him, and it would take Elizabeth Macarthur to write to Foveaux some time later to request that he kindly confirm in writing the agreed grant of land in Sydney to her husband.[247]

As the rebels continued to squabble among themselves through the late summer and into the autumn of 1809, Macarthur was preparing to sail for England with Johnston, to cover his revolutionary tracks. A year had passed since the coup, and soon London would be demanding answers.

15

Turning the Tables

With the Paterson administration in place, Bligh had been checked a third time by the New South Wales Corps. But the game was not yet over. In that last week of January 1809, new hope dawned for him. HMS *Porpoise* had been sailing up and down the coast for weeks ever since delivering Paterson to Sydney. Now with the new regime entrenched, and with the *Porpoise* out of provisions, the ship finally came into port on 20 January. As soon as she dropped anchor, Captain Porteous had himself rowed out to her, climbed her side and, presenting Lieutenant Kent with his Admiralty orders, took over the ship's command.

That same day, Bligh wrote to Captain Porteous, calling on him to refrain from obeying the military ashore and to obey him instead; to run up his commodore's broad pennant, and to place Lieutenant Kent under arrest for previously disobeying Bligh's express orders. There was no response from Porteous so, on 25 January, Bligh wrote to him a second time, saying how disappointed he was in him as a Royal Navy officer for accepting Colonel Paterson's instructions and again calling on him to follow his own directions. This letter changed everything.

Next day, after wrestling with his conscience overnight, Captain Porteous formally refused to accept any further orders from the rebel leadership, although he didn't place Lieutenant Kent under arrest. When Governor Bligh saw his broad pennant being run up by the *Porpoise* he knew he had won Porteous over. There would have been a triumphant cheer at Government House. At last, Bligh had a bargaining chip, courtesy of Captain Porteous. He would have dined well that night, and slept even better.

The defection of Captain Porteous and the loss of HMS *Porpoise* set the rebels back on their heels. Through the day and long into the night there would have been much discussion about what to do. By the next day, pragmatic Major Abbott, who had rejoined the rebel junta and been appointed Engineer, Artillery Officer, and Superintendent of Public Works by his friend Foveaux, and was also currently Officer of the Guard at Sydney, was leading the push to take a hard line with Bligh. As far as he was concerned, the Corps had to force him to back down in relation to control of the *Porpoise*.

Just before noon on the morning of Friday, 27 January, Abbott and Lieutenant-Colonel Johnston drove to Government House in a two-seat chaise, to deliver an ultimatum to the Governor. As they walked from the carriage to the front door of Government House, they could see HMS *Porpoise* lying at anchor in the cove close by. Her Royal Navy crew had orders from Captain Porteous not to permit anyone connected with the rebel administration to board her, and Governor Bligh's broad pennant fluttered from the tallest of her three masts. Her gun ports remained closed, but it would not take long for the crew to run out her cannon and train them on the town, were Porteous to give the order.

The sentries on the path outside the Governor's residence snapped to attention as the two senior officers appeared and strode up the front steps. A soldier inside the house opened the door for the officers, who came in full dress uniform and wearing their swords. As they stepped inside, Johnston and Abbott removed their plumed cocked hats and slipped them under their arms. Bligh's secretary, Edmund Griffin, who had been granted increasing access to the Governor by this time, met the pair and conducted them into the drawing room. Bligh was waiting, clad in his Royal Navy uniform, hands clasped behind his back. On the end wall, a portrait of King George III and Queen Charlotte had been covered with gauze on the Governor's instructions – so that they couldn't witness the crimes committed against their vice-regal representative in the colony.

This was the first that Bligh had seen of Johnston since the evening of the coup, and he hadn't clapped eyes on Abbott since he had withdrawn from the committee searching the Governor's papers. Bligh was not cordial, knowing that his victory with Captain Porteous must inevitably bring a confrontation with the junta.

Johnston had a letter in his hand. He held it out to Bligh. 'Written orders for you from Lieutenant Governor Paterson, sir,' he said.[248]

Bligh took the letter and opened it. The letter required Bligh to give up His Majesty's Ship *Porpoise* and to go under the direction of Lieutenant-Colonel Johnston and Major Abbott to Norfolk Island or any other place of their choosing. Bligh guessed that they were bluffing. To take him to Norfolk Island or even to Newcastle they would have to use a ship, and that ship would have to get past HMS *Porpoise.* Bligh shook his head. 'I will never comply with any orders from you,' he responded. 'And it is at your peril, and at the peril of anyone else to take that ship, with my broad pennant, from me, sir. You shall not have her!'

Johnston sighed. He was not enjoying this. 'Then, I am very sorry, sir, I have orders that unless you comply with His Honour's request, you are to proceed with us to a subaltern's barrack which is prepared for you at the barracks.' He held up another written order.

'Show me that order!' Bligh demanded, holding out his hand.

Johnston declined to hand it over, but agreed to allow Secretary Griffin make a copy of it. In tense silence, they waited while Griffin wrote. The only sound was the scratching of Griffin's nib on paper as he sat writing at the Governor's desk. After reading both copy and original aloud to confirm that he had made an exact copy, to the grim satisfaction of all present, Griffin handed the original back to Johnston.

'Well, sir?' Johnston now said.

Bligh nodded to the covered portrait of the king and queen. 'It is a fortunate thing Their Majesties' faces are covered, that they cannot see this transaction.'

'Sir, you must go with us,' Johnston announced.[249]

Abbott now called in the sentries. As his secretary watched on, looking fearful for the Governor, Bligh calmly put on his Royal Navy cocked hat. Soldiers of the Guard came trotting in. Then, with a soldier on either flank and another behind the Governor, Johnston and Abbott led the way from the room, across the hall and out the front door. Secretary Griffin trailed along behind. The Colonel's chaise was waiting just inside the front gates, and Abbott gave Bligh his hand and helped him up into it. Then Colonel Johnston climbed up beside him and took the reins.

Bligh's daughter Mary now came running from her bedroom, out onto the veranda. 'Papa! Papa! Where are they taking you?'

Colonel Johnston lashed the reins along the horse's back. 'Giddyup!' The chaise rolled toward the open gates, as the bemused sentries there saluted the Colonel and watched the proud Governor pass by. Major Abbott set off to walk back to the barracks, and as he did so Mary Putland ran by him and out the gates, calling to her father.

'You need not go, madam,' said Abbott to her, 'for they will not let you in.'[250]

Mary ignored him, and continued to pursue the chaise. The guards of the Governor's Guard at the gate looked at each other as she passed; no one had said anything about laying hands on a lady, and they let her go. Mary ran from one end of Bridge Street to the other, down one slope, over the bridge, and up the opposite slope, in a tight, full-length dress and corset, under the noonday sun, ignoring the astonished looks of all she passed.

The two-roomed subaltern's barrack chosen for the Governor's close confinement was the barracks' brightest. Up till then it had been occupied by Lieutenant Finucane, Foveaux's secretary. When Finucane had arrived in the colony in July, the barrack had been in a state of disrepair. Some of the other officers' barracks around it were empty because of the shortage of officers, and they were without windows and doors – thieved by rank and file soldiers for their own houses. In August, work had begun on repairing and improving Finucane's barrack. While this was being done, Finucane had moved into the well-appointed Sydney house of John Macarthur's colleague and envoy Walter Davidson while Davidson was in Van Diemen's Land trying to convince Colonel Paterson to come north; Davidson had very quickly befriended Finucane, probably at Macarthur's suggestion. By the time Davidson returned to Sydney in October, the building work had been completed and Finucane moved back into his by then refurbished barrack.

Sergeant-Major Isaac Champion and three soldiers with muskets on their shoulders waited outside the door to the Finucane barrack. Champion had received written orders from Major Abbott on how he was to keep the Governor under lock and key here, indicating that Abbott had expected Bligh to defy the Paterson order and have to be locked up in the town. The soldiers watched as the chaise approached and drew to a halt outside the little ochre-coloured, shingle-roofed barrack. Bligh stepped down. He was about to walk in through the open door to the humble two-roomed abode when he heard his daughter's voice behind him.

Turning, Bligh saw Mary panting up the dirt street, dripping perspiration, toward the barrack. The soldiers held Bligh back. He reached out to Mary, and she proudly took her father's hand, telling him that wherever he went, she went. Arm-in-arm, father and daughter walked into the barrack past the guards. And then Mary, exhausted, collapsed in her father's arms.

Bligh turned to Johnston, who stood looking helpless in the doorway. 'Water, man! For my daughter!'[251]

Johnston backed out, nodding to the soldiers either side of the doorway. The door slammed shut and was locked. Of the barrack's two rooms, one was a bedroom, with a bed, the other a sitting room with a sofa and one or two other items of furniture. Bligh eased his daughter onto the bed. Later, he would give the bed to Mary while he himself slept on the sofa. Outside, Sergeant-Major Champion prepared to carry out Major Abbott's orders. A guard of three soldiers would be mounted on the barrack door day and night. The Blighs were to have no contact with the outside world, and were not to be permitted out, not even for exercise. Lieutenant Finucane's servant and Mary Putland's maid could bring them food, clothing and other necessities. But everything had to be passed in via the guards, to prevent messages or letters being smuggled in or out.

Several minutes after the Blighs had been deposited in the barrack, the door reopened, and Lieutenant-Colonel Johnston stood there. But there was no glass of water in his hand for the Governor's daughter. 'Sir,' said Johnston, 'I am come with an order from the Lieutenant Governor, that you are to prepare yourself to embark aboard the *Estramina*, as soon as she arrives.'

'Where is she going?'

Johnston shrugged. 'I don't know.' Then he bowed extravagantly, and withdrew.[252] Again the barrack door was closed and locked. The Governor was left to stew in his new prison overnight.

The next day, Bligh received a letter from Colonel Paterson proposing that he return to England on a ship provided by the rebel administration. But, said the letter, Bligh must give up command of the *Porpoise*, which continued to sit in the harbour flying his pennant, with Captain Porteous resisting all rebel attempts to seduce him into their camp.

For two days, Bligh made no attempt to reply. He had called the rebels' bluff, and this sent them into a temporary tailspin. After much discussion, the leadership settled on a new tactic. On 1 February, Paterson wrote to advise the Governor that the rebel administration had chartered the *Admiral Gambier*, a recently built merchantmen of 500 tons that had arrived from England the previous 11 October with a consignment of convicts and troops. The ship would take Bligh home to England. The captain of the *Admiral Gambier*, Edward Harrison, had no local owners to contend with and was perfectly happy to accept rebel money for the charter. The ship, Bligh was informed, would be ready to sail within fourteen days. Paterson asked Bligh to nominate those persons whom he required to go home with him to England, and to specify what accommodation he would require on the *Admiral Gambier*.

Bligh considered that while he controlled the *Porpoise*, even if it was via remote control, he had the whip hand. His objective was to get aboard the *Porpoise* and, if he could frustrate the other side sufficiently, he thought he might achieve his goal. So, to string the rebels along, Bligh wrote back that same day, requiring an enormous area in the *Admiral Gambier* for himself, his daughter, his secretary Edmund Griffin, and several servants. He particularly asked for a cabin large enough for Mary to swing a cot to allay the motion of the ship, because of the extreme seasickness from which she suffered. A letter came back saying that the amount of space required by Bligh was too great, owing to the needs of other passengers. Bligh then wrote back that he would not continue this discussion by letter, telling Paterson to send him an officer to negotiate in person.

Bligh had no idea who he was really dealing with here. He knew that Paterson was only a figurehead. Was Macarthur involved again? Was Foveaux still wielding power? Abbott seemed to be playing a leading role, and appeared to be determined to put Bligh on a ship out of Sydney as soon as possible and so wash his hands of the troublesome Governor. The fact that there were so many conflicting personalities and opinions in the rebel leadership was all to Bligh's advantage. Locked in the stiflingly hot two-roomed barrack twenty-four hours a day at the height of summer was not a pleasant experience for either him or his daughter. Yet the Governor felt he had a winning hand, and he was prepared to tolerate this discomfort without cracking. He'd been in far worse situations before this, for far longer. And Mary was prepared to tough it out with him. If they could hold out just a few days more . . .

The rebels gave Foveaux's secretary Lieutenant Finucane the job of negotiating with Governor Bligh. The son of a Dublin attorney, Finucane had joined the army as an ensign in 1796 and had worked his way up to the rank of captain before suddenly and inexplicably resigning his commission in 1807. Later that same year he purchased a lowly ensign's commission in the New South Wales Corps and then a lieutenant's commission in December. Since joining the Corps, Finucane had not done a day's duty with the unit. After spending five months at sea, he had served as Lieutenant-Colonel Foveaux's secretary for five months.

Finucane was not impressed with the fact that Governor Bligh and his daughter had been locked up in two rooms, and was highly embarrassed that it was his own barrack to which they were confined. Each day since their incarceration, he had visited father and daughter to pay his respects and to inquire after their comfort. He was particularly impressed by Mary. 'Her attachment to her father has exposed her to a confinement as rigorous as that imposed on him. She occupies my bed.' He was full of sympathy for the attractive and personable young woman. 'This extraordinary measure has put me to much inconvenience, but how trifling it is when compared to that suffered by the Commodore and his daughter!!!' (His exclamation marks.)[253] It is tempting to think that James Finucane may have fallen in love with Mary. He would not be the first man, or the last, to swiftly become infatuated with the fiery yet beguiling young woman. His journal entry for the next day, 31 January, was all about her. 'I have endeavoured to alleviate Mrs Putland's distresses by the only means in my power, an assurance of very sincere pity.'[254]

Bligh welcomed the young Irishman when he announced on the morning of 4 February that he had been sent to act as negotiator on behalf of the rebel administration. As the pair sat talking on the barrack sofa, with sentries outside the door just metres away, Finucane mentioned that Colonel Johnston and John Macarthur both intended sailing for England on the *Admiral Gambier*. In the *Sydney Gazette*, between 15 January and 2 April, Macarthur even advertised much of his stock for sale – sheep, cows, heifers, bulls, oxen and horses, all going at a low price – but for ready money only. No payment in wine or spirits for John Macarthur. One of his farms, the 2000-acre (810 hectare) property at Seven Hills, he was prepared to sell for two-thirds down, with the remainder of the purchase price later.

As it happened, Macarthur would not receive a single bid for his stock or his land. Too many people in the colony thought that the law was going to catch up with John Macarthur for his role in the overthrow of Governor Bligh and the subsequent rebel rule of the colony. Buying any of his property, colonists thought, would be like buying stolen property. The fear was that the Secretary of State would only order it confiscated, and the buyer would lose the lot.

Bligh remarked to Finucane that it would not be a good idea for his daughter and himself to travel on the same ship as Johnston and Macarthur. 'I should not much mind going with Colonel Johnston,' Bligh added, 'but the presence of Mr Macarthur would be very unpleasant both to myself and to Mrs Putland.'

'I entirely concur with you, sir,' said Finucane. 'It would be very disagreeable for you and your daughter to proceed to England in the same vessel with Colonel Johnston and Mr Macarthur.' Finucane was actually thinking about himself. He could not wait to go home to Ireland, and had been bitterly disappointed when Colonel Foveaux told him they would have to give up their reserved places in the *Admiral Gambier* for the Bligh party and wait for another ship. If Bligh didn't go in the *Gambier*, then Foveaux and Finucane could. There was a pause, and then Finucane said, 'I am convinced, Commodore Bligh, from what I know of Colonel Paterson's disposition, that he will do everything he possibly can to accommodate yourself and Mrs Putland.'

Bligh nodded, and said he would be grateful if that were the case.

Then Finucane made a suggestion. 'It strikes me, sir, that if you would engage to go home in your own ship, the *Porpoise*, and proceed immediately to England, Colonel Paterson would consent to it.'

Bligh seemed interested by the idea.

'Might I take the proposal to Colonel Paterson, on your part?' Finucane asked.

Bligh nodded. 'I would be very thankful if you would.'[255]

Finucane departed the meeting full of enthusiasm, and Bligh was left smiling to himself. He had not suggested sailing on the *Porpoise*. It had been the young Irish lieutenant's idea. And it was exactly what the Governor wanted.

Finucane pushed hard for the *Porpoise* agreement, arguing

to counter opposition from rebel hard-liners who suspected that Bligh would not keep any bargain with them. In the end, Finucane won the day. He returned to Bligh and personally drew up a written agreement. The rebels agreed to Bligh travelling home to England in the *Porpoise*, with the few companions he had nominated, 'on the following conditions, to the strict and unequivocal observances of which Governor Bligh hereby solemnly pledges his honour as an officer and a gentleman'.[256] Under the terms of the agreement, Bligh was to board the *Porpoise* with his family and retainers on 20 February, and would put to sea as soon after that as the weather permitted. He agreed to proceed directly to England and not return to or touch any part of New South Wales. He agreed not to interfere in the affairs of the colony while he remained in it, and he would not do anything to prevent the *Porpoise* being prepared for or making the voyage to England. It was agreed by Paterson that Bligh could return to Government House until he boarded the *Porpoise*, and could communicate with whomever he chose during that period and make the necessary arrangements for his voyage.

Lieutenant Finucane penned two copies of the agreement. Both were signed by Bligh, and Finucane took them away to be sent to Colonel Paterson for his signature. 'Both the Commodore and Mrs Putland expressed themselves thankful for the little attentions I was able to show them and for the successful issue of my treaty,' said Finucane. He added that he was sincere 'in wishing to relieve the distresses of an amiable and interesting woman and in being gratified at their accomplishment'.[257]

That afternoon, Bligh and his daughter were returned to Government House in the Governor's carriage, and instructions were given in Paterson's name for the *Porpoise* to be provisioned for a voyage to England which would commence on 20 February. Bligh was just sixteen days away from achieving his objective – that of regaining control of his warship.

But within three days of the signing of the agreement, junta members were telling Lieutenant Finucane that Bligh would not stick to it. They felt sure that once Bligh was aboard the warship he would drop down to the entrance to Sydney harbour and blockade it. Finucane argued in Bligh's favour: 'I do not partake of those alarms.' He couldn't imagine Bligh breaking 'the promises he has so repeatedly, solemnly and voluntarily made to me'. If Bligh did so, Finucane would consider him 'the most faithless and degraded of mankind'.[258]

16

The Derwent Blockade

On the morning of Monday, 20 February, with the boom of saluting naval cannon in the background, Governor Bligh was piped aboard HMS *Porpoise* and greeted with raised hats by Captain Porteous and a line of officers and midshipmen including Lieutenants Oxley, Ellison, and William Kent the rebel sympathiser. Behind Bligh came his daughter Mary, his secretary Edmund Griffin, his steward Jubb and servant Dunn, and Mary's female servant. Their personal effects had been loaded over the past two and a half weeks and the ship fitted out and provisioned for a voyage of up to six months. Bligh had been anxious to be aboard on the 20th, for he had fears that the rebels would drag their feet, keep him at Government House until the 21st, and then say that the agreement had expired. The rebels had appeared less compelled to meet the boarding date than Bligh, but in the end the guards at Government House had stood aside to let him leave on the appointed day.[259]

Now, with a deck beneath his feet, Bligh informed Captain Porteous that he would be obliged if he would place Lieutenant Kent under arrest, with the liberty of the ship, for previously ignoring his orders. Kent was relieved of duty and informed he could not leave the ship, but could go anywhere on board. And Bligh ordered Porteous to prepare to put to sea as soon as the weather conditions permitted. Bligh was back aboard a warship, and back in charge, with his officers and men obeying his orders. From that moment, he would say, he truly felt that he was once more the legal Governor of New South Wales.[260]

February is the hottest month of the year in Sydney, the equivalent of August in the northern hemisphere. Through these languid southern dog days the *Porpoise* waited for a good wind. Communication with the rebels on shore was limited during this period, and Bligh kept his word about making no attempt to interfere with the rebel administration. The unhappy Lieutenant Kent, seeing a court martial in his future, now complained of feeling unwell and sought permission to go ashore to Sydney's hospital. Bligh denied him permission, suspecting Kent was planning to claim the protection of the rebels once off the ship. Kent's ill-health would improve of its own accord.

On shore, the new administration had quickly settled in. Little had actually changed. With Lieutenant Governor Paterson relaxing at Parramatta, Colonel Foveaux was in Sydney as commandant of the Corps. In reality, Foveaux was still running the colony's affairs, strongly supported by Major Abbott. Sir Harry Hayes, now back at Vaucluse under house arrest, was rich enough to be able to bribe his sentinels to allow him to send and receive mail. Hearing about the state of affairs in Sydney from friends, he would write to Secretary of State, Lord Castlereagh, in England, 'Paterson gets drunk at Government House at Parramatta, and Foveaux is left in Sydney to do as he likes.'[261]

Chaplain Henry Fulton, who had been without employment for a year, was writing to Mrs Bligh in England in a similar vein, at the same time identifying the competing new rebel leadership factions. He said that Paterson was 'drunk the greatest part of the time, so that from imbecility when sober and stupidity when drunk, he is a very convenient tool in the hands of Macarthur, or of Foveaux and Abbott'.[262]

On Sunday, 26 February, the *Porpoise* upped anchor and moved down the harbour under light sail. While friends, lovers and family of crew-members waving along the shoreline were sad to see her go, with the likelihood she would not be back within a year, if she returned at all, the rebel leaders were glad to see the back of Governor Bligh. But it was not the last they would see of him. Not by a long shot. Just inside the heads, the warship dropped anchor.

There she lay, for day after day. Each morning, the rebels on shore would wake to see the *Porpoise* sitting down at the heads like an avenging angel, and curse her and Bligh. Many a local told Lieutenant Finucane that Governor Bligh had no intention of departing. As February gave way to March and summer ebbed into autumn and there the warship remained, they seemed to be proven right. What Governor Bligh was up to became the guessing game of Sydney.

On shore, it was announced on 12 March that the *Admiral Gambier* would be sailing within a few days, and that among her passengers would be Lieutenant-Colonel Johnston and John Macarthur, ordered by Colonel Paterson to go home to England to answer for the rebellion. Sailing with them would be several associates, who would testify in their favour in London. Macarthur, unable to find a buyer for a single sheep, had been forced to drop the idea of selling up and leaving the colony for good. He would be leaving his New South Wales farms and businesses in the charge of his wife Elizabeth. She had successfully run their concerns for close to four years the last time he'd returned to England under a cloud, following his duel with Colonel Paterson, and she would ably do so again. To obtain some benefit from the trip, Macarthur was taking along his two youngest boys, eleven-year-old James and nine-year-old William, to put them into private schools in England.

As the travellers completed their packing, they waited to see what the warship sitting at the heads would do. The fear in some quarters was that Bligh was waiting for the *Admiral Gambier* to sail, and once she was on the water he would pounce, boarding her and arresting Macarthur, Johnston and their rebel accomplices. To be on the safe side, the ship's master, Captain Harrison, and his rebel passengers agreed that the sailing of the *Admiral Gambier* should be put off. Then, attracting the attention of many, on 17 March HMS *Porpoise* raised her anchor and began to move off. Putting on full sail, she cleared the heads, and disappeared out to sea. 'Which proves the public has judged too harshly of Mr Bligh,' a relieved Lieutenant Finucane was to observe that night.[263]

Next day, Saturday, 18 March, the *Porpoise* once more hove into sight, outside the heads. During the night, she had been sitting just over the horizon. 'I was too hasty in the forgoing surmise,' said a disappointed Lieutenant Finucane.[264] No doubt, rebels around him were saying, 'I told you so.' Throughout the 18th, the industrious *Porpoise*, with her gun ports open now, waylaid and stopped every vessel large and small coming in and out of Sydney heads. The master of each was handed a handwritten proclamation. Dated 12 March, and signed by Edmund Griffin on behalf of the Governor, it announced that a state of mutiny and rebellion existed in New South Wales, and forbade all ships' masters from taking out of the colony persons connected with the rebellion, particularly the officers of the New South Wales Corps, plus a list of fifteen civilians. Those civilians were: John Macarthur, Nicholas Bayly, Garnham Blaxcell, Richard Atkins, Gregory Blaxland, John Townson, Robert Townson, Robert Fitz, Thomas Jamieson, Thomas Hobby, Alexander Riley, D'Arcy Wentworth, James Mileham, Thomas Moore, and Walter Davidson.[265]

That same morning, copies of Governor Bligh's proclamation began appearing about the streets of Sydney, distributed by Bligh loyalists. An enraged Colonel Foveaux sprang into action to suppress the proclamation and to find those responsible for its distribution. Directed by Provost Marshal Nicholas Bayly, police constables scoured the town looking for Bligh's agents. Two men were soon arrested for distributing the Bligh proclamation. One was former Commissary 'Little Jack' Palmer. The other was Charles Hook, one of Robert Campbell's most trusted business partners, who was courting a sister of Commissary Palmer. Palmer and Hook appeared in court that afternoon, and were committed to stand trial for sedition. Commissary Palmer would soon be sentenced to three months in the County Jail and fined £50. Hook was also convicted; he was sent to jail for one month and fined £10.

Governor Bligh's proclamation was now the talk of Sydney. Some rebel sympathisers spoke of resisting Bligh with armed force if he tried to return. Not a few of those listed on the proclamation began to show signs of the jitters. That proclamation clearly meant that Bligh intended to try the civilian rebel leadership in the colony for participating in his overthrow. From his later comments, D'Arcy Wentworth would have begun to feel a noose around his neck.[266] And before long, Robert Townson was making unguarded, unflattering remarks about Macarthur, Johnston and the Glorious 26th. This prompted Macarthur, on the eve of sailing on the *Admiral Gambier*, to typically launch a defamation action against Townson on behalf of Johnston and himself.

On 19 March, as the *Porpoise* continued to prowl threateningly up and down the coast within sight of Sydney, Lieutenant-Colonel Foveaux disappointed his secretary by announcing to him that they would not be going home to England after all. In creating panic in rebel ranks, Bligh had played into Foveaux's hands, giving him the excuse to again take up the reins of government. Lieutenant Finucane hastily wrote a counter proclamation to be printed in the *Gazette* that evening. It declared that in 'the present crisis' Colonel Paterson, due to his poor health, had asked Foveaux to make the sacrifice of putting off his departure and giving him 'the powerful aid of his advice and support in saving the colony from anarchy and destruction'. The proclamation also declared William Bligh an outlaw, and announced that any person in the colony assisting him would be guilty of a crime.[267]

On the night of the 19th, Bligh, unaware that his good friend Commissary Palmer and his supporter Hook were paying a high price for their loyalty and were now sitting in the County Jail, set a southerly course for Van Diemen's Land and departed Sydney waters. It seems that he had indeed been waiting for the *Admiral Gambier* to sail, with plans to arrest Macarthur and Johnston. But in the end, apparently, his daughter Mary had been so seasick she had implored him to allow her to go ashore, and it was that which convinced him to sail for Hobart Town.

Toward the end of March, HMS *Porpoise* appeared in the waters off the south-east coast of Van Diemen's Land and ploughed through the perennially rough Storm Bay, to enter the mouth of the Derwent River. Up the broad waterway the ship cruised, passing whalers coming and going. At this point in history, Hobart was becoming the major whaling port in the southern hemisphere, the jumping-off point for the Southern Ocean and Antarctic whaling grounds. Right whales were even caught in the Derwent itself, and along the eastern and western shores of the river were scattered huge iron pots used to boil down whale blubber for its oil. Ahead, towering over the western shore like a brooding giant, sat 1800-metre Table Mount, a flat-topped extinct volcano. Seven years later, once the news of the Duke of Wellington's victory over Napoleon at Waterloo reached this far-flung southern outpost of the British Empire, this huge rocky outcrop would be renamed Mount Wellington.

On Thursday, 30 March, twenty kilometres upriver, the *Porpoise* came upon Hobart Town. The settlement sat on the slopes of the river's hilly western shore at Sullivan's Cove, with a vast harbour spreading before it. This harbour was considered by one English visitor a decade later to be 'superior to any in the known world' and 'sufficiently capacious to hold all the fleets of Europe',[268] Hobart Town was a five-year-old settlement with perhaps 800 residents. Another 500 lived at outstations and on farms in the area. Five-hundred-and-fifty of the settlers had transferred from Norfolk Island, some settling at New Norfolk, further up the Derwent.

The ruler of this little domain was its Lieutenant Governor, David Collins. A fifty-three-year-old native of Devon and a Royal Marines brevet Colonel, Collins had fought the American colonists at Bunker Hill in 1775, had helped settle Sydney in 1788, and had been the colony's Judge Advocate for several years. In 1803, with several French ships exploring the region, two British expeditions had been sent south from Sydney to occupy key sites and forestall French settlement. David Collins had been sent to Port Phillip, site of today's city of Melbourne. But Collins had been unimpressed with Port Phillip, and had soon followed the other little expedition south. On the Derwent, Collins had found that Lieutenant John Bowen had chosen a poor site for his settlement at Risdon Cove and had moved it across the river and made it his own. Although answerable to the Governor of New South Wales in Sydney, Collins had ruled this place like his own little principality ever since.

Soon after the *Porpoise* dropped anchor in Sullivan's Cove, beside an anchored cargo ship from Calcutta that was en route to Sydney, a boat came out from shore carrying Colonel Collins. Having spotted Bligh's broad pennant flying from the warship's mast, he knew that the Governor was aboard. The lord of Hobart Town climbed the warship's side. A short, narrow-shouldered man, his curly hair entirely grey, his black eyebrows thick, Collins had large, inquisitive eyes and a long, intelligent face. With outstretched hand, the Colonel warmly greeted Bligh and his daughter Mary on the deck of the *Porpoise*. When the

Governor told him of all he had been through, Collins appeared horror-struck and pledged his support. At last, it would have seemed to Bligh, the road to his reinstatement was becoming smoother.

Colonel Collins invited Bligh and his daughter ashore to take up residence at Hobart's Government House, and Mary, anxious to have terra firma under her feet once more, gratefully accepted. So, while Bligh continued to live on the ship, Mary transferred ashore. Hobart's then Government House, located where the Hobart Town Hall stands today, was not very grand; it had only three small reception rooms and was in a poor state of repair; but Mary happily occupied a guest bedroom. As a courtesy, Governor Collins posted a New South Wales Corps sentry at her door. The town outside was much like the gubernatorial residence, ramshackle and dilapidated. There were no formal streets; the buildings, mostly of wattle and daub, were scattered haphazardly around the cove as if Hobart Town were a native encampment.

That night, Governor Bligh, Mary, Captain Porteous and Edmund Griffin dined with Lieutenant Governor Collins at Government House. The Colonel invited his subordinate lieutenants and a few local luminaries to join them. Among the town's leading citizens was its only clergyman for many years, Chaplain Robert 'Bobby' Knopwood. Bligh now discovered that the dignitaries of Van Diemen's Land were a colourful lot. Knopwood, for example, much loved locally, was famed for carrying a Bible in one hand and a flask of spirits in the other.

As for the easy-going 'Davy' Collins himself: he had a wife, Maria, back in England but in Sydney he'd kept one convict mistress, Anne Yeats, who'd given him two children; while here in Hobart his latest convict mistress, Margaret Eddington, gave birth to the second of the couple's children this same year, 1809. Unlike officers such as George Johnston and Joseph Foveaux in Sydney, who kept their mistresses away from the gaze of polite society, here in Hobart David Collins openly showed off his mistress as if she were his wife. Bligh's daughter, thinking of how Mrs Maria Collins back in England must be scandalised to hear of such a thing, was unimpressed to see Lieutenant Governor Collins walking around Hobart Town with Miss Margaret Eddington on his arm.

For the next few weeks, the members of the Bligh party were the welcome guests of Colonel Collins, meeting the locals and enjoying their hospitality. Bligh's plan now was to await news of a military force sent out from England to reinstate him. When he knew this was near, he would sail back to Sydney. In Sydney, meanwhile, once it appeared that the *Porpoise* had departed local waters, the *Admiral Gambier* finally prepared to sail. On 30 March, the same day that Governor Bligh reached Hobart, the *Admiral Gambier* left Sydney, carrying Macarthur, Johnston, and their parties. Another rebel figure sailing with them was Assistant Surgeon, Thomas Jamieson.

Several days before, the officers of the New South Wales Corps had held a ball at the now-vacated Government House to farewell Lieutenant-Colonel Johnston. Macarthur, in addition to taking his two young sons with him, was carrying some unusual baggage home to England. Chained to the *Admiral Gambier*'s main deck were a number of wooden cages containing exotic Australian birds, which Macarthur planned to give as gifts to the wives of influential members of the British Government. He saw such gift-giving as altruism, not an attempt to bribe or influence. Macarthur was also taking Governor Bligh's illegally seized papers with him, to assist Johnston and himself prepare the case they would put against Bligh back in England. In the end, these papers would prove of little help to them; in fact, their possession of those papers would weigh against them in court.

After the *Admiral Gambier* had passed out through Sydney heads, the little ship *Venus*, carrying well-wishers, followed her like a dog trailing its mistress. Sixty kilometres out, on a placid sea, Surgeon John Harris transferred from the *Venus* to the *Admiral Gambier* before the *Venus* turned back for Sydney. And then, after less than four years back in the colony following his last enforced departure, John Macarthur, father of the revolution that had unseated William Bligh, sailed away again.

Word of Governor Bligh's location in Van Diemen's Land reached Sydney on 10 April, when the ship from India that had been at Hobart when he arrived there dropped anchor in Sydney Cove. Colonel Foveaux, furious at the news that Bligh was still in the colony and being treated royally in Van Diemen's Land, immediately dispatched a vessel to Hobart. It carried his *Gazette* proclamation outlawing Bligh, and an order to Colonel Collins to cease victualling HMS *Porpoise*.

Foveaux, now guessing that Bligh planned to return with a military force sent out by the British Government, seemed to go into denial. Like leaders during the last days of many a doomed dictatorial regime, in Paterson's name Foveaux, playing Sejanus to Paterson's emperor Tiberius, tightened restrictions on opposition. Among those to suffer was Sir Harry Hayes, who was once more removed from Vaucluse without warrant or trial and sent back to the Coal River mines, for supposed seditious activities. At the same time, Foveaux increased the distribution of largesse to those who continued to support him. During his first five months in office, he had given away 8325 acres (3370 hectares), four times the amount that Governor Bligh had awarded.[269] Now he began to carve up the colony wholesale. 'Oh, it has been charming times!' Sir Harry Hayes was to write to Lord Castlereagh. Of Foveaux, he wrote, 'He gives pardons, grants and leases to the whores and greatest thieves, till there is nothing left.' Hayes considered there to be just one remedy: 'Hang half this worthy set and it will be justice, for they have been the greatest robbers.'[270]

At Hobart, with Table Mount now shrouded in a winter coat of snow, Governor Bligh's idyll was shattered when the proclamation from Colonel Foveaux reached Colonel Collins. Bligh had seen the vessel arrive from Sydney, and suspected that orders had come down from Foveaux for Collins but, at first, Colonel Collins' attitude to him seemed unchanged. Then, going ashore next morning from the *Porpoise* at 8.00, as he did each morning, and walking up the slope to Government House, Bligh arrived at his daughter's room to find that the sentry usually stationed there had disappeared. He immediately guessed that Collins had withdrawn his support of him.

Calmly, Bligh suggested to Mary that they go for a stroll. Once they were away from Government House and walking, at an unhurried pace, toward the ship's boat that waited at the cove, Bligh said, in a lowered voice, 'I will direct the boat's crew, as many as we can muster, to get your things out of your room, for this is so suspicious a circumstance that I will take you on board instantly.'[271]

Once in the boat they were rowed out to the ship. Bligh informed his daughter, to her chagrin, that from now on they would both have to live on board the *Porpoise*. Bligh's suspicions were soon proven correct. Colonel Collins ceased supplying HMS *Porpoise* from the government stores and banned colonists from all contact with the ship, which Bligh now anchored well out in the stream. At first, to counter Collins' ban, Bligh bought food for the ship's crew and passengers from local suppliers who remained loyal to him. One in particular, George Guest, openly defied Colonel Collins' order. Collins cracked down. Guest was arrested and imprisoned, and Bligh was to hear that settlers who had sent mutton and chickens out to the ship expressly for Mary were arrested and flogged. One man by the name of Belbin received 400 to 500 lashes and was then imprisoned.[272]

Bligh was forced to resort to anchoring further down-river and blockading the Derwent. From now on, every ship arriving and leaving was stopped by the *Porpoise*, under threat of being fired on. Dispatches to and from Colonel Collins at Hobart Town were seized, and supplies commandeered. The warship regularly moved her anchorage. Sometimes she lay at the choppy entrance to the D'Entrecasteaux Channel, at a place later named Bligh's Retreat by locals. Other times it was at sweeping Adventure Bay on Bruny Island, where Bligh had landed in years past on three separate missions with the *Resolution*, the *Bounty*, and the *Providence*, and where he had reputedly twice planted fruit trees, among them Tasmania's first apple trees.[273]

Bligh's spirits would have received a lift when news came down from Sydney that on 14 August the merchantman *Boyd* had arrived in Sydney carrying a detachment of several hundred troops from the 73rd Regiment, the 2nd Black Watch, Major Abbott's old regiment, from their previous station at Cork in Ireland. But while this signalled that the home government had at last sent out forces to replace the New South Wales Corps in the colony, frustratingly, these troops came without their commanding officer and without orders to sideline the Corps or to arrest any rebels. In Sydney, nothing changed. These Scottish troops from the 73rd Regiment simply set up a tented camp three kilometres outside the capital, and there they sat. Colonel Foveaux and the New South Wales Corps continued to rule the colony.

Foveaux, learning that the Black Watch soldiers would eventually be joined by the remainder of their regiment, knew that his days in charge of New South Wales were numbered. That knowledge simply spurred him into dividing up the spoils even more lavishly. By the time he was finished, Foveaux had Paterson approve the distribution of 68,101 acres (27,560 hectares) to 292 individuals, thirty times more than Governor Bligh had granted.[274] One of the recipients had a connection to Foveaux himself – on 10 September, 'in their eagerness to have the grant completed before the troops arrived', the surveying department surveyed 500 acres (200 hectares) for a grant to Ann Sherwin, Lieutenant-Colonel Foveaux's de facto wife.[275]

In Van Diemen's Land, the uncertain and seemingly aimless

existence aboard the *Porpoise* went on for month after month. With characteristic grit and determination, not to mention stubbornness, Bligh was not budging. For those around him, it was a difficult time. Secretary Edmund Griffin, the Governor's only male confidante, had no choice but wait it out with his chief. With the ship rocking to and fro at anchor, Mary Putland was frequently seasick, but she was determined to stick it out, for her father's sake. For conversation, she only had her father, Griffin, and her maid. The officers of the *Porpoise* – Porteous, Oxley, Ellison, and the still under-arrest Lieutenant Kent – were by now completely fed up, and only spoke to Governor Bligh or his daughter when they had to. A cheerless Christmas came and went. And then, New Year's Day brought in the year 1810. The *Porpoise* had been playing this waiting game here on the Derwent for nine months.

By the second week of January, Bligh's patience finally snapped. The coup was now two years old yet not a word had reached him from London in response to his dispatches about the rebellion and the subsequent rebel administrations. He knew that unless the *Admiral Gambier* had foundered, Macarthur and Johnston must have reached England well before this time. The British Government had to be fully aware of what was going on in New South Wales, and the remainder of a relief force must be on its way. Bligh gave orders for the *Porpoise* to weigh anchor and sail back to Sydney.

His new plan was to wait at Sydney until substantial support arrived from England, continuing to seize provisions from passing ships until that support arrived. By this time, his dander was well and truly up and he was in a fighting mood. 'I went to Sydney, not only to wait there, but to defend myself when I was there. Because, had there been no change of government, they would have attacked me the moment I arrived.'[276] If need be, Bligh was ready to go to war with the New South Wales Corps.

17

Bligh's Return

Governor Bligh came sailing back into Sydney on 17 January, 1810. In noting his arrival, Lieutenant Finucane, who had begun referring to him as 'Mr Bligh' ever since being hoodwinked and embarrassed over the *Porpoise* agreement, was once more calling him 'Commodore Bligh'.[277]

As Bligh sailed HMS *Porpoise* into Port Jackson, he saw to his joy that the British frigate HMS *Hindostan* and the 20-gun Royal Navy storeship *Dromedary* lay at anchor at Sydney Cove. The relief force had arrived at last! The two ships had in fact arrived in Sydney on 28 December, carrying 400 more officers and men of the 73rd Regiment.

Once Bligh dropped anchor, a senior army officer was rowed out to the *Porpoise*. Lieutenant-Colonel Maurice O'Connell, a native of County Kerry and commanding officer of the 73rd Regiment, stepped onto the deck of the newly arrived warship, returned the salutes of the assembled ship's officers and, with a smile and an Irish twinkle in his eye, saluted and welcomed William Bligh and his daughter. O'Connell, with large, lively eyes, dimpled chin, well-proportioned features and long hair tumbling over his ears, had rock star looks. A bachelor, he was forty-two years old, but looked much younger.

O'Connell informed Bligh that Lieutenant-Colonel Lachlan Macquarie, formerly the 73rd Regiment's Commanding Officer, had been sent out from England to become the new Governor of New South Wales. Macquarie had come with instructions from the Secretary of State to formally reinstate Bligh as Governor – for one day – and then take over from him. Finding that Bligh was not at Sydney when he arrived, Macquarie had not been able to reinstate him before he assumed control of the colony. So, Macquarie had taken the necessary oaths and was now Governor of New South Wales in Bligh's stead.

This was a crushing blow to Bligh. Like a good sea captain, he had been determined not to give up the ship. He had come out to New South Wales to do a job, planning to give it at least five years. Until he had set the colony on a solid, corruption-free footing, he considered that he had unfinished business here. While he was still in the colony, even if it was at its southernmost extremity aboard the *Porpoise*, he had believed that he retained the governorship. But London had felt otherwise, and had taken it from him.

Balancing this news, to some extent, was the confirmation from Lieutenant-Colonel O'Connell that the New South Wales Corps was being recalled to Britain in disgrace. The 73rd Regiment now replaced the unit in the colony. To Bligh's satisfaction, Macquarie had arrived with orders to arrest Lieutenant-Colonel Johnston and send him back to England in close confinement, to be tried for leading the overthrow of His Majesty's Governor. Macquarie had also carried orders to arrest John Macarthur and try him in the colony for High Treason, on the basis that London believed Macarthur to have been the instigator of the rebellion. Both men had been lucky to leave New South Wales when they did, before Macquarie arrived, thereby avoiding arrest.

Yet, despite all this positive news, Bligh was still stunned by the sudden loss of his governorship, and when Lieutenant-Colonel O'Connell issued an invitation for Bligh and his daughter to join him for dinner ashore that evening, and Mary nodded her encouragement, Bligh dazedly accepted the invitation. As Colonel O'Connell escorted Bligh and his daughter ashore, cannon on the warships in the harbour boomed out a salute to the former governor. Putting a brave face on his bitter disappointment at being officially replaced, Bligh, back on Sydney soil, walked arm-in-arm with Mary through a 73rd Regiment guard of honour on the road from the Government Wharf to Government House. At the Government House door, 73rd Regiment sentries presented arms to Bligh. How different this reception was from the surly one he had received the last time he'd stepped onto this veranda.

The Blighs were ushered indoors to confer with Governor Macquarie. Bligh had met Macquarie once before, at Cape Town in 1788, when the *Bounty* had been on the outward leg of her fateful voyage. Then, Macquarie had been a bright-eyed, if deeply religious twenty-eight-year-old Scottish lieutenant with the 77th Regiment on his way to serve in India. Now he was taciturn, craggy-faced, and just days short of his forty-eighth birthday. Macquarie had not been London's first choice for this job. The Secretary of State, realising at last that it had been a mistake to send navy men to command army men, had appointed Brigadier-General Sir Miles Nightingall to replace Bligh. Macquarie had initially been coming to the colony as commander of the 73rd Regiment and Nightingall's deputy, but when Nightingall backed out at the last moment Macquarie had been offered the post. Macquarie now shook Bligh's hand and introduced Elizabeth, his thirty-one-year-old Scottish wife of two years. Plain but personable, Elizabeth was Macquarie's second wife; his first had died from tuberculosis in 1796. Elizabeth Macquarie, too, made Bligh and his daughter welcome – to the house that had been both their home and their prison for several years.

Treating Bligh with the utmost respect and consideration, Macquarie handed him a letter from Lord Castlereagh, in which the Secretary of State formally advised Bligh that while the government fully approved of his conduct, circumstances made it expedient for Macquarie to replace him so that Bligh could return to England to participate in the prosecution of those responsible for the rebellion. Macquarie then showed him a proclamation he had issued in Sydney on New Year's Day, when Bligh was still sitting unhappily at the mouth of the Derwent. That proclamation, drawn up in accordance with Macquarie's orders from Lord Castlereagh, announced his appointment as Governor and made plain 'His Majesty's high displeasure and disapprobation of the mutinous and outrageous conduct displayed in the forcible and unwarrantable removal of his late representative, William Bligh, Esq.'[278]

Macquarie also showed Bligh a copy of another proclamation, issued by him on 4 January, also in accordance with his orders from London, in which he declared all official appointments made by the rebel administrations illegal and invalid, and announced the reappointment from 8 January of all those who had held office during the Bligh administration and who had not subsequently gone over to the rebels. All grants of land and stock and leases made in the name of Johnston, Foveaux or Paterson were declared null and void and were cancelled. At a stroke, the rebel giveaways, totalling upwards of 100,000 acres (40,000 hectares), had been annulled. The new governor had the power to ratify some of those grants and leases if he felt they were given for reasons of 'impartiality and justice', but no grants or leases to officers of the New South Wales Corps could be ratified under any circumstances. In addition, Macquarie had declared all trials and investigations held since Bligh's overthrow 'to have been before an incompetent jurisdiction, and to be illegal'.[279]

As a result of these proclamations, Sir Harry Hayes, Provost Marshal Gore, George Crossley and Lawrence Davoren were all released from their chains at the Coal River mines and brought back to Sydney and allowed to go home. Gore and Crossley had spent close to two years as prisoners in the underground mines. Commissary Palmer, Charles Hook, George Suttor, and the four other defiant Hawkesbury farmers had all served their illegal sentences by this time. The Macquarie proclamation was too late for the five men unlawfully hanged on Joseph Foveaux's signature and James Finucane's countersignature. By the time that Bligh returned to Sydney, Palmer, Campbell, Gore, Oakes and other Bligh officials had been reinstated in their former positions. Because the Principal Chaplain, Samuel Marsden, a friend and supporter of Bligh, had returned to the colony at the same time as Macquarie and resumed his post, Reverend Fulton again took up his original role as Assistant Chaplain.

'I hope you approve of what has been done, sir,' said Macquarie to Bligh, knowing that he was disappointed to find Macquarie occupying his post with London's blessing.

Bligh sighed. 'I know the reasons, which you have stated in your proclamation, Colonel, for taking upon yourself the government of the colony.'[280]

While implementing the home government's orders relating to the rebellion, Macquarie was careful not to let his personal feelings about his predecessor's overthrow be known. Supporters of John Macarthur would later read this as condemnation of Bligh and tacit support for the rebels, but we now know what Macquarie truly felt, from the journal of his wife Elizabeth. As it happened, the Macquaries, on their way out to Australia, had come across Harris and Jamieson in the *Admiral Gambier* at Rio de Janeiro, when the rebels were going the other way, to England. Macarthur and Johnston, impatient to beat Bligh back to England, had left the *Admiral Gambier* at Rio and sailed for England via Ireland in the *Lady Warburton* only days before the Macquarie convoy reached Brazil. Harris and Jamieson, who were no longer the friends of either Macarthur or Johnston, had been content to remain with the *Admiral Gambier*.

Macquarie had been relieved not to find Lieutenant-Colonel Johnston at Rio, for Macquarie and Johnston were old friends. The two Scots had known each other in their younger days in the army when, as Mrs Macquarie revealed in her private journal, Macquarie had been 'an intimate companion' of Johnston. Mrs Macquarie said, referring to her husband and herself, 'We felt sorry' that Johnston 'should have committed himself as he had done, by an act of the most open and daring rebellion, by which as far as it appears to us he will probably forfeit a life, which has, till this unfortunate period, been spent in the service of his King and country.'[281] Had Macquarie come across Johnston there at Rio de Janeiro, he would have had no choice but make that arrest in Rio and send Johnston home with an escort from his 73rd Regiment. As for Macarthur, Macquarie would have also arrested him, and brought him back to New South Wales to stand trial.

Both Drs Harris and Jamieson talked with the Macquaries several times in Rio, using the opportunity to profess their innocence of any wrongdoing in the coup. Mrs Macquarie says that Dr Jamieson spoke to her husband and herself at length, explaining the events and causes of the rebellion from the rebel perspective. Despite the one-sided accounts, the Macquaries didn't accept the rebel story: 'It appeared to us that even by their own account the conduct of those persons who had acted against the Governor was not to be justified, or even excused.'[282] By the time Lieutenant-Colonel Macquarie landed in New South Wales, he believed that the leaders of the rebellion had been at fault, not Governor Bligh, and that Johnston, and probably others including Macarthur, would hang for it.

Despite his personal feelings, Macquarie had made up his

mind to steer a middle course and put an end to the factionalism in New South Wales. He was even taking Lieutenant-Colonel Foveaux's advice on how to run the colony for the time being. Incredibly, Macquarie would praise Foveaux in a May dispatch to London, saying that Foveaux's measures as dictator 'reflect the greatest credit on him'. He even recommended Foveaux as 'eminently qualified' to run another colony.[283] Another former rebel who proved useful to Macquarie was Isaac Nicholls, son-in-law of Macquarie's old friend Johnston. Only recently a fervent revolutionary, Nicholls now became a regular visitor to Government House and a useful tool of the new governor. Macquarie was also inviting Bligh's reinstated officials to Government House so, as far as he was concerned, he was being even handed.

But increasingly, it was former rebels who had the new governor's ear, and Bligh was not happy. Macquarie's friendly attitude toward Foveaux particularly incensed Bligh. Foveaux had disobeyed orders from the Secretary of State to go to Norfolk Island. Without authority, he had assumed the post of Lieutenant Governor. He had continued Bligh's illegal arrest. He had breached laws and human rights with equal abandon. It would transpire that the leading legal minds of the British Government would determine that Foveaux was just as guilty of treasonable acts as Johnston. Had London known about Foveaux's activities earlier, he too would have been ordered home under close arrest. But, apparently because he had no orders concerning Foveaux, and finding him 'a man of business', Macquarie now made use of him.[284]

As Bligh wrote home to his wife, he considered it a slight to himself that Macquarie would take the advice of a man who had illegally kept His Majesty's Governor under lock and key. 'It is a hard trial of my temper for me to be here just now,' he told Betsy.[285] It was also a hard trial for Governor Macquarie. The bitter Bligh, not only forced to live among his enemies but seeing them at Government House filling Macquarie's head with their propaganda, was close to cracking under the strain of the past two years. The ancient Romans had a saying: anger is a brief madness. And Bligh was a very angry man indeed as a result of all that he had gone through as a prisoner and as a fugitive. This was all now being compounded by the humiliations he was suffering in Governor Macquarie's Sydney. As far as Bligh was concerned, Macquarie was sleeping with the enemy. Certainly, Macquarie seemed to thumb his nose at Bligh's successful measures to regulate the colony's economy, allowing the illegal bartering of wine and spirits to continue. He even personally purchased 100 acres (40 hectares) from a rebel, Lieutenant Minchin, via Minchin's agent, using spirits to pay for it.[286]

In support of Bligh, Macquarie told London on 10 May that he had been unable to find 'any act of his which could in any degree form an excuse for' Governor Bligh's overthrow. 'Very few complaints had been made to me against him, and even those few are rather of a trifling nature.'[287] On the other hand, according to one report that was quite at odds with the picture of Bligh that Macquarie gave London, Macquarie wrote to his brother that Bligh had become 'a most disagreeable person to have any dealings or public business to transact with'. According to this account, Macquarie agreed with members of the civilian rebel leadership who increasingly had his ear, expressing the view to his brother that Bligh was a most unsuitable vice-regal representative.[288]

Meanwhile, adding to Bligh's disgust, Macquarie was permitting the officers and men of the 73rd Regiment to openly fraternise with their counterparts of the New South Wales Corps. In one thing at least Bligh was approving – London had finally, belatedly accepted his recommendation to send out a proper lawyer to replace Richard Atkins as Judge Advocate. Macquarie had brought out Ellis Bent to fill the post. Slight, in poor health, and only twenty-six, Bent had been practising at the bar for less than four years, but he had legal training, unlike all his predecessors in the post of Judge Advocate.

Macquarie now told Bligh that London wanted the ex-governor to command the convoy that would take the New South Wales Corps back to England. In addition, Bligh could choose as many witnesses as he needed, within reason, for the trials of New South Wales Corps officers that were planned to take place in England, and the government would pay for their passage. Bligh would also be permitted to collect all necessary documents in the colony to aid the prosecution. It would be a month or two before the convoy was ready to sail, so Macquarie offered to provide rooms for Bligh and Mary at Government House. But, rather than be under Macquarie's feet, and in his shadow, Bligh decided to rent a house in the town, if His Excellency would be so kind as to place an armed sentry at his door to ward off the attentions of rebel sympathisers. Macquarie readily agreed.

The Macquaries invited Bligh and Mary to dinner that first evening, but Bligh had to decline because he had already accepted Colonel O'Connell's invitation. So, with his head spinning with all that had transpired during the day, and consumed by thoughts of which witnesses he should take home and what letters and proclamations he needed to reclaim from rebel hands, Bligh went with Mary to dine at Lieutenant-Colonel O'Connell's quarters – Johnston's former barrack, until recently the rebel headquarters.

Colonel O'Connell proved to be charming, and quite cheeky. Mrs Macquarie was to tell a story about him which illustrated that cheek. A month after leaving Rio de Janeiro on the way to New South Wales, the Macquaries' ships had reached Cape Town. When the Macquaries went ashore, Mrs Macquarie had found herself having to climb up the stone jetty steps on all fours. Colonel O'Connell, laughing, had said, 'I see you were not brought up in the Highlands for nothing, Mrs Macquarie.'[289]

Within a few days, Bligh rented a house in Bridge Street, beside the Tank Stream, for £10 a month. He, Mary, Edmund Griffin and their staff took up residence there, with a sentry at the door. In this temporary home, Bligh reunited with supporters including Palmer, Campbell, Gore, Fulton, Suttor, Caley, Dr Mason, Hayes, Hook, Arndell, Hassall and numerous others, and heard the stories of their trials and tribulations during the almost two years of rebel rule. As the weeks passed, there was a whirl of social events, starting with the postponed dinner with the Macquaries. There followed numerous Government House soirées, private and regimental dinners, Governor Macquarie's birthday dinner, a fête put on for Bligh by the Macquaries, and a ball aboard HMS *Porpoise* to which even Elizabeth Macarthur was invited, and which she attended. Bligh pointedly declined any Government House invitation also extended to officers of the disgraced New South Wales Corps. To him, those officers, including young Lieutenant Finucane, were traitors who should be under arrest and put on trial.

To add extra drama, on 8 March a fire broke out aboard the storeship HMS *Dromedary* as she lay in the harbour, just as the captains of the merchant ships then in Sydney and several senior military officers were sitting down to dinner with Governor Macquarie at Government House. As the captains of the ships in port – several of them substantial East India Company merchantmen – dashed back to their vessels to move them away from the smoking *Dromedary*, Commodore Bligh hurried from his rented house, pulling on his uniform jacket. Smoke was pouring from the *Dromedary*'s stern windows as he reached her. The fire had begun near the ship's magazine but, fortunately, all her powder had earlier been transferred ashore.

Being senior naval officer in the port, Bligh quickly took charge. As he joined the *Dromedary*'s Captain Samuel Pritchard, his 102 sailors, and volunteers from on shore struggling to counter the blaze below decks with buckets of water, Bligh gave orders for the *Dromedary* to slip her cables and run to the Government Wharf. There, he deliberately scuttled her in the shallow water beside the wharf, dousing the flames. The *Sydney Gazette* would report that Bligh that evening fought the fire alongside colonels Foveaux and O'Connell.[290] It was the one and only time that Bligh and Foveaux were on the same side.

On 17 March, with the projected departure date of the convoy for England not far off, Colonel Foveaux and his secretary, Lieutenant Finucane, slipped out of Sydney with their retinue. Foveaux was keen to arrive back in England before Bligh so he could gain the ear of the Secretary of State and muster as many friends as possible to put a case against Bligh and for himself. He was also planning to lobby for appointment as Colonel David Collins' replacement as Lieutenant Governor in Hobart Town. Colonel Collins' position did indeed become vacant this very month, but not through any intervention from London. When Foveaux left Sydney, he was ignorant of the fact that, a week before, Davy Collins, perhaps anxious about his future after he had sided with the rebels, had suffered a heart attack at Hobart and died. So desperate was Foveaux to gain the march on Bligh, he sailed for New Zealand waters in the little 140-ton brig *Experiment*, which was heading for the Bay of Islands, hoping to find a more substantial whaler there that was returning to England and on which he could buy a passage.

The Sydney that Foveaux and Finucane left behind was gearing up for the departure of Bligh's convoy. HMS *Hindostan* and HMS *Porpoise* were ready to sail, and on Monday, 10 April they were boarded by rank and file members of the New South Wales Corps and their families. Ongoing repairs to the storeship *Dromedary*, which had been refloated after the 8 March fire, meant that her departure and that of the convoy as a whole was delayed by several weeks. A few soldiers of the Corps had transferred to the 73rd Regiment and were staying behind, among them Corporal Michael Marlborough, the man who claimed to have dragged Governor Bligh from under a Government House bed that fateful evening, and his colleague, Private William Wilford. Members of the Corps going back to Britain offered their homes and chattels for sale to the newcomers, but many Corps officers retained their properties, renting them out or putting in managers, implying that they had plans to one day return.

Through late March and early April, the locals held a string of farewell dinners for Bligh, the grandest being those of Commissary Palmer and Robert Campbell, both of whom would be accompanying him on the voyage back to England to give evidence against the rebels. Campbell, as loyal as he was to Bligh, was reluctant to leave Sydney. The rebel regimes had done significant damage to his business interests, and he had made it clear he preferred to stay behind to rebuild them. It took a written order from Governor Macquarie for him to change his mind. Accepting the order, Campbell appointed Charles Hook to manage his affairs while he was away.

In the second week of April, Bligh loyalists led by Commissary Palmer, Assistant Chaplain Fulton, Reverend Hassall, and Campbell partner James Birnie decided to send the former governor away with a written address of support, for publication in the London papers, 'as a token of the veneration and esteem in which we have ever held your character'.[291] So, Provost Marshal Gore sought permission from Governor Macquarie for a public meeting at the New Church. Macquarie was nervous about the meeting, worrying that it would stir up the pro- and anti-Bligh factions and reopen the wound he was trying to heal, but gave his permission just the same, and the meeting was advertised in the *Gazette*.

At noon on Tuesday, 11 April, a crowd gathered at the church. Predictably, remaining rebel leaders and their sympathisers also turned up to the meeting in force. Chaired by Provost Marshal Gore, the meeting passed a resolution in support of Bligh, condemning the 'unwarrantable mutiny and outrageous conduct' of 26 January 1808, and disavowing Lieutenant-Colonel Johnston's claim that he had no alternative but to depose Bligh.[292] As Gore read this part of the resolution aloud, he could see shaking heads in that part of the church occupied by the rebel group. So he asked, provocatively but pertinently, 'Is there any person or persons at the meeting who will avow [declare] that he or they had a design to massacre the Governor and the officers in whom he confided, if Colonel Johnston had not seized and imprisoned the Governor?' In his first dispatch to London, Johnston had claimed that would have been the outcome had he not acted against Bligh.

'No! No!' came calls from the rebel quarter.

'There was no such intention!' added someone among them.

Then D'Arcy Wentworth exclaimed, 'What, man! Do you think we are going to put a rope round our own necks?'[293]

The resolution was passed unanimously by the Bligh supporters, without the rebels voting for or against. Palmer, Fulton, Hassall and Birnie signed the resolution and left. Then Simeon Lord and Gregory Blaxland stood and asked to put a counter resolution. Gore refused to allow it, so Blaxland and Lord grabbed the first resolution and went storming off to Government House. The meeting broke up. Shortly after, Gore was summoned before Governor Macquarie.

Macquarie was fuming. 'I expect on such an occasion, Mr Gore, you should act impartially, in putting to the meeting such questions as they wished to have proposed.'[294]

Tail between his legs, Gore returned to the church, where only the pro-rebel party remained. Lord was there, along with Blaxland, Wentworth, Bayly, Blaxcell, Kable, Underwood, Captain Anthony Fenn Kemp, Lieutenant Lawson, Lieutenant John Oxley of HMS *Porpoise*, and William Cox Senior, the former paymaster of the New South Wales Corps who had recently returned to the colony from England as a civilian after resigning his commission. At 3.00 pm, Gore reconvened the meeting and allowed Blaxland and Lord to propose their resolution, which was passed unanimously by their supporters, and put in writing. This resolution declared that the original meeting had only been convened to 'provoke and renew animosities', and declared full support for Governor Macquarie's proclamation of 1 January 'recommending harmony and a conciliatory spirit'. It also called on Gore to sign this latest resolution as the meeting's chairman and to have it published twice in the *Gazette*.[295]

As Gore was signing the resolution, Lord, Blaxland and Cox told the others that they would go to Parramatta and the Hawkesbury to counter any pro-Bligh addresses being presented to public meetings there. Once Gore had signed this second resolution, he held it out to Blaxland, Wentworth, Lord and their friends to sign. Not one of them was prepared to put their name to it. Apart from Gore's signature, it remained unsigned. Gore took both the pro-Bligh resolution and the rebel counter resolution to Macquarie, suggesting that His Excellency allow the publication of both. Macquarie chose to publish neither.[296]

On 4 May, just before Bligh left his rented Bridge Street house for the last time, the original loyal address passed by the 11 April meeting was presented to him by his supporters. By this time, it had been signed by 460 colonists. In contrast, the infamous requisition drafted by John Macarthur on 26 January 1808 calling on Johnston to overthrow Bligh had, after weeks and months of cajoling, threats and promises in 1808, only been signed by 150 individuals.

18

The Greatest Shock of All

It was Friday, 5 May 1810, and Commodore Bligh, his daughter Mary Putland and their small staff boarded HMS *Hindostan* and settled into their quarters for the voyage home to England. The *Hindostan*, a heavy frigate of 50 guns, promised to provide the most comfortable quarters for Bligh, and particularly for the seasickness-prone Mary, on the long excursion across the world. The prospect of that voyage, after Mary's hellish eleven months aboard the *Porpoise*, and knowing that it had taken the Macquaries seven months to come out from England, must have been daunting for her.

That afternoon, Bligh received a visit aboard the *Hindostan* from Lieutenant-Colonel Maurice O'Connell, with whom he and Mary planned to dine ashore that night. The Irish colonel now stunned Bligh by asking for his daughter's hand in marriage. Bligh had not seen it coming, just as he hadn't seen the *Bounty* mutiny of 1789 or the Macarthur coup of 1808 coming. So focused was he on his own business, he had missed the signs that the handsome, attentive colonel had fallen in love with his daughter.

Bligh didn't have to think about his answer. He showed O'Connell the door. 'I gave him a flat denial for I could not believe it,' he would write to Betsy. But he hadn't counted on Mary's reaction, when father and daughter retired behind a closed door. It turned out that the feelings were mutual – Mary had fallen in love with Colonel O'Connell. 'She had approved his addresses and given her word to him.' Mary had promised to marry the Colonel. Bligh asked his wife to feel for him as he'd tried to come to terms with the situation. 'Nothing I could say had any effect.'[297]

Ellis Bent, the colony's young new Judge Advocate, was not a fan of Mary Putland. 'I don't like her,' he would write to his brother.[298] Of a similar age to Mary, Bent noted that while she was quite pretty, with a good figure, he considered her conceited and affected. Bent claimed that Mary was known to throw plates and a candlestick at her father when she was angry with him.[299] On 5 May, feisty Mary was very angry indeed, and she let her father know it. She wanted her own way, and she was determined to get it. Bligh adored Mary, as he adored his wife and other daughters, and he caved in to her. 'At last overwhelmed with a loss I could not retrieve,' he wrote to wife Betsy, 'I had only to make the best of it. My consent would only be extorted, for it was not a free gift.'[300]

That evening at dinner, Maurice O'Connell announced to his dinner guests that he and Mary were to be married. Because Bligh was due to soon sail, the marriage was rushed through three days later. The couple was married by Bligh family friend Chaplain Samuel Marsden at the New Church, with Bligh giving his daughter away. As his wedding gift, Bligh gave the couple his land in the colony. This comprised three properties. The first two had been given to him by the home government as part of his salary package. He had named both after famous sea battles in which he had fought – one, at Box Hill, was Copenhagen; while the other, Camperdown, would eventually become the Sydney suburb of that name. The third, Blighton, the rundown property on the Hawkesbury visited by Lieutenant Finucane, had been granted to Bligh by his predecessor, governor King, on his arrival in the colony and before he took office. All three now formed part of Mary's dowry.

A large Government House reception followed the 8 March wedding ceremony, hosted by Governor and Mrs Macquarie and attended by many of the colony's notables, except 'a few malcontents'.[301] The decorated ballroom was full of well-dressed colonists who danced the night away to the Black Watch's regimental band. To crown the greatest social event in the colony's short history to date, there was a display of fireworks over the harbour, entertaining all of Sydney. To Bligh's apparent surprise, the Macquaries showed 'an extraordinary degree of pleasure and even exultation' in the wedding.[302]

Perhaps Bligh was only trying to console his wife when he told her this. The Macquaries, like Bligh, were putting the best possible face on the event. Neither Lachlan Macquarie nor Judge Advocate Ellis Bent was in favour of the union. They believed the marriage would split the colony. In marrying Colonel O'Connell, Mary would be staying behind in New South Wales with her new husband. The couple would live in the Sydney commandant's barrack for a year, and then for several years more would rent Vaucluse Estate from Sir Harry Hayes, who returned permanently to Ireland. Macquarie felt that in remaining in the colony Bligh's daughter would become a focal point for the former Bligh loyalists and a source of antipathy for the former rebels and their friends. This would, he felt, continue to divide New South Wales into two camps and hamper his attempts to move on and leave the rebellion behind.

Four days after the wedding, on 12 May, Bligh sailed from Sydney in HMS *Hindostan*, with HMS *Porpoise* and HMS *Dromedary* following close astern. In many respects, to both Bligh and Macquarie, the departure came not a moment too soon. Lining the decks of the three departing ships were the hundreds of men of the New South Wales Corps, sadly watching their home of the past twenty-two years recede from view. Private John Gray, the Parade Ground sentry on the day of the coup, was among them, as was Private Gillard, the gunner who'd had Government House in his sights. And Sergeant Bremlow, the NCO sent to stiffen the resolve of the Governor's Guard on that fateful day. And Sergeant-Major Whittle, the rock of the rebellion, with his wife and tribe of children, glumly saying goodbye to Sydney, their shop, and their comfortable Antipodean way of life.

With Johnston, Foveaux, Finucane and Minchin already returned to England, there was a depleted complement of New South Wales Corps officers making the journey back to Britain with their troops – Abbott, Kemp, Brabyn, Lawson, Moore, Laycock, Draffin, Bell, and their commander, the ailing, increasingly befuddled Poor Pat, Lieutenant-Colonel Paterson. Paterson would not survive the journey – he would die in his wife's arms aboard HMS *Dromedary* when the convoy was off Rio de Janeiro. In addition to carrying away the disgraced officers and men of the New South Wales Corps and their families, heading for an uncertain future in England, the ships were taking Bligh and his civilian witnesses back to the mother country.

Among the thousands who farewelled the little fleet from the foreshore and a flotilla of small boats that day was Bligh's daughter Mary, now Mrs Maurice O'Connell. As she disappeared from his sight, waving sadly from the shore, Bligh, on the deck of the *Hindostan*, consoled himself with the thought that, 'If I had forced her away and had lost her on the voyage (to illness) I could never have survived it.'[303] He would never see Mary again. Once before, William Bligh had returned to England after losing a ship. Now, he was returning after losing a continent. And a daughter.

19

The London Trial Begins

King George was mad, or so his doctors had declared. Now, to the relief of the nation, his son, the Prince of Wales, had taken the reins as Prince Regent. Meanwhile, the French army was retreating out of Portugal as General Arthur Wellesley, the future Duke of Wellington, settled into his Iberian stride. Over the past few years Britain had been through a difficult period marked by a Dunkirk-like evacuation of British forces from the Iberian Peninsula following the Battle of Corunna, and rampant inflation, strikes, and civil unrest at home.

Now, by the late spring of 1811, there were good reasons for Britons to be optimistic. In this atmosphere, news of the general court martial of a senior British army officer as a consequence of a 'mutinous outrage' in Australia that had 'caused the greatest sensation'[304] in Britain rivalled the exploits of General Wellesley in the newspapers and in public conversations. This New South Wales affair hadn't been just any mutiny, said its critics, it was 'a mutiny so unprecedented in the military annals of this country' and 'so dangerous by its example'[305] that it threatened British military discipline everywhere.

It was 10.00 o'clock on the morning of Tuesday, 7 May 1811. The members of the vast audience in the Great Hall at Chelsea's Royal Hospital rose to their feet. This military hospital, designed by Sir Christopher Wren to house soldiers unfit for duty – today's red-coated 'Chelsea pensioners' – had been established by King Charles II in 1681. The Great Hall, with its soaring ceiling, dangling chandeliers and chequerboard stone-tile floor, had been built four years later. Today, it was serving as a courtroom.

Scotland's *Edinburgh Advertiser*, one of the many newspapers throughout Great Britain that would print ongoing updates of this trial, would report that 'the court was much crowded' on the day of commencement.[306] The vast majority of those present in the gallery were male: army and naval officers, retired military men, civil servants, members of the nobility, gentlemen of the press; all in their best uniforms or hand-tailored suits and silk top-hats. For those present, and for countless newspaper readers following this trial featuring the famous Captain Bligh, about whom even West End plays had been written since the *Bounty* mutiny, this promised to be both entertaining and enthralling – for the incredible New South Wales military coup was universally considered to be all about Bligh. It was, in the words of navigator Captain Matthew Flinders, 'Captain Bligh's extraordinary business'.[307]

The members of the gallery now fell into a hush as a military jury trooped into the Great Hall. Fifteen in all, the members of the Court included six lieutenant generals, two major generals, and seven colonels – none of them junior in rank to the Accused. The officers, all clad in tailored crimson uniforms glowing with gold braid, white gloves and cocked hats, were accompanied by the Judge Advocate General of His Majesty's Forces who wore ermine-trimmed robes and a fussy white wig of office. His role would be similar to that of a judge in a civil trial. In 1811, the Judge Advocate General, the JAG in modern terminology, was the surprisingly young thirty-one-year-old the Honorable Charles Manners-Sutton. He was a rising star in British society. A son of the Archbishop of Canterbury, Manners-Sutton would soon enter parliament. By 1817, at the age of just thirty-seven, he would be Speaker of the House of Commons and in 1835 he would be elevated to the peerage, being created Viscount Canterbury.

At the insistence of the highest authority in the land, the British Government was treating this military court martial with great seriousness. The forty-eight-year-old Prince Regent, the future King George IV, had only received his kingly powers via the enacting of the Regency Act three months before, in February, after his father King George III had been declared insane the previous November. Prince George was best known for his interest in the arts and architecture, and under his influence Regents Street and Regents Park would be developed, and Windsor Castle restored. But once he became Prince Regent, he surprised many with a vigorous interest in government affairs and matters military, and in this court martial in particular.

Over the next few years, the Prince Regent would prove such a militarist that he would dissuade the government from following the line pushed by many in the Whig party, who wanted to end the war with Napoleon and let the French have Europe. He would receive much of the credit for keeping up the pressure on the French and ultimately bringing about Napoleon's final downfall by 1815. It is clear that a decisive outcome in this very public court case now opening at the Kings Hospital was considered by the Prince Regent to be essential, for the sake of military discipline, public morale and British prestige, and he would go to extraordinary lengths to keep abreast of its proceedings.

As the Judge Advocate General and officers of the court took their seats at a series of tables at one end of the rectangular hall, the officers setting their hats on the felt covering the table in front of them, members of the audience and the trial's participants resumed their chairs. It was not an intimate setting. In the vast hall, not unlike a church, every scrape of chair on stone floor or audience-member cough was amplified, and the voices of participants would echo around the walls.

At a table opposite his judges, the Accused, uniformed and bareheaded, also took his seat, with two civilian lawyers at his side. The man facing the charge of mutiny was Lieutenant-Colonel George Johnston, the former Major Johnston, previously deputy commander of the New South Wales Corps. Johnston's two attorneys were John Adolphus and Charles F. Williams, a pair who would work well in tandem, with one dashing off written questions while the other interrogated witnesses. Johnston himself looked too innocuous a character to have master-minded a military coup, leading 300 troops, with bayonets fixed, colours flying, and fifes and drums playing, to surround Government House in Sydney and arrest His Majesty's Governor on 26 January 1808. Too genial a man to have set up the revolutionary government which had subsequently controlled New South Wales for almost two years as a vicious little police state.

Yet, while the official focus was on Johnston, who was now on trial for his life, in reality two others were on trial. One was the former Governor of New South Wales, Commodore William Bligh. The other was John Macarthur who, in sharp contrast to his colonial status, was a complete unknown in Britain. His one-time friend Major Edward Abbott, now in England, wrote to mutual friend Captain John Piper back in New South Wales: 'Mack makes a very little figure in this part of the world.'[308]

Ex-governor Bligh was in court, sitting at the front at a table with his own legal counsel, Frederick Pollock, and Francis Seymour Larpent, counsel for the Crown. Bligh, who was to serve as Prosecutor in the case against Johnston, was now fifty-six years of age, although he looked older. He had become a sad yet driven man. At home in his Lambeth terrace house, his dear wife Betsy was dying. His favourite daughter Mary, the light of his life, was across the world in New South Wales. And here he was having to defend his name and reputation in front of the nation, not for the first time. Bligh wanted Johnston convicted for his part in the Sydney coup of 1808. If Johnston were to be found Not Guilty, then Bligh knew he would be damned for all time as the cruel, corrupt tyrant that Johnston and his fellow coup leaders claimed he had been. And all the efforts that Bligh had put into clearing his name after the *Bounty* affair would have been for nothing. While there would be no hangman's noose for him if he lost this prosecution, public opinion, and history, would serve as his executioners.

Bligh was so convinced that Johnston would be found guilty of mutiny, and so determined to make sure the whole world knew about the verdict, he had employed a Mr Bartrum, a shorthand writer from Clement's Inn, to take down every word said during the trial. Mr Bartrum's notes would be turned into longhand for Bligh and his counsel to study during the trial. But, most importantly, Bligh intended having the word-by-word record of the trial published in book form following its conclusion. Yet, while the prosecution of Johnston was important, to Bligh it was only a step toward convicting his chief foe, the man who above all had been responsible for his overthrow in New South Wales: John Macarthur.

Macarthur wasn't in court, but he was not far away; he was sitting outside the Great Hall in an anteroom reserved for witnesses for the Defence. Macarthur sat with army officers, naval officers including an elderly retired admiral, rank and file soldiers, and civilians. Most of the faces were familiar: Abbott, Kemp, Minchin, Finucane, Lawson, Laycock, and Harris from the New South Wales Corps, a regiment that no longer existed – the shamed unit had been renamed the 102nd Regiment.

Assistant Surgeon Thomas Jamieson was not present; he had died in England over the winter of 1809–1810. Young Lieutenants Kent and Ellison from HMS *Porpoise* were there, as were civilians John Blaxland and Charles Grimes, and a grinning Sergeant-Major Whittle. Macarthur, immaculately dressed, with his dark hair combed up at the front, lips pouting, glowered at a wall.

Many of these men had once been his friends, but Macarthur had fallen out with almost every one of them over time. Minchin and Grimes he had banished from New South Wales. Harris, he had tried to banish. Blaxland hated him with a passion. Abbott and Laycock had turned against him. Finucane was allied to his enemy, Foveaux. Still, since arriving in England the previous year, Macarthur had worked hard to paper over the cracks in his relationships with his fellow rebels, for the sake of this court case and the cases expected to follow. Macarthur had even tracked down Lieutenant-Colonel Joseph Foveaux, his successor as dictator of the colony and a man he had tried to shoot not so long ago. In the way that only Macarthur could, he had convinced Foveaux that they should cast aside old enmities and be allies in the cause of self-preservation.

Once in England, Macarthur had wasted no time before attempting to ingratiate himself with their lordships in Whitehall. He had brought several emu, the Australian flightless bird, for the wife of the Secretary of State, and black swans for the Under Secretary's wife. He also had a number of other smaller birds which he planned to present to further influential members of the government, but friends in England suggested this was going too far. Furthermore, Macarthur had darkened the doors of every potential influential backer. His eldest boy Edward had done the early legwork, and between them father and son had racked up a collection of well-placed officers, gentlemen and members of the nobility to provide Macarthur with moral support.

Colonel Johnston was better-connected than Macarthur. He

had as his patron the Duke of Northumberland, under whom he had served in the American War of Independence. Through Northumberland, Johnston had an avenue to the Commander in Chief of the army, the Duke of York. This connection was not enough to prevent Johnston being called before a general court martial, but it might have some influence on the members of the court who heard his case.

Lord Castlereagh and his Under Secretary Edward Cooke had been determined to prosecute the New South Wales rebels to the full extent of the law; the rebellion had, after all, been as much against their authority as it had been against Bligh's. Castlereagh had sought an opinion on the rebellion from senior government legal adviser T. G. Harris, who had expressed the view that the rebel leaders' actions had constituted an act of treason. But shortly after Lord Castlereagh received this advice, in an episode that would have pleased John Macarthur in more ways than one, Castlereagh challenged Foreign Secretary George Canning to a duel after learning that Canning was secretly trying to have him removed from office. A scandal erupted over the duel, fought with swords but without a fatal wound, and both men resigned. Castlereagh would return to government in 1812 and become one of Britain's most celebrated foreign secretaries.

The man who replaced Castlereagh as Secretary of State at the War and Colonial Offices, Lord Liverpool, was less enthusiastic about the New South Wales prosecutions. The pragmatic, unimaginative Liverpool, who would become Prime Minister in 1812, had not been personally involved at the time of the rebellion as Castlereagh had been, and he currently had a war with Napoleon to worry about. Liverpool asked both Attorney-General Sir Vicary Gibbs and Solicitor-General Sir Thomas Plumer for their opinions in the matter. Both these gentlemen agreed with T. G. Harris' assessment and recommended legal action – at a minimum, Johnston and Foveaux must be prosecuted for instigating and continuing a mutiny. Had

Colonel Paterson survived the journey home, it was intended that he would also have been prosecuted for allowing the mutiny to continue.

Plumer and Gibbs had also provided the Secretary of State with a list of civilians who should be tried for conspiracy to commit treason. Topping that list was John Macarthur, who had, in the opinion of T. G. Harris, 'excited the mutiny' and 'instigated the arrest of Governor Bligh'. Macarthur's name was followed by that of Nicholas Bayly, Dr Robert Townson, John Blaxland, Garnham Blaxcell, and Dr Thomas Jamieson as 'having previously concerted together with Major Johnston the arrest and imprisonment of Governor Bligh'.[309]

This list was slightly different from Bligh's 12 March 1809 list of fifteen civilian rebels (Gregory Blaxland was off the list, John Blaxland was on it), and considerably shorter. This suggests that the Attorney-General and Solicitor-General may have been in possession of evidence from sources additional to Bligh which confirmed, to their mind, the identities of the true instigators of the revolt. It is possible that Charles Grimes or Lieutenant William Minchin, who had both been exiled by Macarthur and had been in England since the autumn of 1809, had secretly revealed to the authorities who the rebel movers and shakers had been, in return for immunity.

During the course of the trial it would become apparent that Minchin cooperated with the Prosecution to a degree, but only in respect to John Macarthur; Minchin stayed loyal to his fellow serving officers and did not desert Johnston. Grimes seems the most likely to have collaborated fully with the authorities. Of the civil magistrates appointed by the junta immediately after the coup, his was the only name that did not appear on the Plumer–Gibbs list, and he would later be very contrite about his role in the coup. Tellingly, Grimes would never return to the colony – where former rebels might have taken out savage revenge on him for informing on his colleagues. Grimes had the opportunity and the motive to change his tune and sing to the government, and it is highly likely that he informed on Macarthur and the others.

As for other rebels whose names had not found their way onto the list after Bligh had named them as conspirators, it seems that Plumer and Gibbs may have excluded a number of them as a result of the approaches of their connections in England. Despite their connections, neither Macarthur nor his fellow junta members knew at this point precisely who was to be prosecuted and who could breathe easily; this information would only emerge later. But, like everyone else involved with the case, Macarthur would have guessed what road the government would take, and Johnston's court martial was the first step down that road.

Macarthur was a cold, humourless man at the best of times. Yet, shining through the granite there was a glow of certainty and confidence. Macarthur had every reason to believe that Johnston would be acquitted. Among other things, a court martial in January, brought by the Admiralty against Lieutenant William Kent for failing to follow Governor Bligh's orders when Bligh was under arrest in Sydney, had ended in young Kent's acquittal. This acquittal was said to have been due to the extraordinary circumstances that had prevailed in New South Wales at the time. Macarthur would also have had reason to believe that, through Johnston's connections and his own, at least one of the officers now sitting in judgment on Johnston, and probably more, was very sympathetic to Johnston. And then there was Bligh's past record on the *Bounty* to consider. In Macarthur's book, all this, and twenty witnesses to the tyranny of Governor William Bligh, added up to a powerful case for the Defence.

Macarthur could not afford a verdict other than Not Guilty. If Johnston were to be found guilty, then Macarthur could expect his own conviction to be a priority for the authorities. In his case, it would be a trial for conspiracy to commit treason, with the prospect of a very unpleasant death – hanging, drawing and quartering.[310]

Having worked closely with Johnston and his legal team leading up to the trial, Macarthur knew that Johnston would not be denying that he and the New South Wales Corps had overthrown Governor Bligh. The Defence would contend that Johnston and the Corps had been forced to act, to end Bligh's despotic rule, which had, they would say, left all good men in fear for their property, their freedom, and their lives. They had also acted, they would say, to prevent a bloody civil uprising against Bligh. Far from being rebels and traitors, they would declare, they had been British patriots, acting in the interests of king and country.

All the rebel players from the Glorious 26th knew precisely what they had to say to defend Johnston and protect themselves. A catalogue of accusations against Bligh, coloured with falsehoods and exaggerations, had been crafted by Macarthur and shared around so that all the members of the rebel chorus would learn their lines and sing the same tune, over and over again. As much as Macarthur had come to be despised by his former allies, they knew that together they would prevail, while divided they would fail.

For Macarthur, the lead-up to the trial had been very stressful, and he was feeling the effects of it. For years, he had suffered from severe indigestion; he had turned to a vegetarian diet, was drinking water instead of wine and also downing large quantities of milk which he was convinced would soothe the gastric pain. Since he had been back in England his liver had been playing up, he'd suffered severe colds, and he had been plagued with congestion of the lungs. Then he had been 'seized with violent spasms in my side', and now suffered from 'a terrible nervous affectation' – a nervous twitch.[311] After his journey back to England in 1809, he had confidently predicted that from the date of his arrival he would be 'in three months after on my way back'.[312] Now, more than two years later, the battle was only just beginning and a return was not in sight.

Still, Macarthur was prepared to put up with the pain and discomfort if it meant that he could finally deal with William Bligh and get back to New South Wales and resume the business of building his fortune. For all the months of preparation, Macarthur knew that there was a good possibility that the case might be thrown out long before it reached the point of defending Johnston's actions. But he would have to wait, with his painful stomach and nervous twitch, for the first adjournment and news from inside the courtroom before he would know if that stratagem had succeeded.

Inside the Great Hall, the trial had begun. But the initial proceedings lacked the excitement promised by a general court martial for mutiny. The charges were read, awash with legalese: 'whereas', 'on or about', 'forthwith', 'aforesaid'. The oath was administered to the President of the Court, in effect the foreman of the jury, Lieutenant General William Keppel. The commander of the 67th Regiment for the past three months, Keppel had previously been governor of the island colony of Martinique in the Caribbean for six years, and so knew about the difficulties of colonial government. The names of the fourteen other members of the court, Johnston's jury, were read aloud, and Colonel Johnston was given the opportunity to object to each of them. Johnston made no objections. The Judge Advocate took the oath.

And then: 'Lieutenant-Colonel Johnston, are you guilty or not guilty of the charge which is preferred against you?'

Johnston, whose sheathed sword would lay on the table in front of the president, impounded, throughout the hearing, came to his feet. In a controlled though soft voice he replied, 'Not guilty.' He resumed his seat.[313]

But before the trial could go any further, several officers on the jury interrupted proceedings, asking if the crime with which Johnston had been charged had not occurred more than three years before. This was an interruption that John Macarthur would have been expecting, coming from supporters of Johnston. There was an act of parliament, a Statute of Limitations, which prevented a man from being charged with a crime more than three years after the event. Lengthy and sometimes heated debate now followed between the fifteen officers of the court, with one officer in particular arguing that the trial could not and should not proceed.

'More than three years having elapsed before the prosecution is commenced,' said the unidentified general or colonel. 'I wish to know the reason why it was not brought on before.'

General Keppel, President of the Court, tried to brush the objection aside, saying, 'That can be inquired into in the course of the investigation.'

But his colleague would not be put off. 'How can we investigate a charge that ought not be investigated?' He went on to say that Captain Bligh should be asked why the prosecution had not been brought earlier.[314]

Here, the young Judge Advocate General stepped in. Manners-Sutton suggested that the case be proceeded with. When Governor Bligh was giving evidence, he said, the question of why the prosecution had taken so long could be asked, and decided. The members of the court concurred, and the trial proceeded.

With a document in his hand, William Bligh came to his feet. The commodore and former governor, a little portly now in his late middle age, walked to the witness chair. For many in the large gallery, this was their first sight of Captain Bligh, made famous by his epic voyage in an open boat with eighteen members of the crew of the *Bounty*. Bligh would have preferred his fame to have rested on his exploits as Captain James Cook's hand-picked protégé and sailing master, on his own dangerous missions on far-flung oceans, on his battle honours under famous commanders such as Lord Nelson. But it had not been fated to be.

Bligh took the oath, and then read a prepared opening speech which succinctly, within ten minutes, established the events, from his point of view, leading up to the insurrection of the New South Wales Corps, and then of the military coup itself. He spoke calmly, deliberately. Back at home with Betsy and his four unmarried girls for the past six months, Bligh seemed to have recovered his spirits and his self-control. As recently as the previous November he had still been signing his letters as Governor Bligh. It was an honorary title to which he was entitled, and during this trial he would be from time to time addressed as such. But the shock of losing his position to Macquarie had left him feeling as betrayed by the Secretary of State as he had been by the rebels in New South Wales, and it took him a long time to come to terms with it. Surrounded by people who loved and respected him, he had entertained Palmer, Campbell, Suttor and the other supporters who had come home from New South Wales with him, and had been comforted by good friends such as Sir Joseph Banks. The rage, it seemed, had subsided, to be replaced by a determination to see justice done and to clear his name.

Bligh's counsel now received the court's permission to put questions to his client. Bligh had chosen the young, bright and up-and-coming Frederick Pollock quite purposely. Only in his twenties, Pollock had at this time been at the bar for less than three years. But his great skills as a lawyer were already apparent, especially to Bligh, who had a good eye for young talent. This case would in fact launch the glittering career of the later Sir Frederick and later still Chief Baron Pollock. It helped that Pollock liked Bligh, as his letters to the commodore and his wife make clear, and Bligh was fond of and respected him. Pollock now set out to quickly quash the argument that the case should be dismissed due to the Statute of Limitations, by establishing the date of Bligh's return to England – 25 October 1810; six months prior to the court's sitting. As Bligh had been detained in New South Wales prior to that, Pollock proposed, it would have been impossible for him to initiate the charge of mutiny against Johnston any earlier.

The garrulous Judge Advocate General, decades younger than the Accused, the Prosecutor, and the officers of the court, now spent many minutes addressing the court about how they might determine whether or not a prosecution could have begun earlier than it did. He then turned to several matters regarding procedure, before finally inviting the Defence to cross-examine Captain Bligh, who had remained in the witness chair all this time. Colonel Johnston's counsel John Adolphus eagerly came to his feet and addressed his first question to Bligh.

'What was the earliest period that you could have demanded a court martial on Colonel Johnston?'

Bligh had thought he had settled that question with his responses to his own counsel, and looked up to the Judge Advocate General for direction. But Manners-Sutton allowed the question with a nod. So Bligh replied, 'I had no power to demand any court martial, that I know of, until the 25th of October 1810, when I arrived in England. Unless I had ordered Colonel Paterson to try him in New South Wales.'

'Had you written to Colonel Paterson or applied to His Majesty's Government for a court martial on Colonel Johnston,' continued Johnston's lawyer, 'might not such an investigation have taken place two years ago?'

Bligh saw red. To his mind, it was a damned fool of a question, the answer to which was patently obvious. 'I could not write to Colonel Paterson. I considered him a [expletive deleted] rebel! That was the reason I could not [expletive deleted] write to him. His Majesty's Governor to write to a [expletive deleted] man who had put him under [expletive deleted] arrest?' Obviously, Bligh's rage still simmered.

The Judge Advocate General quickly intervened. 'I believe the court will think the facts have been ascertained,' he said to

Adolphus, before turning to Bligh. 'It would preserve the general decorum of the proceedings better if the witness was rather more cautious in the language which he uses.'[315]

When John Macarthur learned of this outburst, he would assuredly nod with satisfaction. It was true that the court would now rule that the Statute of Limitations did not apply in this case; the law provided for 'some manifest impediment [which] arises to prevent the prosecution being brought'.[316] Such an impediment had obviously existed, in the form of Bligh's illegal state of arrest, so the three-year limitation did not apply. But the Defence must have been expecting this outcome. As Macarthur would have known, Adolphus had quite deliberately continued to flog the proverbial dead horse to provoke Bligh. And, in the estimation of those on Johnston's side, he had succeeded admirably. From his own mouth, Bligh had condemned himself as a man whose temper was close to the surface, a man whose language could be crude and objectionable.

Macarthur, the experienced duelist, could claim first blood in this, his latest and most deadly duel with William Bligh.

20

The Case for the Prosecution

With the matter of the Statute of Limitations out of the way, the Prosecution case began with Governor Bligh now questioned by his counsel Frederick Pollock to fill out the details of his earlier statement. When Pollock asked him if the regulations that Bligh had implemented in the colony regarding the distribution of wine and spirits had discontented anyone, Bligh said that his control of their distribution, on London's orders, had certainly discontented John Macarthur and the officers of the New South Wales Corps, as they had previously monopolised that distribution.

Some later writers would suggest that Bligh's measures regarding wine, spirits and currency, like Prohibition in the USA in the 1930s, were destined to lead to problems. Yet Bligh did not prohibit the import of wine and spirits. Wine and spirits continued to be distributed in the colony; Bligh had merely taken the distribution (and the profits) out of the hands of the military officers, and regulated it. Even the rank and file soldiers of the New South Wales Corps had sent Bligh an address of thanks for increasing their liquor ration in 1807.[317]

Bligh then described for the court, from his point of view, the events leading up to 26 January 1808 and then of the coup itself that evening. Before leaving New South Wales, Bligh, as meticulous as ever, had commissioned Assistant Surveyor James Meehan to draw up a large map of Sydney, showing the key streets and buildings. He'd had this map pasted onto a piece of board and now, with the map propped on an easel, he was able to point out for the members of the court the location of Government House in relation to the barracks, the location of the guns on the Parade Ground that were aimed at Government House, the line of march of the Corps on the evening of 26 January, and so on.

Pollock next brought Bligh to the contentious matter of how he gained control of HMS *Porpoise* in February of 1809. The rebels, before and during this trial, were highly critical of the fact that Bligh had broken his word and had not gone back to England in the *Porpoise*. Bligh critics over the subsequent 200 years have also used this as an example of what they've considered Bligh's duplicity, untrustworthiness and wickedness. In answer to this, Bligh began by pointing out that he had been locked in a subaltern's barrack by the rebels for seven days because he would not give up control of the *Porpoise*. Bligh's critics seemed to think that this ungentlemanly and illegal close confinement of the Governor by an illegal regime, along with his daughter, was acceptable, but that his method of escaping it was not. Bligh's conscience was untroubled. To him, no bargain with rebels and traitors was worth the paper it was written on. He told the court, 'The moment I got the command of the *Porpoise* I took care to keep it, and would not suffer any of their terms.' He stated, 'I considered myself, the moment I got on board my ship, as the legal Governor of the country, and so I considered myself to the last.'[318]

The second day of the trial resumed with Bligh still in the witness chair. At this point, the Prosecution had several lengthy documents read to the court, in particular the dispatch of 11 April 1808, sent by Johnston to London describing how and why he had led the overthrow of the Governor, and the attached copies of letters relating to John Macarthur's Criminal Court trial of 25–26 January 1808. At this tedious juncture, several members of the court raised questions about that colony's Criminal Court, and Judge Advocate General Manners-Sutton expressed the view that no person brought before the Criminal Court in New South Wales had the right to challenge the Judge Advocate, as Macarthur had done, and that Governor Bligh had no power to replace the Judge Advocate, as Macarthur had demanded. This was an early and unexpected point against Macarthur and for Bligh, and destroyed the validity of the actions of Macarthur and the six officers sitting on the Criminal Court in his case on 25–26 January.

Bligh testified for the Prosecution until the morning of the third day of the trial, Thursday, 9 May when the Defence was given the opportunity to cross-examine him. After establishing that Bligh had not commanded land forces apart from Marines prior to arriving in New South Wales, Adolphus and Williams went straight for the jugular. They asked how many times Bligh had been previously involved in courts martial for mutiny. Bligh turned to the officers of the court. 'Really, gentlemen, it is hard for me to answer such a question. The whole world knows perfectly well that in 1787 there was a mutiny on the ship *Bounty*. I presume that is what they allude to. I don't know any other mutiny that I have had anything to do with, except that dreadful mutiny at the Nore, in which, of course, I was not particularly concerned.'[319]

The Nore mutiny of May–June 1797 and Bligh's involvement in it were to confuse some historians and provide ammunition for more recent critics of Bligh who cite this as an example of his tyrannical character. The *Encyclopaedia Britannica*, for example, was among the confused. In its 1987 edition, it said of Bligh,

'As captain of the *Director*, he was put ashore when his crew joined the crew of the *Nore* (1797) in another mutiny.'[320] The eminent *Britannica* got it very wrong. The Nore was not a ship, but a place, at the mouth of the River Medway, near Sheerness, close to the mouth of the River Thames. At the Nore, the crews of the twenty-four warships of Britain's North Sea Fleet followed the example of the Channel Fleet at Portmouth in raising the red flag of rebellion and going on strike for better conditions. Bligh's ship, HMS *Director*, had recently joined the fleet at the Nore. Those officers considered by their crews to be the most cruel and oppressive, including three of Bligh's subordinate officers, were either sent ashore or locked in their cabins by the mutineers. Bligh himself was not numbered among these unpopular officers, and was allowed to stay aboard the *Director* by the mutineers, who continued to obey his day-to-day orders. Meanwhile, Captain John Bligh, commander of HMS *Latona*, another ship at the Nore, was among those immediately sent ashore by its crew.

William Bligh remained on the *Director* for another week. But when he refused to continue to lock up his three unpopular subordinate officers or to give the mutineers access to the ship's small arms, the rebels also put him ashore. The British Government thought so much of Bligh's opinion that they sent him to Yarmouth, where a third fleet was anchored, to gauge whether the sailors there would obey orders to threaten the Nore fleet with their guns. After going aboard many of the ships at Yarmouth and talking with their crews, Bligh had reported back that it would be unwise to expect sailors in one British fleet to go against comrades in another. Supporting Bligh's assessment, shortly after, eight ships of the Yarmouth fleet sailed to the Nore as their crews threw in their lot with the Nore mutineers. To resolve this mutiny, the government took a hard line, refusing to give in to the sailors' demands or even to negotiate, and after several weeks the mutiny collapsed. The leaders of the strike faced court martial. The 'president' of the mutineers' governing council, seaman Richard Parker, a former officer, was convicted of mutiny and hanged from a yardarm, as were thirty-five of his fellow ringleaders.

Following the Nore Mutiny, Bligh lobbied on behalf of twenty-one members of his crew and had them excused from punishment for involvement in the mutiny. The crew of the *Director* would shortly after perform heroically under Bligh at the Battle of Camperdown. Ironically, several dozen other leaders of the Nore Mutiny were transported to New South Wales as convicts after being court-martialled for their part in that affair, and had been in the colony at the time that Bligh was overthrown in 1808.[321]

Lieutenant-Colonel Johnston's defence team was aware of Bligh's favourable connection with the Nore Mutiny. They didn't pursue that matter; they were more interested in focusing the Court's attention on the *Bounty* mutiny, and in unsettling Bligh. They succeeded on both scores. When asked about the *Bounty*, Bligh, feeling the need to defend himself, launched into a detailed account of that mutiny. After several minutes, the Judge Advocate stopped him, saying that Bligh's lengthy answer was 'perfectly immaterial to the case we are now trying'. Bligh was incensed by this ruling. He felt that he should have the right to answer the implied accusation contained in the Defence question about the *Bounty*.

A member of the court felt the same way, and voiced the opinion, 'The question being put to criminate Captain Bligh, he has a right to answer it.'

The President, General Keppel, spoke up. 'It is no imputation against an officer that he has brought persons to court martial.'[322]

The other member persisted with the view that Bligh should be given the opportunity to fully explain the *Bounty* affair now that the Defence had raised it. The Judge Advocate relented and allowed Bligh to give a short account of the *Bounty* mutiny and the subsequent court martial of several of Fletcher Christian's fellow mutineers who had been caught in the Pacific, three of whom were subsequently hanged for their part in the mutiny. The point that Bligh now made was that *he* had not brought those mutineers to court martial. The *Bounty* court martial had taken place in England while he was on the other side of the world completing the *Bounty*'s original mission, the transfer of breadfruit plants from Tahiti to the Caribbean, in the *Providence* – without a hint of mutiny from that crew, he was proud to say.

The Defence now asked Bligh whether he had ever been personally court-martialled. Bligh replied that he had faced a court martial for the loss of the *Bounty*, and had been totally exonerated. He also said that he had been before a court martial in 1804 when commander of the 74-gun HMS *Warrior.* His senior lieutenant, John Frazier, had claimed to be unfit for duty because of a sprained ankle, but Bligh was convinced he was malingering and ordered him to take his watch, allowing him to sit on a chair while on duty. When Frazier refused to take his watch, Bligh had him arrested and court-martialled. When the *Warrior*'s surgeon, Dr Cinnamon, testified at this court martial that he had not felt Frazier had been fit for duty, Frazier was acquitted.

In quest of revenge, Frazier had then requested that Bligh be brought before a court martial, accusing him of 'tyrannical and oppressive and unofficerlike behaviour' for ordering him to do duty when unfit, and of 'calling me rascal, scoundrel and shaking his fist in my face'.[323] Several members of the *Warrior*'s crew backed his side of the story. Other members of the crew had supported Bligh's version of events and felt that, while their captain could use colourful language and wave his hands about, they took his behaviour with a grain of salt. And none of Bligh's witnesses had seen him shake his fist in Frazier's face.

Bligh himself had candidly admitted to that 1804 court martial that he may have at times appeared over-anxious for his orders to be obeyed and had used language and gestures 'peculiar to myself', but denied victimising Frazier. From the evidence of some witnesses, it seemed that Frazier had gone out of his way to annoy and provoke Bligh over a period of several months. The upshot was that the court had found the charges against Bligh 'in part proved' and reprimanded him, adding that he was 'admonished to be in future more correct in his language'.[324] Bligh had returned to the command of the *Warrior*, and Frazier soon after left the Royal Navy; Bligh told the Johnston Court Martial that he believed Frazier had been dismissed from the service.

The Defence then moved on to accuse Bligh of having favoured Andrew Thompson, his bailiff in New South Wales, who had since died in a Hawkesbury River flood while trying to help fellow colonists. The accusation was that Bligh had returned to Thompson a fine of £100 imposed for selling spirits. Bligh answered that although he had kept Thompson in his employ, he had urged the Judge Advocate to prosecute him for illegally selling spirits, and he had definitely not ordered the fine refunded. To his knowledge it had not been refunded, and Johnston's lawyers were unable to prove that it had been. Nor did they mention that Bligh's successor, Governor Macquarie, had thought so highly of Thompson he'd made him a magistrate.

The Defence next accused Bligh's late son-in-law, Lieutenant Putland, of being in business with Robert Campbell, but Bligh stated that to the best of his knowledge this had not been the case. This was the extent of the Defence's accusations against Bligh for corruption, despite all the earlier bluster by Macarthur, Johnston and Foveaux that Bligh had pillaged the colony.

Now, with the appetiser out of the way, the Defence moved to the juicier subject of John Macarthur. Bligh was asked, 'Did you not damn the Privy Council and the Secretary of State, and say that Macarthur should not keep the grant of land which he held by the order of the Secretary of State?'

Bligh vehemently shook his head. 'No, I declare to God I never did.'

'Did you not, in the hearing of Major Abbott, use these words, or others to the like effect? "Damn the Secretary of State. What do I care for him? He commands in England and I command here".'

'I know nothing about it,' said Bligh.

'Did you not say, in the presence of Lieutenant Minchin, "I don't care a damn for the Secretary of State. He is but a clerk in office – in today, and out tomorrow"?'

Both Major Abbott and Lieutenant Minchin would later personally testify that Bligh had used these words, and supporters of Macarthur to this day have repeated them as fact. Yet Bligh's response, under oath, was unequivocal, when asked if he had said this. 'I did not!'[325]

Both Abbott and Minchin would prove to be lying when they testified about other matters in this case, which doesn't exactly give a concrete foundation to their evidence. But the Defence had very cleverly, just prior to this, established that Bligh had been reprimanded by a court martial for improper language, making it quite credible that such colourful statements as Abbott and Minchin attributed to him had come out of his mouth. But the Defence attorneys seemed taken aback by Bligh's emphatic denial. They had obviously taken the word of Macarthur, Abbott and Minchin that their statements were truthful, but here was Bligh denying he had used these expressions. In all his career, Bligh had been accused of a number of things, but never before now had he been accused of lying, especially not of lying under oath. Just to be sure there was no mistake, the surprised Defence now asked: 'Will you venture to restate upon your oath, that you never did utter any of those expressions, or any words to the like effect?'

To which Bligh gave the considered response, 'To the best of my recollection, I know nothing of this kind of conversation taking place.'[326]

Bligh didn't even suggest that similar conversations had occurred, after which Abbott and Minchin might have distorted his words. His testimony was firm, and by implication made liars of Macarthur, Abbott and Minchin. In his defence, it does seem strange that Bligh, always the faithful servant of his naval commanders and the Admiralty for forty years, without ever being on record uttering an unflattering word about this captain or that admiral despite his proclivity for colourful language, would have said such demeaning things about Lord Castlereagh, a man for whom he seems to have had, at the time, the greatest respect. It would remain to be seen whether or not the court believed Bligh, but by introducing the Abbott and Minchin statements so early in proceedings the Defence was aiming to sow doubts in the minds of members of the court about Bligh's style of government in New South Wales.

Having opened this chink in Bligh's armour, the Defence continued to hammer him on the matter of the alleged conversations between Abbott, Minchin and himself, until the Judge Advocate General stepped in, declaring that these questions had nothing to do with the case. The only way they could be relevant, he said, was if these expressions were so important they could not possibly be forgotten by the man who uttered them, and that he was denying them 'in cool deliberate perjury'. Yet, even if the Defence could prove that Bligh had said these things, said Manners-Sutton, he believed that it would not help their case one bit.[327]

Bligh now spoke up, saying that even if in the navy, or in a remote colony, such expressions might be excused, he could not understand why the Defence had put such questions to him, in the light of his well-known loyalty to the Crown and its ministers. 'I could never utter a word disrespectful to them, and I disavow the charge in the strongest possible manner. I know nothing of such speeches.' It was true, he admitted, that if someone had asked him for something which he had no power to grant, he might have said, 'Damn it, get out of my way,' or used a similar expression. But as for damning the Secretary of State or the Privy Council, 'I cannot persuade myself I ever did.'[328]

The Defence moved on, aiming to prove that Bligh had deprived men of their property. John Macarthur continued to loom large, as Bligh was asked if he had ordered a fence that Macarthur was building on his Sydney lease pulled down. Two weeks before his Criminal Court trial in January 1808, in addition to compiling his excuses for the removal of Judge Advocate Atkins, Macarthur had deliberately tried to stir up trouble with the Governor. For the first time in the two years since being granted the lease beside the New Church, Macarthur had begun to build a fence around it, using off-duty soldiers as his labourers, knowing that Bligh would take the bait.

Sure enough, Superintendent Divine had been sent with a gang of convicts to remove the posts and fill in the holes. This land was then in dispute. Bligh wanted to return it and several other leased blocks to public use, and had offered to swap it for land elsewhere in the town nominated by Macarthur. Macarthur had nominated three other blocks, one of which was occupied by the quarters of the government boats crews. Bligh had turned down each of these as being impractical and asked Macarthur to nominate a more realistic parcel. Macarthur had then said he'd keep the original block, thank you very much, and had provocatively commenced to build the fence.

After Bligh established the facts relating to Macarthur's block of land, the Defence questioned him about the homes of six men nearby, all of which had been built on government leases. Had Bligh not ordered these homes pulled down? Bligh replied that he had personally gone to the six men in question and told them that their land was required for public use, as had been set down by the colony's first governor, Arthur Phillip, whose blueprint for Sydney had been faithfully followed by his successors. Bligh had offered these men new land elsewhere in the town, and freehold as opposed to leases, at that. He'd also offered the help of the Superintendent of Convicts in demolishing their huts and rebuilding them at the new sites, and offered material from the government stores for the construction of new houses on the new freehold sites. Some of the men involved, said Bligh, had agreed to the arrangement, and had thanked him once they had set up their new residences. No houses had been pulled down on Bligh's orders. Several had been demolished by their owners in accordance with the agreement with the Governor. No one had been forcibly deprived of their land or property. The Defence, unable to prove otherwise, had to move on.

Bligh was now accused of taking a valuable English bull, the property of his rival in England, Captain William Kent, for his own use, and against the will of Kent's agent, Surgeon Harris. Bligh flatly denied it. The Defence next spent some time on Judge Advocate Atkins and his 'adviser', George Crossley. One of Johnston's attorneys read out Bligh's far from complimentary report about Atkins to the Secretary of State.

Bligh was appalled. 'That paper, sir, which you have now read, was a secret document transmitted by me to the Secretary of State in sure confidence.'

'There has been a breach of trust somewhere!' complained a member of the court.

'This is a confidential paper!' exclaimed another indignant general.[329]

Bligh agreed, and told the court that the rebels had seized many of his confidential documents after the coup. He had asked Governor Macquarie for their return but, just prior to his departure from Sydney, Macquarie had advised him that as a result of his inquiries he had established that either Macarthur or Johnston had taken these papers and Bligh's personal items including his sword back to England with them. Bligh never did have any of this material returned to him.

The Defence, realising it had stepped onto dangerous ground by using a stolen government document, quickly put away the Governor's confidential report and turned to the matter of George Crossley. The Defence established that Bligh knew that Crossley had been sent out to the colony as a convicted perjurer, and that Bligh had spoken with him several times on legal matters. But Bligh maintained that it had been Judge Advocate Atkins and the Governor's secretary, Edmund Griffin, who had mostly dealt with Crossley. The Defence was pursuing the rebel mantra that Crossley had been employed by Bligh's administration contrary to the act of parliament which prevented ex-convicts from practising in a court of law. As it would turn out, because that act only referred to England, it would be ruled to not apply in New South Wales. During the administration of Bligh's successor, Lachlan Macquarie, George Crossley and several other ex-convicts with legal training would be permitted to appear in the colony's courts from time to time, until free attorneys migrated from Britain. All John Macarthur's hullabaloo about Crossley's employment by the Bligh administration being illegal had been either ill-informed or a deliberate and premeditated lie.

Defeated on this score, the Defence now accused Bligh of interfering with the administration of the colony's courts. Bligh countered by stating that not only had he not interfered in the running of the courts, but Colonel Johnston had himself done so by, in late 1807, trying to insist on nominating the military officers who would sit on the bench. Bligh had pointed out to Johnston that the act of parliament relating to the colony's courts required the Governor to nominate those officers. Bligh testified that Johnston, peevishly, had asked him if he also intended taking command of the regiment from him. To settle the argument, Bligh had offered to either write to London for a final decision on the matter or to allow Johnston do so. At the same time, he told the court, he'd said to Johnston, 'Whatever answer comes out from home shall settle the matter between us. But on our parts, let us be constantly amicable and quiet together.'[330] Bligh stated that, apart from this issue, his relations with Johnston had been cordial, and Johnston had usually visited him at Government House whenever he came into Sydney from his property.

The Defence then brought Bligh to the events of the coup. 'Did you not express to Colonel Johnston, at the time he placed you under arrest, that you were very much obliged to him for the handsome manner in which he carried the wishes of the colony into effect?'

Here was Bligh's facetious comment of the night of the 26th coming back to haunt him. His actual words were sufficiently misreported to give an entirely different slant to that which Bligh had intended. He had not told Johnston that he was 'very much obliged to him' or made reference to the wishes of 'the colony'. Bligh had been far from obliged to Johnston, and had facetiously spoken of 'the inhabitants', referring to Johnston's letter and its reference to 'the inhabitants', not 'the colony'. He was able to answer the question with an adamant, 'No, sir.'[331] This reference now alerted Bligh to the ways in which his opponents would distort and misrepresent his conversations and statements. It would not be the last time this happened during the course of the trial.

In his opening statement, Bligh had claimed that victory salutes had been fired by the rebels around noon the day following the coup, in the form of three volleys of musketry and twenty-one from the cannon on the Parade Ground. The Defence now asked him, 'On recollection, do you persist in this statement?' When Bligh said he did, he was asked, incredulously, 'But it really did take place?'

'The guns were fired, and it was reported to me there were twenty-one. I cannot say I counted the guns myself.'[332] And Bligh was adamant this took place on the 27th. This question of a salute by the guns on the Parade would have seemed inconsequential to some observers, but the Defence was determined to prove that it had not taken place, or certainly not when Bligh said it had. If they could prove this point, they would establish that at the very least Bligh's memory was unreliable, or, worse, he was lying. And if his memory could be proved to be unreliable in one instance, it could be unreliable in others. The question of the salute from the guns would come up several times again later, ultimately in spectacular fashion.

The fourth day of the trial began with Bligh and the Defence still locked in combat. Bligh agreed that when Lieutenant-Colonel Foveaux took over from Johnston he had maintained the same rebel measures as Johnston. When asked why he had included Walter Davidson on the list of rebels, even though he had arrived back in the colony after the coup, Bligh replied that Davidson's actions had justified his inclusion on the list. Bligh was being very careful, knowing that Davidson was the nephew of the Prince Regent's physician. He had his suspicions that Davidson had been the rebels' envoy to Colonel Paterson, but could not prove it. The Defence, no doubt hoping to perhaps get Bligh to say something that would not go down well with the Prince Regent, persisted with its question. But Bligh would say no more than that he considered Davidson's conduct justified his inclusion on his list of rebels.

The Prosecution was now permitted to re-examine Bligh. Frederick Pollock quickly established that Bligh had been honourably acquitted by the *Bounty* court martial. And he established that Bligh did not derive any personal advantage from the removal of houses from government land in Sydney or from the removal of the fence-posts on John Macarthur's Sydney lease. With that, after three and a half days in the witness chair, Bligh was excused.

Commissary John Palmer was now called to give evidence for the Prosecution. 'Little Jack' testified that on 26 January 1808, the colony had been thriving under Governor Bligh, and he had never known the colonists in general more satisfied. Asked if there was any danger of a revolt if the military had remained obedient to their officers, he answered that there had been no danger whatever. He went on to tell of the coup, and his treatment by the rebels, including his questioning by the rebel committee. The Defence, in its cross-examination, questioned Palmer about the machinations of 25–26 January, and tried to have him agree that Bligh intended charging the six officers of the Criminal Court with treason for refusing to sit with Judge Advocate Atkins. Palmer said he didn't remember any such thing being resolved.

After the Prosecution re-examined him briefly, Palmer was questioned by the Crown's counsel, Francis Seymour Larpent. With considerable experience in courts martial, Larpent would, within a year, be attached to the headquarters of the future Duke of Wellington as Judge Advocate General of all British forces in Portugal and Spain for the remainder of the Peninsula War, a job he would perform with great efficiency, prosecuting deserters, thieving soldiers and corrupt commissary officers. When Larpent asked about the celebrations that followed the 26 January coup, Palmer testified that a salute of twenty guns had been fired by the rebels on the 27th.

On a member of the court asking whether Palmer knew if Johnston and his officers had been involved in the barter of spirits prior to Governor Bligh's control of their distribution, Palmer said that it was generally believed so, but he had no specific proof of it. But, when it was suggested that Bligh's wine and spirits proclamation had led to the rebellion, he expressed the view that this proclamation had been a long time before the rebellion and was not the cause of it. When asked if Colonel Johnston had told Governor Bligh prior to the insurrection that inhabitants were discontented with his rule, or had proposed that Bligh step down, Palmer said that neither had been the case.

Robert Campbell was next called. The little Scotsman was not a happy man. Not only were his businesses in New South Wales still in difficulties following the two years of rebel rule, he had arrived in England to find that his English agent had gone bankrupt, owing him £30,000, the equivalent of millions of dollars today. For the moment though, Campbell focused on the business at hand. Like Palmer, he related what had taken place at Government House on 26 January. Of more interest was his testimony about 16 December 1807. On that day, Campbell had sat as a magistrate when John Macarthur was brought up for committal. Macarthur had objected to him, so Campbell had stepped down, being replaced by another magistrate when Macarthur was committed next day. On the 16th, as Campbell was leaving the courthouse, the then Major Johnston, who was senior officer on the bench that day, had remarked to him that Macarthur had a very turbulent character and as a result had done himself a great deal of harm when a captain in the New South Wales Corps. A month and a half later, Johnston would appoint this same turbulent character to run the colony.

The Defence, in cross-examination, asked if Campbell had been in business with the ex-governor's son-in-law, Lieutenant John Putland. Campbell said that Putland had intended buying a share of the *Rose*, the ship in which Campbell had a third interest, but had died before doing anything about it. Apart from that, Putland had no business connection with him. The Defence, which was still obsessed with the employment by Bligh's administration of convict lawyer George Crossley, read the transcript of the statement that Campbell had given to the rebel committee on 27 January. In this statement, he was quoted as saying that 'Crossley was the principal adviser to the Governor'. In response, Campbell now said, 'I scarcely knew what I said. If I said that Crossley was the principal adviser, I certainly must have been mistaken.'[333] As Campbell never signed this statement, it is not impossible that this line about Crossley had been inserted later and the whole unsigned statement rewritten by his inquisitors. Not that it mattered; in the end, the Crossley affair would have no bearing on the outcome of the case.

Chief Constable Francis Oakes was called next. As Oakes took the stand in his pocket he carried a writ; he was being sued for £500 by John Macarthur for attempting to arrest him in December 1807. Oakes testified about that failed arrest attempt, and to what he saw and heard on the day of the coup and the days following. The Defence tried to have Oakes agree that there was a vast, highly agitated crowd outside the military barracks when Major Johnston arrived with Lieutenant Minchin on the afternoon of 26 January. But he responded, 'I don't believe there was a single person more than common on the Parade when I saw Major Johnston driven there.' When it was suggested that it was due to the military that the public peace was restored on 26 January, Oakes exclaimed, 'Public peace restored! I don't know that it was ever broke, unless they were the military who broke it!'[334]

Provost Marshal William Gore followed Oakes. Gore testified that, on Governor Bligh's orders, and unlike under previous administrations, no man could be lodged in jail in the colony without a magistrate's warrant, and no man could be freed from jail without the Provost Marshal's approval. After he testified to what happened at Government House on 26 January, the Defence, in cross-examination, again focused on the George Crossley affair, to no advantage to Johnston's case.

Chaplain Fulton followed Gore, and he told of his experiences during and after the coup, including facing a rebel inquisition. Fulton particularly remembered John Macarthur reading aloud in the Criminal Court a confidential letter to Governor Bligh from the Secretary of State concerning relations with the United States of America. Secretary Edmund Griffin came next, and told a similar story about the coup. Like others before him, he stated that at no time prior to the coup had Johnston or anyone else approached the Governor with complaints about the way he was running the colony.

Four enlisted men from the former New South Wales Corps followed. The regiment had been through unhappy times; on the voyage home, a measles epidemic had broken out aboard ship. The sickness had returned once the unit moved into barracks at Horsham in Sussex. More than 100 women and children, members of soldiers' families, had died at sea or back in England. It was as if the regiment was being made to pay for its behaviour in New South Wales. Private John Gillard, the gunner, was the first soldier to give evidence. He testified that he had, on the orders of Lieutenant Minchin, loaded the two Parade Ground cannon on the evening of 26 January and aimed them at Government House as the Corps was marching to topple the Governor. He also testified that he had tampered with the guns outside Government House on Lieutenant Minchin's orders, to prevent them being used in Government House's defence. The Defence asked whether Colonel Johnston had known the Parade Ground guns had been pointed at Government House.

'Why, sir,' Gillard responded, 'he certainly must know it. He passed close to the guns as he went with the regiment up to Government House.'[335]

Private John Gray, the sentry on duty at the Parade Ground at the time of the coup, told of all he'd witnessed on the afternoon and early evening of 26 January. Asked about the state of the colony leading up to the coup, he said, 'I thought it was in a peaceable state.'[336]

Isaac Champion, the former acting sergeant-major, who had been reduced to the ranks by the rebels, told of his part in the coup and of supervising Governor Bligh's guard at the subaltern's barrack on the orders of Major Abbott. When the Defence asked Champion if he had been a sergeant when he left the colony, he said, 'No, sir. I was reduced a few months before by my friend Colonel Johnston there.' He pointed to the Accused.[337]

Private Robert Davis testified to seeing the painting of the Governor's arrest in Sergeant-Major Whittle's house. Then Sergeant William Bremlow told of his part in the coup. This included seeing the officers become drunk at the 24 January mess dinner and also what was said by them at that time. He told of his going to the Guard House on the afternoon of 26 January with a message from Lieutenant Minchin, and joining the Governor's Guard for the invasion of Government House. Private William Hutton testified next, and told of being in Sergeant-Major Whittle's search party at Government House at the time the Governor was located in John Dunn's room.

Private Thomas Finnegan described seeing an effigy of Governor Bligh on 27 January. When asked by the Prosecution where he saw it, the Irish soldier answered, 'I see one, sir, at Sergeant-Major Whittle's.' After much discussion, he decided that it was the size of a window pane. Finnegan stated that at the time he had been perfectly happy with Governor Bligh's administration, and had no reason to change his mind since.[338]

Next, Bligh's servant John Dunn, settler George Suttor, and clerk Thomas Tait all told of their experiences on 26 January. Of these last ten witnesses for the Prosecution, only one, Champion, was cross-examined by the Defence, and he only briefly. Dr Martin Mason was next, and his lengthy testimony, which included the story of his harassment by the Foveaux administration, carried over into the trial's sixth day. In relation to his so-called illegal still, Mason stated that he had previously informed local magistrate Thomas Arndell and the district's chief constable that he was operating the still for medicinal purposes. The fact that the Order declaring him guilty had been dated prior to his court appearance was remarked upon with disapproval by a member of the court.

Superintendent of Convicts, Nicholas Divine, testified next, freely admitting that he had gone over to the rebels to save his own skin. He told the Court that there had been no danger of insurrection in the colony leading up to the coup, and that a number of convicts had expressed their regret to him at Governor Bligh's overthrow. Shipwright James Dowse Harris testified to what he had seen in Sydney on 26 January, also stating that, from what he knew, there was no danger of a revolt in the colony at the time the New South Wales Corps acted to supposedly forestall such a revolt by arresting the Governor. To counter his testimony, all the Defence could do was remind the court that Harris had previously been a convict.

The final witness for the Prosecution was sea captain and former Macarthur employee Charles Walker, who told of the rebel celebrations in Sydney on 27 January. Captain Walker also testified that under a written order from Nicholas Bayly he had been prevented from leaving Sydney on the American brig, *Jenny*. He said that the *Jenny* had been given six hours to leave Sydney by the rebels, and that troops had been sent aboard to 'smoke' her – fill the below decks with smoke to flush out stowaways – but her American master had steadfastly refused them permission to do it. Days later, the *Jenny* had been arrested at Broken Bay, accused of smuggling spirits ashore. The *Jenny* had been brought back to Sydney by the rebels, under military guard.

Subsequently, said Captain Walker, John Macarthur had proposed in one of his kangaroo courts to confiscate the ship as punishment for smuggling. The *Jenny*'s fiery skipper, forty-five-year-old Bostonian, Ebernezer Dorr Jnr, son of a Revolutionary War hero and friend of the legendary Paul Revere, had exploded, apparently declaring such a confiscation an act of war. Realising that sparking war between America and Britain was not such a good idea, Macarthur had backed down, and Dorr had been permitted to pay a bond, reclaim the *Jenny* for her Boston owners, Dorr & Sons, and sail for China.

This concluded the case for the Prosecution. Johnston's attorneys now sought more time to prepare their defence, and the members of the court indicated their willingness to agree to an adjournment of several days. Judge Advocate General Manners-Sutton now informed the court that he expected to be granted an interview by His Royal Highness the Prince Regent the next day, Tuesday, or on Wednesday the 22nd at the very latest, at 1.00 pm, and so adjourned the court until Thursday, 23 May.

The Judge Advocate General's interview with the Prince Regent, who was in effect now King of England, in the middle of the Johnston Court Martial, was an exceptional occurrence. What took place at that meeting is unrecorded. Perhaps the Prince Regent and his Judge Advocate General discussed the weather, or architecture. But it is more likely that Manners-Sutton gave His Highness, at the Prince Regent's request, his appraisal of the case put by the Prosecution in the Johnston trial and the cross-examination by the Defence, and forecast whether or not there was the likelihood of a conviction.

21

The Defence

Lieutenant-Colonel Johnston opened his defence by presenting a written statement, which was read to the court. From the beginning he said, 'I admit as an undisputed fact that I did remove Captain Bligh from the government of New South Wales, and put him under arrest.' But he would set out to prove that this was not mutiny, but a necessary and patriotic act designed to prevent an insurrection in the colony against a tyrannical and corrupt governor.[339] Johnston's statement, which had the ring of John Macarthur's rhetoric about it, wasted several pages arguing that the Statute of Limitations should still be applied to the case, even though the Judge Advocate General had already declared otherwise. He then moved to make some interesting claims.

One of them was that had Governor Bligh arrested the six officers serving on the Criminal Court on 26 January 1808, just two officers would have been left to run the Corps at Sydney. This was untrue. Including Johnston, there were ten officers on active duty with the Corps at Sydney and Parramatta, not eight. In addition, there were two officers of the Corps who had submitted their resignations which had yet to be accepted. One was Nicholas Bayly. The other was Robert Anderson, a thirty-seven-year-old ensign from Donegal. Anderson had submitted his resignation in Van Diemen's Land and gone to Sydney in 1805. Like Bayly, Anderson was granted leave from the Corps. At the time of the 1808 coup, Anderson was living with his convict mistress, Mary Franklin, in Sydney.

With the resignations of both Bayly and Anderson being finally accepted later in 1808, technically, in January 1808, Johnston could have recalled both these men to duty. There were also several more officers of the Corps in Van Diemen's Land, and Captain Piper on Norfolk Island, who might have been summoned to Sydney. Even if Bligh had arrested the six troublesome officers – and there is no evidence that this was Bligh's intention – the Corps would still have had its share of officers.

Continuing with his statement, Johnston claimed that the colony had been in fear and trepidation of George Crossley, the ex-convict lawyer. He then turned to defending his actions on 26 January. He declared that 'an immense number of people, comprising all the respectable inhabitants, except those who were immediately connected with Captain Bligh, rushed into the barrack and surrounded me'. These people had implored him to take the government from Bligh, he said, and this was why he had acted as he did. He claimed that Bligh had been 'very sorry that he had incurred public displeasure' and had thanked Johnston 'for the handsome manner' in which he had conducted his overthrow. Johnston also claimed that the condition in which Bligh was found in John Dunn's room at Government House 'would make the real heroes of the British navy blush with shame and boil with indignation'.[340]

Bligh would have been the one boiling with indignation on hearing such a statement.

Johnston also claimed that it was coincidental that Bligh's overthrow took place in the middle of John Macarthur's

Criminal Court trial. As for the charges faced by Macarthur at that time, Johnston claimed that he had consulted legal experts in England who were of the opinion those charges were 'shallow, absurd and wicked'.[341] Astonishingly, Johnston then went on to deny that Bligh had been confined in a subaltern's barrack in January–February 1809. 'The fact is,' he told the court, 'that he was lodged in the Surgeon's barrack, the very best in Sydney except that which was occupied by Colonel Paterson himself.'[342] This claim verged on the insane, and again has John Macarthur's stamp on it. The subaltern in question, Lieutenant Finucane, was due to be called as a Defence witness, and the Defence attorneys must have known that he would testify that Governor Bligh had been kept in his lowly barrack, not in the Surgeon's handsome house. Johnston closed by declaring that his witnesses would be far superior in character to Bligh's and would irresistibly contradict Bligh's evidence.

The first witness for the Defence was none other than Richard Atkins, the former Judge Advocate. He had gone into hiding the moment he arrived back in England, and both the Prosecution and the Defence had sought him to testify for their side. When Atkins took the stand, he told the Defence that Governor Bligh had not attempted to influence his opinion in cases before him. But, Atkins said, he had been in such fear of the Governor that he had sometimes sanctioned measures that were contrary to his feelings and judgment. Yet, when the Defence wanted him to state that Bligh had interfered with the operation of the colony's courts by personally choosing the magistrates for each case, Atkins pointed out that under act of parliament the Governor was required to do so.

The Defence then mentioned a number of legal cases in the colony and sought Atkins' agreement that the Governor had some improper involvement in them. In each case Atkins either denied that Bligh had any such involvement or he declined to comment on the basis that he had no personal knowledge of them. He also stated that it was at his own request that George Crossley had been employed on legal business for the administration, but that Crossley had played a leading role in offering advice to himself and the Governor on 25 and 26 January. He also expressed the view that Commissary Palmer and Robert Campbell were 'most respectable gentlemen' and 'men of honour' who had acted 'very fairly' when sitting as magistrates.[343]

To this point Atkins had proven to be an excellent witness for the Prosecution rather than for the Defence, but when asked to express an opinion on the character of Prosecution witness Dr Martin Mason, Atkins told the court that Mason had been dismissed from government service by Governor King for overworking convicts at the Coal River, and did not resign. He also told a story of Mason tying a female convict to a post overnight when she refused his advances. Yet Atkins offered no proof of either claim, and admitted that Mason had not been either dismissed or even reprimanded after the supposed incident with the female convict.

Atkins also disparaged the loyal address to Governor Bligh of 1 January 1808 from Hawkesbury residents, which had carried 833 signatures, saying that the signatures of most of them could have been bought with a glass of gin. Atkins further said that Prosecution witness, Captain Charles Walker, had been heavily in debt, and that his debts had been paid by his mistress, the Sydney prostitute who was now Walker's wife. He also claimed that houses had been pulled down in Sydney on the orders of the Governor, and he had heard men say, 'My turn will be next'. Atkins did admit that he had no direct knowledge of any order to pull houses down.[344]

On the other side of the ledger, Atkins acknowledged that on the evening of 26 January he had been shown Governor Bligh's confidential and unflattering letter to Lord Castlereagh about him, by Nicholas Bayly. He also conceded, when asked by Crown Counsel Larpent, that Governor Bligh had conducted himself 'as an honourable, honest man' throughout his time in office. Nor, he said, had Bligh altered the decision of any court in the colony, and in fact had no power to do so. Atkins testified that to his mind there had been great discontent in Sydney at Bligh's rule, but added, 'Whether it would have amounted to insurrection, I am of the opinion it would not, because the military could certainly have quelled and put a stop to it immediately.'[345] But, he said, had the six officers of the Criminal Court been arrested and imprisoned – as Atkins had urged Bligh to do at the time, which didn't say much for Atkins' judgment in 1808 – he now felt that in that event, the soldiers of the Corps could have been induced by their officers to join an insurrection.

When Atkins left the witness stand, he was replaced by the Defence's star witness, John Macarthur, the man accused of being the mutiny's prime mover. The entire court became a little more attentive as Macarthur, relaxed and self-confident, seated himself in the witness chair and took the oath to tell the truth, the whole truth, and nothing but the truth, so help him God. He was so certain that Johnston would win this case that he planned to personally sue Bligh for £20,000 for false arrest in New South Wales.

On the stand, Macarthur proceeded to paint a picture of himself as a successful pastoralist with 4600 sheep, 300 horned cattle, and 50 horses. Appearing before the Privy Council in 1804 after being sent back to England following the duel with Colonel Paterson, Macarthur had impressed the members with his projections for the production of fine wool in New South Wales to enable the colony to one day replace Spain as the main supplier to British woollen mills. Consequently, the Council had recommended he be given an additional 5000 acres (2025 hectares) of grazing land in the colony. Now, Macarthur testified that shortly after Bligh had arrived in the colony, Macarthur had approached the new Governor in the garden of Government House at Parramatta. There, he said, while alone with Bligh, he had asked if the Governor had been informed of the home government's support of his ambitions for his sheep and cattle.

According to Macarthur, Governor Bligh had exclaimed, 'What have I to do with your sheep, sir? What have I to do with your cattle? Are you to have such flocks of sheep and cattle as no man ever heard of before? No, sir!'[346]

Did Bligh really say this? It was, at the time, British Government policy to encourage the smaller farmers of the colony as opposed to the larger landholders such as Macarthur. And Bligh had come out from England briefed that Macarthur would prove to be the greatest thorn in his side in the colony. In light of this, it is not unlikely that the sometimes hot and hasty Bligh said something of this sort. But were these his exact words?

Macarthur testified that he then told Bligh he believed the home government had instructed the Governor to support his farming efforts. To which, according to Macarthur, Bligh had retorted, 'I have heard of your concerns, sir. You have got 5000 acres in the finest situation in the country. But by God, you shan't keep it!'[347]

Again, were these Bligh's words, or did Macarthur distort or add to them? We know from Macarthur's previous court ventures and associated documents that he had a very inventive turn of phrase and was expert at manipulating words. There is also the question of whether Bligh actually had the power to take away a government land grant, as opposed to a lease, from any settler. Macarthur would himself testify that these grants were in perpetuity and could not be revoked. If Bligh didn't have the power to revoke a grant, why would he threaten to do so? Macarthur went on to testify that he had persisted with the Parramatta conversation, to the Governor's obvious annoyance, by stating that, as he had the 5000 acres on the orders of the Privy Council and Secretary of State, he assumed his right to the land was indisputable.

According to Macarthur, Bligh had exploded, 'Damn the Privy Council! And damn the Secretary of State, too! What have they to do with me? You have made a number of false representations respecting your wool, by which you have obtained this land.'[348] We only have Macarthur's word that Bligh said this. They were alone in the garden. No witnesses could back him up.

As a result of this outburst, said Macarthur, he had invited Bligh to inspect his flocks and see the quality of his wool for himself. According to Macarthur, once they were inside the house, Bligh had mentioned their conversation to the retiring Governor King, in such language that King had burst into tears. Two hours later, said Macarthur, Bligh, King, and the then Captain Abbott had visited Elizabeth Farm and inspected Macarthur's sheep. Bligh then questioned the need for this inspection, declaring that no one doubted the possibility of raising fine wool in New South Wales. Macarthur testified that he had reminded Bligh of their earlier conversation and said that he felt Bligh had doubted his claims.

'No such thing!' he said Bligh had returned. 'And I desire, sir, you will never attempt to attach any such meanings to my words.' When Macarthur persisted, again bringing up the Secretary of State, Bligh had exclaimed, according to Macarthur, 'Damn the Secretary of State! He commands at home. I command here.'[349]

Bligh was by this point in the trial penning nightly letters to his patron, Sir Joseph Banks, giving him a summary of what had taken place in court that day. The night of 23 May he wrote with horror of Macarthur 'charging me with *damning the Secretary of State* and other untruths'.[350] The emphasis was Bligh's; he was mortified by the accusation, and totally denied it.

Macarthur returned to the witness chair next day. As his testimony continued, he settled into his loquacious stride, and was providing a narration of events that went beyond what the Defence asked him, when the Judge Advocate General cautioned him to confine his answers to the questions put to him. When asked for his opinion of Provost Marshal Gore, Macarthur launched into a hearsay story about something Mary Putland had supposedly told him about Gore, and again Manners-Sutton had to intervene, instructing him to give a direct answer to questions put to him. When subsequent questions ranged over Macarthur's Criminal Court trial and his actions on 25–26 January 1808, even Johnston's counsel had at one point to chide Macarthur for failing to answer the question put to him.

Macarthur denied ever having spoken to his former employee, Captain Walker, about Governor Bligh, and said that he had once employed the witness Thomas Tait, the Commissary clerk, but had dismissed him. He did agree that he'd had differences with all the governors who had preceded Bligh. On one occasion, he said Governor Phillip had flown into a violent rage with him and had threatened to arrest him. He admitted that Governor Hunter had withdrawn his confidence in him, while Governor King had publicly censured him, but Macarthur said that he considered all this unjust. He also conceded that he had never personally complained to the authorities in London about Governor Bligh prior to the coup. And he admitted to having written both the 26 January 1808 requisition calling on Johnston to depose Bligh and the 11 April 1808 dispatch sent by Johnston to the Secretary of State telling of the coup.

When the Defence and Prosecution had finished their questioning of him, both Crown Counsel Larpent and a member of the court questioned Macarthur in depth about his part in the coup. That member was General Sir David Baird, who was famous in Britain for capturing Cape Town from the Dutch in 1806. Wounded three times during his career, Baird had lost his left arm at the bloody 1809 Battle of Corunna where, as second-in-command, he had taken charge of British forces when the commanding general was killed, despite his own serious wound. Probably unbeknownst to Baird, John Macarthur's eldest son, the Australian-born Edward Macarthur, had been a raw junior officer in his army at Corunna.

General Baird's Corunna wound was still troubling him as he sat with the other senior officers at the Johnston Court Martial, but not as much as John Macarthur's testimony. Baird repeatedly asked Macarthur to identify the leading inhabitants who had gathered at the barracks on 26 January, pinning the number down to just a handful, not the huge crowd that Johnston had claimed was present. He also wrung an admission from Macarthur that the majority of the colony's civil magistrates had sided with the Governor, not with the rebels, in contradiction of his claim that all the leading inhabitants had supported the coup.

Several times, Macarthur was forced to correct himself in the face of this unfriendly barrage from Larpent and Baird: 'What I mean . . .', 'I mean to say . . .', 'I meant to say . . .'[351]

That night, Bligh wrote to Banks, 'Mr Macarthur has been proved to be a very bad character.' He told of how Macarthur had admitted to writing the requisition and the dispatch and added, 'The charges of my pulling down houses and taking away the property of individuals is all come to nothing, and I think the court now begin to see into the whole.'[352]

When Macarthur returned to the hot seat for a third day, he began by correcting several statements he'd made the previous day. Crown Counsel Larpent then asked, 'Was there any instance in which you were not concerned in the causes of the arrest of Governor Bligh?' Macarthur claimed not to understand the question. Larpent rephrased it, saying he wanted to ascertain if there had been any other causes of the rebellion.

'None at all,' Macarthur swiftly replied.

Larpent looked at him in astonishment. 'Don't answer that in haste,' he cautioned, but Macarthur repeated his answer.

Crown Counsel Larpent then remarked that it therefore seemed that the revolt had been all about the forfeiture of Macarthur's £900 bond for the *Parramatta*, about the pulling down of a fence being built on his Sydney lease, and about his personal court dispute with the Governor on 25–26 January. And, incredibly, either through egotism or derangement, Macarthur agreed that the coup had been all about him.[353] A pro-Johnston member of the court now tried to help Macarthur by suggesting other reasons for the revolt, and this generated a lively discussion between members of Court before Larpent's questioning of Macarthur resumed.

The Crown's counsel asked Macarthur why he had refused the 15 December 1807 warrant which Chief Constable Oakes had attempted to serve on him. Macarthur replied that he had considered it merely a private letter from the Judge Advocate, not an official communication, and so had ignored it. In response to this, one of the members of the court, apparently General Keppel, the former governor of Martinique, declared, 'I was once at the head of a colony myself, and if the orders which I sent were disobeyed, how could I govern the colony?' The General took up a copy of the warrant itself, which had been tendered in evidence. Impatiently, he pointed to the first line on the summons: '"I have it by command of His Excellency the Governor." That is official as can be!'

Macarthur mumbled that he had meant no disobedience.

'No disobedience!' roared General Keppel. He reminded Macarthur of the note that he, Macarthur, had given to Chief Constable Oakes declaring that he refused to acknowledge or accept the summons.

Macarthur tried to excuse himself. It had been 11.00 at night, he said. He had been worked up. And he'd no longer considered himself an owner of the *Parramatta*, so he hadn't felt he needed to appear before Judge Advocate Atkins.[354]

On that unconvincing note, Macarthur's testimony lurched

to a conclusion. In the end, he had seemed very much out of his depth. No longer was he in a colonial court where his friends sat on the bench and where he could say pretty much what he pleased. In this court of law, his word play, distortions and chicanery had not gone unchallenged. In fact, Macarthur had proven to be such a bad witness for the Defence it would soon become apparent that Johnston's attorneys immediately decided to cut him adrift.

22

Going After Bligh

The Defence had much ground to make up in the wake of Macarthur's disastrous appearance. If Johnston was to be acquitted it was now imperative that Governor Bligh be proven to have been tyrannical and corrupt, with the result that the colony was on the verge of a civil revolt.

Lieutenant Finucane, Foveaux's right-hand man, was called next. But not for any tactical reason; he had requested an early appearance as he said he had urgent business in Ireland to attend to. Finucane immediately set the Defence back by confirming that Governor Bligh had been imprisoned in his subaltern's barrack, not in the Surgeon's barrack as Johnston had testified. Hastily moving on, the Defence set out to put distance between its client Johnston and the embarrassing Macarthur, asking Finucane if Governor Bligh had made any distinction between Colonel Johnston and John Macarthur. Finucane stated that Bligh had said he wouldn't mind going back to England with Johnston, but not with Macarthur. No questions were put to Finucane about the nature of Colonel Foveaux's tyrannical rule or Finucane's supporting role during that period. Neither would Joseph Foveaux himself be called.

Captain Anthony Fenn Kemp was next to take the stand. He would launch the assault on Governor Bligh's credibility. Kemp was soon claiming that Bligh, 'Threatened to pull down houses in every direction, and to take leases away.' He told the court that he had warned the Governor in November 1807 that Simeon Lord, D'Arcy Wentworth and others were talking about raising £1500 to send John Macarthur to London to represent them in complaining about Governor Bligh to the Secretary of State. He said Bligh had responded, 'They might represent, and be damned! I am irremovable as Mount Ararat.' He also testified that Bligh had threatened, at the Government House dinner table, to make 'a broken merchant' of John Blaxland 'if he did not take care'.[355] He also testified that Bligh had said that leases in the colony were not worth a damn.

Asked to characterise Prosecution witnesses, Kemp said that Dr Martin Mason had been in poor financial circumstances. As for Commissary Palmer, Kemp said he himself was currently being sued by Palmer for the way he'd been treated by the rebel courts, and so he could not comment on him. Kemp considered Sergeant Bremlow, who had given revealing testimony on behalf of the Prosecution, 'a very troublesome character' and 'a great drunkard'.[356] Despite this characterisation, Kemp was unable to explain why Bremlow had not only been trusted by but was very much in the confidence of the rebel leadership in 1808.

In cross-examination by the Prosecution, Kemp was embarrassed when Frederick Pollock produced a letter Kemp had written to Provost Marshal Gore only a month or so before the coup. In that letter, Kemp had asked Gore to make representations to Governor Bligh on his behalf about keeping Kemp in Sydney. Kemp had recently been sent up from Van Diemen's Land, where he'd been stationed for three years, after falling out with Colonel Paterson. He was obviously hoping not to be sent to some out-of-the-way posting, as he had business interests in

Sydney. At the end of this letter, Kemp had said that Governor Bligh had 'behaved in so handsome a manner towards me that I trust I shall ever entertain a grateful remembrance of'.[357] Only weeks later, on 26 January, Kemp had been a leader of the coup against that same governor who had, in his words, previously behaved so handsomely toward him.

Lieutenant Minchin was up next. Of Bligh, the efficient Adjutant of the Corps said, 'He was generally supposed to be a very violent and arbitrary man.' He also testified that once, in a meeting with Bligh and Assistant Surgeon Jamieson, the Governor had declared, 'He did not care a damn about the Secretary of State's instructions. He was but a clerk in office, in today and out tomorrow.'[358] Jamieson, now dead, could not corroborate Minchin's claim that Bligh had belittled the Secretary of State. Despite this, the Defence would be hoping that Minchin's claim would combine with the evidence of Macarthur and Johnston to suggest that a pattern was emerging about both Bligh's language and attitude. On the other hand, such testimony could also suggest that the rebels, desperate to prove their contention that Bligh had been a tyrant, had colluded prior to the trial to create a collection of unflattering statements that they could attribute to the Governor. Statements that Bligh had already emphatically denied.

Minchin also testified that Governor Bligh had severely reprimanded him in the presence of Lieutenant-Colonel Paterson – for acquitting an Irish convict of sedition, when Minchin had been serving on the bench of magistrates. Again, Minchin's only witness, Paterson this time, was conveniently dead. Minchin went on to contradict the evidence of his artilleryman, Private Gillard, testifying that the guns at the Parade Ground were not aimed at Government House on 26 January. He also positively asserted that no 21-gun salute or volley of muskets had been fired the following day. Minchin next claimed that seven convicts who had been caught after escaping in a small boat had been tried twice for the same crime – because Governor Bligh had been furious that they had been acquitted the first time.

That night, Bligh wrote to Sir Joseph Banks of the testimony of Kemp and Minchin, 'I have been severely attacked by the two . . . Every word of theirs I hope to prove ill-formed.' He commented, with some surprise, 'Their whole evidence seemed to have been prepared to prove everything bad in me, or to invalidate my witnesses.' He told Banks that he was beginning to regret not having been more forceful with the Prosecution.[359] He had assumed the evidence about the coup would speak for itself, but now he was realising the sad fact that a crafty lawyer can make truth immaterial in a court of law.

Minchin was back in the witness chair the next day. Under cross-examination by the Prosecution, he revealed that when Macarthur had appointed him to take home rebel dispatches in April 1808, Macarthur had tried to bribe him into leaving his wife Ann in Sydney and to induce him to stay faithful to the rebel cause – with promises that Minchin could keep his salary, barrack and servants in the colony while he was away, and would receive of a new grant of 500 acres (200 hectares) plus government cattle. The Prosecution had obtained a copy of the letter in which Macarthur had made these offers to Minchin – only Minchin could have given it to them, clearly with the intention of embarrassing and even incriminating Macarthur. Frederick Pollock was now able to reveal that Macarthur had ended this letter to Minchin by saying, 'If in any other manner I can contribute to your comfort and Mrs Minchin's you have only to say what your wishes are.' Minchin told the court he had treated Macarthur's offer with contempt, adding, 'I laughed at it.'[360] Nonetheless, Minchin's wife had indeed remained behind in Sydney in Minchin's barrack when Minchin left for England.

Frederick Pollock now presented Minchin with copies of the *Sydney Gazette* which detailed the two trials of the seven escaped convicts that Minchin had referred to the previous day. When the Defence protested that the *Gazette*, being published by the Governor, could contain whatever falsehoods the Governor wished to print, Pollock then produced the official records of the trial proceedings. Faced with this evidence, an embarrassed Minchin had to agree that the first trial of the seven had been on the charge of stealing a boat, which had led to an acquittal, while the second trial was for attempted escape, for which all seven were convicted. The two trials had not involved the same charge, as Minchin had testified.

All the Defence witnesses had and would testify that no 21-gun salute to celebrate Bligh's overthrow had been fired on 27 January, or on any day close to it. Minchin now said the same. Johnston was maintaining that the Corps had arrested Bligh to protect him from a civil revolt; this claim could be shown to be suspect if it was proved that the Corps had officially celebrated Bligh's overthrow, and so the Defense witnesses had to say there had been no salute. Minchin had been Artillery Officer in Sydney at the time, so, if anyone knew whether the artillery had fired a salute, he should. And Minchin had emphatically denied that a salute had been fired. Pollock now presented a record book to Minchin. It was the official day-book of government storekeeper, John McGowan.

In the book it was recorded for Wednesday, 27 January 1808: '*Government use* – 84 lbs gunpowder, Royal salute on account of Major Johnston taking the government of the colony'.[361] This revelation brought gasps from the gallery. Minchin, obviously taken by surprise, claimed he could not recognise McGowan's handwriting and so could not be sure of the authenticity of the record. Despite the clear evidence of the record, Minchin steadfastly held to the story that no salute was fired that day. To admit to it would have made perjurers not only of himself but of Johnston and numerous other Defence witnesses.

Bligh, who would have found the day-book during his thorough search for records relevant to the case prior to his departure from

Sydney – it had obviously been overlooked by the rebels – was able to report to Sir Joseph Banks that Minchin had in court that day 'proved he was the most competent false witness that ever existed, to the great abhorrence of everyone present'.[362]

Lieutenant William Ellison of HMS *Porpoise* was next sworn for the Defence, and testified that he would not put any confidence in Provost Marshal Gore. He was quickly followed by Charles Grimes, Surveyor-General and Acting Judge Advocate in the rebel administrations. Grimes' testimony was that government leases in Sydney were for a maximum of fourteen years. In cross examination, the Prosecution produced an unrepealed regulation of Governor King's which had stipulated that leases of the land marked out for public use by Governor Phillip were for a maximum of five years. This was the land on which stood the six houses that Governor Bligh had said should be demolished. This proved that those leases had expired, and were being occupied unlawfully by the householders in 1808. When Grimes was asked about his signature appearing on the requisition to arrest Governor Bligh, he said he'd signed it at 11.00 pm on 26 January, after the coup had taken place. Under pressure from Crown Counsel Larpent, he conceded that he'd intended it to appear that he had signed prior to the Governor's overthrow.

John Blaxland now took his turn on the stand. After being arrested at Cape Town at Bligh's request, he had spent months in Wandsworth Prison in England leading up to the Johnston trial. His woes had not ended there – his former ally, John Macarthur, was suing him for an unpaid bill for £630. Blaxland's evidence was focused on his claim that he had been promised 8000 acres (3240 hectares), plus stock, by the home government on his migrating to the colony. He said that Governor Bligh had refused his full grant, on the basis that he had not invested the required £6000 in the colony. Blaxland contended that he had invested the £6000 and that Bligh had deliberately prevented him from receiving his grant and had no intention of giving it to him.

Blaxland presented pages of figures in support of his claim, but when the court examined them in fine detail the figures didn't seem to add up. The Prosecution was then able to show that, contrary to Blaxland's assertion that Bligh had no intention of giving him his grant, just four days prior to the coup the Assistant Surveyor had, on the Governor's orders, surveyed the proposed grant for Blaxland so that he could receive it once he did meet the financial qualifications. Bligh was to tell Banks, 'I think we have rebutted Mr Blaxland's evidence today in the most complete manner.'[363]

Lieutenant Minchin was now recalled. Since Minchin had given his evidence, Bligh and Pollock had been poring through the records every night for days. So engrossed in that search had Bligh been, he had neglected to write to Sir Joseph Banks for several days – for which he was to apologise. The effort was worth it. Bligh had come up with some interesting evidence. Armed with this information, Crown Counsel Larpent reminded Minchin, who was still under oath, that he had testified that following a particular court case he had been severely reprimanded by Governor Bligh for a particular judgment, in the presence of Lieutenant-Colonel Paterson.

Larpent now asked if Minchin stood by that testimony, as Larpent was now aware that Colonel Paterson had been in Van Diemen's Land at the time Minchin said he was with him and Governor Bligh at Government House in Sydney. The ancient Romans had a saying: a liar should have a good memory. Minchin, caught out lying, tried to duck and weave his way out of a perjury charge by saying that it must have been another, earlier case, but he couldn't remember which, or when.

Judge Advocate General Manners-Sutton was totally unimpressed with this excuse, as he informed the court: 'Mr Minchin recollects distinctly the reprimand, he recollects distinctly his own observation in answer to it, he recollects Governor Bligh's reply, and he totally forgets the case to which the whole applied!'

Minchin, sweating hard, responded, 'Upon my oath, I do.'

A disbelieving member of the court frowned across the courtroom at Minchin. 'Why do you say "Upon my oath"? Don't you know that *all* you say is upon your oath?'[364]

Minchin slunk from the courtroom. With a mixture of satisfaction and disgust, Bligh would tell Banks that night, 'Minchin was sufficiently proved perjuried'.[365]

Surgeon John Harris was called next, and pompously took his place. When Elizabeth Macquarie met Harris in Rio de Janeiro in 1809 she had noted that he 'seemed indeed to think himself a very great man, and to think that other persons should think the same'.[366] Asked by the Defence for his opinion of Governor Bligh, Harris answered, 'A passionate man, but otherwise I heard nothing against him.' He testified that on one occasion when he had been with the Governor, 'He said "Damn Mr Cooke", or "the Secretary of State" – I am not certain which – "What does he know about land or stock?" '[367]

Harris remembered Governor Bligh applying to him for the use of Captain Kent's bull, and his own refusal. He said that he had later seen the bull in Sydney. But strangely, he admitted never approaching Governor Bligh about this supposed theft of Captain Kent's bull, even though he was Kent's agent. When asked if the people of the colony had been dissatisfied with Governor Bligh, he said that an order issued by the Governor for the shooting of stray dogs had dissatisfied a great many people in Sydney. The Prosecution, in cross-examination, then embarrassed Harris by producing a notice placed by him in the *Sydney Gazette* in which he'd announced that any stray dogs found on his own property would be shot.

Harris also confirmed that in the case raised by Lieutenant Minchin regarding the seven escaped convicts, there had been two trials on separate charges. He also said that in 1806 he had overheard the retiring governor, King, warn Governor Bligh to be wary of John Macarthur. Asked his own opinion of his one-time close friend Macarthur, Harris said, 'I always considered him a troublesome character.'[368]

Bligh would comment to Banks, 'Harris gave fairer evidence than any of them, but he united in particular points of falsehood with his party'.[369]

Lieutenant William Kent was the last witness of the day. He began by saying that in 1807 he had been sent to Norfolk Island in HMAT *Lady Nelson* to transfer settlers from there to Van Diemen's Land, and that Governor Bligh had given him verbal orders for the island's commandant, Captain Piper, to round up and shoot any settlers who resisted leaving.

Next day, Lieutenant Kent's testimony resumed with his story of Bligh ordering him to batter down Sydney on 29 July 1808. He also claimed that Bligh had wanted Captain Porteous to do the same, but no proof to support this hearsay statement was tendered then or later by the Defence, and Porteous himself was not called by the Defence. Kent could not explain why Bligh did not himself use the guns of the *Porpoise* to 'batter down' Sydney once he gained control of the ship in 1809, or even threaten to do so. Likewise, Bligh could have battered down Hobart Town with the *Porpoise*'s guns to force David Collins, who had perhaps eighty soldiers at his disposal, to supply him with food once Collins turned against him. Bligh neither threatened nor molested Hobart. Instead, he peacefully played pirate down-river for nine harrowing months.

When Lieutenant Kent went on to tell the court that he had been acquitted by a court martial brought against him by Bligh in January, the Judge Advocate General said that information was irrelevant to this trial, other than it tended to show that Kent may now be biased against Governor Bligh.

The Prosecution, to counter Kent's claim about verbal orders to shoot Norfolk Island settlers, produced Governor Bligh's written orders to Lieutenant Kent and Captain Piper in which Bligh had spoken about caring for the islanders in terms such as, 'you will contribute every comfort to the settlers' and 'grant them every protection'.[370] Nowhere was there any evidence to corroborate Kent's testimony that Bligh had been prepared to treat settlers heavy-handedly or even murderously. Verbally battered and bruised, his evidence discredited, Kent left the stand. He would serve aboard the man-o-war HMS *Union* under his scheming uncle, Captain Kent, until the latter died at sea in 1812. In 1816, Lieutenant Kent would attempt to secure the 1000 acres (400 hectares) granted to him by the rebel administration in New South Wales; the government would turn down his application.

Major Edward Abbott came next to the stand. Despite having fallen out with Macarthur and Johnston, Abbott, who had played a leading role in Foveaux's rebel administration, kept to the rebel line in all respects. But, to disassociate himself from the original coup conspiracy, he told a barefaced lie. He was asked. 'Had you, before the arrest of Governor Bligh, any communication or information that such an event was likely to take place?'

'No,' Abbott emphatically replied.[371] He was committing perjury. We know now, but the court didn't know then, that Abbott had written to ex-governor King on 13 February 1808, admitting that not only had he known in advance about the planned overthrow of Bligh by the Corps, but that he'd counselled Johnston on how to go about it. Of course, that letter was by then safely concealed among the late Governor King's papers, and would only come to light much later. If Abbott was prepared to lie under oath to that question, his entire testimony was suspect.

David Dickinson Mann, formerly a secretary to Governor King, then testified that Governor Bligh had ordered him to tear down his house, which was on reserved government land behind Government House. He said that when he had protested to Bligh at Government House, the Governor had declared, 'I will make the laws for this colony, and every wretch of you, son of a bitch, shall be governed by them!'[372] To counter this, the Prosecution produced a letter of 1 January 1808, from Mann to

Governor Bligh's secretary, Griffin, in which Mann nominated an alternative home site elsewhere in Sydney that he proposed to purchase using the money that Commissary Palmer had agreed to pay him, on Bligh's orders, for his existing house. Mann's original claim had been that he was being heartlessly thrown off his land by the Governor. This letter made a liar of him.

Vice-Admiral John Hunter, the colony's second governor, now followed. In fifty scant words, the elderly Hunter gave a character reference for Johnston.

Then Sergeant-Major Thomas Whittle took the stand. Whittle, a cogwheel of the revolution, testified that Governor Bligh had come to his front gate at 7.00 o'clock one morning and threatened to demolish his house, which stood on the reserved ground, so Whittle had signed his house over to Colonel Johnston. Speaking of the evening of 26 January, Whittle told the court that he had seen Governor Bligh shortly after his capture, 'All dirty with feathers and cobwebs, one stuff and another.'[373]

Whittle denied displaying a painting of Governor Bligh's capture in his house, denied ordering wood brought for bonfires, and denied ordering men to attend John Macarthur's trial. He thought he might have helped chair Macarthur around the town after his acquittal, but denied saying that on the 26th, 'The men should have had the other half pint, and the House would have been about the Governor's ears'. He admitted that on 23 January, three days before the coup, Macarthur had told him he was soon to make a purchase of wine cheaply. At Macarthur's request, Whittle had provided a list of soldiers deserving of a distribution of cheap Cape wine for just five shillings a gallon.[374] A shipment of Cape wine had recently been unloaded into the government storehouses from the *City of Edinburgh*.

The Prosecution now quizzed Whittle about the alleged threat by Governor Bligh to knock down his house. Frank Larpent asked on what date this confrontation supposedly took place.

'Upon my word, I cannot tell,' the Sergeant-Major responded, looking a little uneasy. When asked the year, he said it was 1808.

'Was it a few days before the Governor's arrest?'

Whittle had broken out in a sweat. 'It was four or five months.'

'How could it be four or five months before the arrest of the Governor, and yet in 1808?'

'I think it was in 1808.' Whittle, perspiring profusely, was looking around the courtroom for help.

'Who was present besides yourself and the Governor?'

Whittle's eyes rolled up into his head, and he fainted away, toppling from the witness chair, to the astonished gasps of the audience. The brash and bold old soldier of forty-two years' experience was carried from the courtroom, and never came back to face a continuation of Frederick Pollock's questioning.[375]

Once decorum had returned to the courtroom, Sergeant John Sutherland was sworn. He testified to finding Governor Bligh hiding under the bed in John Dunn's room. In cross-examination, the Prosecution demanded to know how high the bed was from the floor.

'This is to prove the impossibility of the thing, I suppose,' remarked General Sir David Baird. 'It is a matter of no consequence if it was so. With two or three hundred soldiers about the house, who would not have done the same?'[376]

Manners-Sutton didn't see the relevance to the case of such a question anyway, but the examination on this point was allowed to continue. Sutherland would not estimate the distance between bed and floor. He would only say there was room enough for Bligh to hide there. He also claimed that none of the soldiers in the room had bayonets on their muskets.

Sergeant Richard Mason, who had been a dragoon in New South Wales, next testified that he had been asked to be transferred from the Governor's detail because Bligh had continually called him, strangely, 'tremendous buggers', 'wretches', and 'villains'. (His own pluralistic words.)[377] It was as if he and other soldiers had been schooled to use these words, with an instruction along the lines of, 'When they ask you men whether the Governor cursed you, you are to say he called you tremendous buggers, wretches, and villains.'

Sergeant-Major James Cox followed Mason, testifying that he had thought there might have been bloodshed if the six officers of the Corps had been jailed by Governor Bligh, but the Prosecution had him admit that he felt that the men would have obeyed Major Johnston if he had ordered them *not* to take any action against the Governor.

Both Lieutenants Laycock and Lawson had been prepared to give evidence, but the Defence, apparently thinking they might say something to prejudice Johnston's case, didn't call them. So, Cox became the last witness for the Defence. The court was adjourned until Wednesday, 5 June.

When the court resumed for the final day of sitting, General Sir David Baird was not among its members – he had to undergo urgent surgery on his most recent battle wound, and sent his apologies to the President. Before both Johnston and Bligh were permitted to sum up, Edmund Griffin was called to authenticate some documents, and then Bligh's servant John Dunn was called to testify to the height of his bed from the floor. The Defence objected to Dunn being questioned on this, but Manners-Sutton ruled that, as the matter of Bligh and the bed had been introduced by the Defence, even though it was immaterial, the Prosecution should be able to answer it. Bligh was, of course, anxious to dispel the impression that he had acted in a cowardly manner on the evening of 26 January, and was determined to prove he could only have hidden behind the bed, not under it. Dunn told the court that the clearance between the floor and the bottom of his bed had only been four or five inches, making it physically impossible for Bligh to have hidden under the bed as Sergeant Sutherland had testified.

Now came the summing up. Both Johnston and Bligh presented written summations, which were read aloud by the Judge Advocate General, starting with Johnston's. The Colonel, in his summation, contended that he had proven his case on every salient point – that Bligh was a foul-mouthed tyrant who did interfere with the courts and did terrify people with the threat of destroying their homes. He acknowledged that the officers of the Criminal Court in the Macarthur case may have been wrong in excluding the Judge Advocate, but said that had nothing to do with himself. He couldn't avoid mentioning Macarthur, whose affairs, as the Crown Counsel had caused Macarthur himself to admit, had been the root cause of the mutiny. 'I am not fond of dwelling on the case of Mr Macarthur,' Johnston said. 'He is represented as a troublesome man, and perhaps he was so. But at least toward him Captain Bligh was the aggressor.'[378]

Even though Johnston's dispatch to Lord Castlereagh of 11 April 1808 and subsequent letters claimed he would prove that Bligh had been corrupt and had personally profited during his brief term of office, this claim didn't figure in Johnston's summing up. He had presented not a single witness or piece of evidence of it, apart from the vague, unproven claim that Bligh had taken Captain Kent's bull. It was truly astonishing that the rebels could have claimed that a man such as Bligh, who never in his career showed the least interest in making money, had plundered New South Wales. If you are going to accuse someone of a crime, you need to produce solid evidence, or at least fabricate convincing evidence. The rebels had done neither.

The one area where they might have accused Bligh of greed, they ignored. Bligh's third land grant, rundown Blighton on the Hawkesbury River, had been given to him by Governor King in King's last days in office. In return, Bligh, during his first days in office, had given the King family a similar grant, which they'd called Thanks. It was all quite legal and above board, but it was still a little unsavoury, and showed poor judgment on the part of both Bligh and King. In 1817, the Bligh family would actually voluntarily give Blighton back to the government. Yet Johnston and Macarthur failed to even mention this grant.

Bligh, when he presented his summation, quite correctly felt that the Defence had attempted to put him on trial, as opposed to defending Johnston. He said of the Defence case, 'My whole life has been searched for occasions of censure.' One by one, Bligh countered the claims against him, and then pointed to Johnston's guilt as the leader of a mutiny against him. Finally, he referred to Johnston's witnesses, the members of the 26 January junta. 'If he be guilty, which of them does not share his crime? If he be worthy of punishment, which of them can hope for impunity?'[379]

With the end of Bligh's summation, the court was cleared. The officers of the court immediately began their deliberations. No one in this case had been entirely innocent. Bligh could be said to have contributed to his own downfall with his bad language and blinkered focus on ending the corruption in the colony. Macarthur, the officers of the New South Wales Corps, and a handful of settlers – mostly former army officers – who had joined the rebel junta, had all come out of this trial disgraced and incriminated. If Lieutenant-Colonel Johnston had been Macarthur's tool, as his friends would privately claim, then he had been his willing tool. It was now up to the court to decide whether George Johnston was guilty of leading a mutiny, and whether he should swing for it.

The court agreed a verdict in less than an hour. That verdict and the court's recommendations were then put in writing and sent to the Commander-in-Chief, who in turn would take them to the Prince Regent.

23

The Outcome

The officers and soldiers of the 102nd returned to their morbid Horsham barracks. The court martial witnesses went back to their London lodgings. Bligh went home to Durham Place, confident of the trial's outcome: 'I think it is fully evident to the Court that Johnston is guilty.'[380] Many other people shared this view and, like Governor Macquarie and his wife Elizabeth, felt that Johnston would pay for his crime with his life.

While awaiting the announcement of the verdict, Bligh filled the days reading and correcting Mr Bartrum's transcript of the trial. Encouraged by Earl St Vincent, First Lord of the Admiralty, who had always taken a hard line on mutiny, Bligh placed an order with Sherwood, Neely and Jones of Paternoster Row to print and bind 900 copies of the 484-page trial transcript for publication, at his own expense. All Bligh needed was the brief last chapter – the verdict and, he hoped, a punishing sentence.

The trial had, by the time it concluded, given Bligh the satisfaction he had sought. His wounded pride had healed somewhat, his rage was at last contained. His desire for savage revenge had subsided. In his closing address, he had said, 'I care very little what the sentence may be.' He'd added, 'I entertain no vindictive feeling towards Colonel Johnston.' The truthfulness of that statement was born out by Lieutenant Finucane, who had testified that Bligh was prepared to go home in the same ship as Johnston, but not with Macarthur. Bligh seems to have felt a little sorry for Johnston, whom he saw as Macarthur's dupe. A Guilty verdict was all Bligh claimed he now wanted for, with that would come 'vindication of my honour and reputation'. Because, said Bligh, reflecting the gentleman's code of the day, 'Reputation is dearer than life.'[381]

For four long weeks the parties waited for the verdict. And then on 2 July, it was announced by the office of the Commander-in-Chief at Whitehall: 'The Court having duly and maturely considered the whole of the evidence adduced on the Prosecution, as well as that offered in defence, are of the opinion that Lieutenant-Colonel Johnston is *Guilty* of the act of Mutiny as described in the Charge.' The sentence of the court was that Johnston was 'to be *Cashiered*'.[382] That is, he was to be dishonourably discharged, with his charge and sentence read at parades of every regiment in the British army. But that was all. There was no other penalty, no prison sentence, and certainly no death sentence.

For Bligh, this was a victory, but a bitter one. He didn't agree with the reason that was given for the leniency of the sentence. The Commander-in-Chief's announcement of the verdict noted that the sentence was 'so inadequate to the enormity of the crime of which the prisoner has been found guilty', but remarked that it had apparently been due to 'the novel and extraordinary circumstances' which the evidence suggested had existed 'during the administration of Governor Bligh'.[383] Many would read this as meaning that the court believed that, while Johnston had led a mutiny, Bligh had in some respects brought that mutiny on himself.

Still, the Palace was unimpressed with the sentence. 'The

Prince Regent admits the principle under which the Court has allowed this consideration to act in mitigation of the punishment which the crime of Mutiny would otherwise have suggested, yet no circumstances whatever can be received by his Royal Highness in *full* extenuation of an assumption of power, so subversive of every principle of good order and discipline as that under which Lieutenant-Colonel Johnston has been convicted.'[384]

One of the members of the court was also far from impressed with the sentence. Lieutenant-General Sir David Baird had missed the last day of the sitting due to surgery so had not been present to vote on verdict or sentence. In Baird's opinion, which he later expressed to Governor Macquarie, his absence that crucial day 'was very fortunate for Johnston', for he considered that Johnston did not deserve the slightest degree of mercy.[385]

Johnston now removed his uniform for the last time, and gratefully returned to New South Wales. He went back in debt, and unable to pay all the £6000 that his defence had cost him. After he sent his attorney John Adolphus a begging letter, Adolphus, in letting Johnston off part of the bill, said that he had always believed that the parties who led him into the coup would have removed from his shoulders the expense of his defence. Macarthur was to claim that he loaned Johnston £400 to get home, but otherwise he donated no part of his fortune to Johnston's cause, contrary to his written promise of 26 January 1808.

Back in the colony, Johnston would live quietly at Annandale as a reclusive gentleman farmer, becoming the welcome guest at Government House of his old friend Lachlan Macquarie. At the urging of the religious Macquarie, Johnston married Esther Julian in 1814 and legitimised their offspring. In 1817, Macquarie gave Johnston a grant of 1500 acres (600 hectares) at Cabramatta, taking Johnston's total holdings in the colony to over 4000 acres (1600 hectares). Johnston would die at Annandale in 1823.

There would be no more military trials for the 1808 rebellion in New South Wales. The new Secretary of State for War and the Colonies, Lord Liverpool, seems to have felt that the army was unhappy at dealing out punishment to its own for the overthrow of a navy man. In light of this, further courts martial were seen to be only a waste of time. What followed has a very modern political ring to it. With the Johnston case out of the way, the Secretary of State wanted to sweep the whole affair under the carpet. The file on the military coup in New South Wales was closed. Bligh was promptly promoted – on 31 July, four weeks after the Johnston verdict was announced, Bligh was made a Rear Admiral, his appointment being backdated twelve months.

Bligh's civilian witnesses were dispensed with, informed that if they weren't aboard the ship *Mary* by a certain day in late August, they would have to find their own way back to New South Wales, at their own expense. 'I cannot help feeling very much for unfortunate loyal and good men,' Bligh wrote to Banks on 13 August. He was particularly concerned for Suttor, Oakes and Mason. 'Their families are in great distress and suffer much neglect from the persons in power.'[386]

The now Admiral Bligh tried to put the best public face he could on this outcome, but it wasn't easy. Not even the unstable Lieutenant-Colonel Joseph Foveaux, Macarthur's venal successor as dictator of the colony, would now be prosecuted, despite the recommendations of the highest law officers in the land. Not that Foveaux's superiors had been fooled by his excuses for taking charge in the colony, or were in any way influenced by Macquarie's extraordinary support of him. Foveaux, an embarrassment now, was not considered for the lieutenant governorship of Van Diemen's Land, or anywhere else. He was shunted to an Irish backwater as inspector of recruiting, and subsequently made commander of the Greek Light Infantry, one of the lowliest regiments in the British Army, formed from Greek refugees in 1810. After that unit was abolished in 1816, Foveaux would never again be given a command, although his connections would be good enough to ensure he ended up a lieutenant general.

Yet, for other complicit officers of the Corps, the army offered no future of any kind. Major Edward Abbott quickly resigned his commission and returned to Australia. Despite his involvement in the Macarthur coup, he served as Deputy Advocate General in Van Diemen's Land and later as administrator of Launceston, where he would die in 1832. Captain Anthony Fenn Kemp also left the army and likewise went to Van Diemen's Land. For a year he was ignored, but in 1816 he was given a large grant in the Midlands region, near Green Ponds, today's Kempton, which was renamed for him. He named his property Mount Vernon, in honour of George Washington, whom he had met as a young man while briefly farming in the US. Bankrupt for a time during his new life in Van Diemen's Land, Kemp would go on to argue with every governor of the colony.

Lieutenant William Lawson also left the regular army. He had let his farm at Concord, planning to return, which he did in 1812, with a commission as a lieutenant in the Veteran Company militia. He would become one of the colony's largest landholders. In 1813, Lawson, Gregory Blaxland and D'Arcy Wentworth's teenaged son Charles succeeded in finding a route across the Blue Mountains, opening up the western plains. Towns in the Blue Mountains are named after each of them. Charles Wentworth later purchased Sir Harry Hayes' Vaucluse Estate and built Vaucluse House. For years after their return to New South Wales, the Blaxland brothers were continually in dispute with Governor Macquarie.

Lieutenant William Brabyn was promoted to captain in late 1808 and became commandant in northern Van Diemen's Land until the recall of the New South Wales Corps to England.

He returned to New South Wales in 1812 with Lawson and former ensign, Archibald Bell, with all three of them serving as lieutenants in the Veteran Company. Brabyn farmed at Prospect. Bell headed a military detachment at Windsor for six years, and in later life was appointed to the colony's Legislative Council.

Lieutenant William Moore stayed with the 102nd Regiment and was promoted to Captain. Never returning to the colony, he sold his Sydney house to the government. Lieutenants William Minchin and Thomas Laycock both remained with the 102nd Regiment until its abolition in 1816, serving in Canada during the War of 1812 against the United States. Laycock returned to New South Wales in 1817. Having lost his Sydney farm, Home Bush, in the cancellation of rebel grants, he ran a hotel and a butchery in Sydney. Adjutant Minchin returned in 1818, and Governor Macquarie gave him a 1000-acre (400 hectare) grant the following year. This property, Minchinbury, would later form part of the Minchinbury wine estate. In 1820, Macquarie made Minchin his Principal Superintendent of Police, but Minchin died within a year.

Charles Grimes remained in England, sacked from the post of Surveyor-General and bemoaning his 'one fatal error' in supporting John Macarthur and his coup.[387] Grimes' job eventually went to Lieutenant John Oxley, who asked Macarthur for the hand in marriage of his once sickly daughter, Elizabeth. Macarthur turned him down flat, declaring that Oxley had limited prospects. Elizabeth died unmarried, while Oxley went on to achieve fame as an explorer on land and sea. Surgeon John Harris returned to his Sydney farm, Ultimo, which later formed the basis of the inner-Sydney suburb of that name.

All but one of the supporters of William Bligh who had testified at the Johnston Court Martial soon returned to New South Wales. The exception was Dr Martin Mason. When the *Mary*, the ship carrying the Bligh supporters back to Australia, docked at Portsmouth in 1811, Mason went ashore, and disappeared. He was never seen again. Whether or not he was murdered is open to question. 'Little Jack' Palmer was demoted to Assistant Commissary by London; the bureaucrats felt he had been in the top job long enough. He held that post at Parramatta until 1819, and was a magistrate until his death in 1832.

Robert Campbell came back to Sydney to find his businesses in disarray; they were liquidated in 1814. He rebuilt, and in 1817 co-founded Australia's first bank, the Bank of New South Wales, which grew into Westpac, today one of Australia's largest banks. One of his bank employees, as cashier, was Nicholas Bayly who, as a rebel junta leader, had harassed him in 1808. Bayly ended his days in financial difficulties, while Campbell was once again very prosperous by the time he died in 1846. William Gore resumed duties as Provost Marshal, the post having been filled during his absence in England by Commissary Palmer's son George, a former lieutenant with the 61st Regiment. Gore lost his job in 1819 when he fell into debt. Increasingly erratic, later accused of attempted murder, he lived to the age of eighty, dying insolvent, at Artarmon, his farm on Sydney's North Shore which became the suburb of that name. Nearby Gore Hill is named after him.

Despite the hysterical accusations by Macarthur and other rebels, neither William Bligh nor any of his senior officials including Palmer, Campbell, Griffin or Gore were found to have been guilty of graft. Palmer's account books were investigated by the authorities in London, who unearthed no evidence of corruption. Despite the claims of Bligh and three reports by Palmer, no charges were brought against Macarthur or other rebels for graft by London or by Governor Macquarie in the colony. Macarthur never did pay the £900 *Parramatta* bond that had been a catalyst of the coup.

There were numerous legal writs floating around at the time of the Johnston Court Martial. Most of them came to nothing. An exception was a case for unlawful imprisonment which

George Crossley, the ex-convict lawyer, brought against Kemp, Moore, Laycock, Minchin and Lawson, who had sat on the bench that had sent him to the coal mines for two years. Crossley won his case, and was awarded £500 in damages. There is no record of him ever receiving his money.

John Macarthur had threatened to sue William Bligh for £20,000 for his arrest in Sydney, but the threat came to nothing after the outcome of the Johnston trial. For both Macarthur and Bligh, the real central figures in the case, the Johnston Court Martial was the beginning of difficult times. Despite his promotion, Bligh's career came to an abrupt halt. At the same time, while further military prosecutions were abandoned, the British Government persisted in its determination to bring John Macarthur to trial in a civil court, for High Treason. Macarthur was not off the hook.

24

Mad Mack

Firmly believing that John Macarthur had been the chief instigator of the Sydney coup of 1808, Lord Liverpool let Lord Castlereagh's instructions to Governor Macquarie stand – Macarthur was to be arrested and tried for High Treason, in the colony. This meant that Macarthur could not return to New South Wales without risking arrest, trial, conviction, and possible execution. 'Plunged in a state of mental despondency', in his own words, Macarthur became an exile in England.[388]

At first, Macarthur wanted his wife Elizabeth to sell up and join him in England. She ignored him, remaining in New South Wales, raising their daughters and raising their sheep. With no interest in fashion or building a grand home, Elizabeth ran the Macarthur properties with hard-headed efficiency. Unafraid to get her hands dirty, she was out with the shepherds and the shearers. She personally supervised the export of Macarthur wool to England. Macarthur continued to urge her to come to England, but when this proved pointless, he urged her to get close to Governor Macquarie. She didn't need any prompting to do that – she and Elizabeth Macquarie were old acquaintances.

Macarthur's wife became a regular guest at Government House, and as a result the Macarthur estates were within a few years being allocated newly arrived convict labour by Macquarie.

When Macarthur sent his nephew Hannibal back from England to take charge of their businesses, Elizabeth would not relinquish the reins, instead bringing Hannibal in as a partner. For a period of two years, Macarthur didn't receive a single letter from his wife. But she continued to send him money. 'Exert yourself to remit me all you can,' he instructed her.[389] He bought goods on credit and sent them out to the colony in his ship the *Isabella*. It was wrecked on the way, and he fell deeply into debt. He urged both Elizabeth and Hannibal to send him more money, and began forging Elizabeth's handwriting on her cheques so they would be paid 'to order' rather than to Macarthur himself, so that his bankers couldn't claim the money against his large debts to them.

Year after year, Macarthur lobbied the British Government to allow him to return to New South Wales. By 1817, the government indicated it would relax its attitude to him if he acknowledged in writing that he had acted improperly in 1808. Macarthur refused to acknowledge any wrongdoing, but finally agreed to confine himself to farming and to keep out of public life. On this basis, his return was approved. On 30 September 1817, he arrived back in Sydney, eight and a half exiled years since he'd left, bringing a large number of vine cuttings he'd collected while wandering in France. To secure a free passage back to Sydney for his vines and for himself, he had used his powers of persuasion to convince the home government that winegrowing could take off in Australia and that he and his vines would launch the new industry.

Through the efforts of his wife Elizabeth, Macarthur's wool estates were flourishing. Back at Elizabeth Farm once more, Macarthur came up with numerous schemes for new businesses: an agricultural company, a bank, a newspaper. Some ideas materialised and succeeded, others fizzled. He actively opposed trial by jury and any business involving former convicts. George Johnston never had anything to do with him again. Soon at odds with Governor Macquarie, Macarthur cultivated the friendship of the visiting Commissioner John Thomas Bigge, who was writing a report on the colony for London. That report's unfavourable assessment of Macquarie brought about the end of his governorship. In the 1820s, Macarthur outfitted his household staff in grandiose royal blue livery with brass buttons, and threw himself into feverish periods of architectural design – extensions for Elizabeth Farm, and grand houses for his other estates. As his landholdings grew to 60,000 acres (24,300 hectares) he became increasingly rich, and increasingly unstable.

In 1825, with Macquarie recalled, Macarthur convinced Governor Darling to appoint him to the colony's new Legislative Council but, in constant dispute with the governor, he rarely attended its meetings. In 1829 he was appointed to the reconstituted Legislative Council, but within three years Governor Bourke had him removed. For, by early 1832, Macarthur was evidently going quite mad. He had thrown wife Elizabeth out of the house, accusing her of infidelity, and turned her room into a bedroom for royalty, whom he expected to visit any day. Elizabeth moved into their Sydney house. Their daughters, whom he commanded to remain at Elizabeth Farm, were banned from his sight, while he accused them and household staff of stealing his clothes. Then, in September, after he raved that his sons had been poisoned and were planning an armed insurrection in a remote part of the colony, he was declared legally insane. Confined to his bedroom at Elizabeth Farm for the last years of his life, he finally died in a cottage at his Camden estate on 11 April 1834. His death barely rated a mention in the press.

Thus quietly passed the turbulent man who had engineered the overthrow of Governor Bligh in 1808; the man who had masterminded the only military coup in Australia's history; 'a man of the most violent passions, his friendship strong and his hatred invincible', according to contemporary colonist Robert Scott.[390] In the end, Macarthur was shunned and forgotten by his own generation. Wife Elizabeth returned to Elizabeth Farm where she lived unassumingly until her death in 1850. It was Macarthur's sons who revived the family name. Eldest son Edward, who in December 1807 had tried to retrieve his father's inflammatory note from Chief Constable Oakes on the Sydney road, rose to become a lieutenant general in the British army and was knighted. Brother William was also knighted, and served as Acting Governor of Victoria for a time.

Through the efforts of the descendants of fourth son James, the Macarthur Onslows, the name of John Macarthur was redeemed in the twentieth century. Macarthur's face even found its way onto the Australian $2 note in the 1960s, not as the instigator of the only military coup in the country's history but as the so-called father of the Australian wool industry. Yet if any Macarthur is to be credited with parenting the wool industry in Australia, it must be his wife, Elizabeth. For more than twelve crucial years, during Macarthur's two sojourns in England as a consequence of a rash duel and an equally rash rebellion, it was Elizabeth who built the foundation of the Macarthur wool empire.

Even then, other colonists, such as the Reverend Samuel Marsden, who had maintained extensive landholdings in the colony which ran large flocks of sheep even while he was in England for some years, were sending better quality wool to England up to 1814. It was only in the 1820s, when Macarthur wool was awarded three gold medals in England, one for quality and two for quantity – John Macarthur receiving sole credit for it, without a mention of Elizabeth – that Macarthur began to be portrayed as Australia's leading wool baron.

There is no question that John Macarthur should be given

credit for seeing the potential for both wool and wine in Australia's economic future. But ultimately, his fame, like his fortune, was built primarily by the efforts of others. On a personal level, apart from a genuine early affection for his wife and children, whom he seems to have misled about his plots and plans for many years, he had no redeeming qualities.

In taking on Macarthur, William Bligh had locked horns with a wily opponent who had a talent for manipulating words, and people. As Macarthur himself had acknowledged at the Johnston Court Martial, the triggers for the rebellion of 1808 had all related to Macarthur. Without Macarthur, there would have been no rebellion. His insanity was evident even then. His plot for using the Criminal Court as a means of forcing a showdown with Bligh that would inevitably lead to the Governor's overthrow was crazy, if ingenious. His spurious legal arguments might have had a ring of authenticity that fooled some colonials, but they fell apart in a real court of law in London. His wild, unsupportable accusations that Bligh had threatened colonists' lives and had plundered the colony for personal gain were doomed to be exposed as inventions. And then there was his embarrassing performance on the stand at the Johnston Court Martial.

Two centuries after the event, it is now possible, from letters of participants and from testimony at the Johnston Court Martial, to piece together how the coup of 26 January 1808 came together.

In December of 1807, Macarthur, frustrated by Governor Bligh's successes in curbing the power of the officer cartel, and with the members of the cartel beginning to accept that they couldn't beat Bligh, decided to take on the Governor in spectacular fashion. Whether he had decided in advance to reject the warrant that Chief Constable Oakes attempted to execute, or whether it was a spur of the moment action on the night of 15 December, Macarthur very quickly saw how he could turn his court appearance to his advantage.

On 16 December, 'Mack' seems to have gone to his two close friends at Parramatta, Captain Edward Abbott and Nicholas Bayly who, with Captain John Piper, had formed a tight-knit group in the early days of the colony. This Macarthur–Abbott–Bayly *troika* conceived the idea of arresting Bligh after trapping him into a confrontation with the officers of the Criminal Court, from which the notoriously stubborn Governor would not back down. They also planned a Corps mess dinner on the eve of Macarthur's Criminal Court appearance to bring all key players into the loop and to shore up support.

Following Macarthur's 17 December hearing, Captain Abbott had approached Major Johnston on behalf of the *troika* and proposed that he arrest Bligh and then take him back to England. This was the plan on which Abbott believed the rebels were embarking but, behind Abbott's back, Macarthur and Bayly subsequently convinced Johnston to make himself Lieutenant Governor and rule in Bligh's place.

All the officers of the New South Wales Corps at Sydney had been swiftly brought into the plot. Lieutenant Minchin testified that a month or six weeks before the coup he had stopped going to Government House to dine with the Governor. Minchin fell out with Macarthur shortly after the coup. These two facts suggest that the plot was in place before the end of December 1807 and Minchin, a waverer, was ordered by the chief plotters not to go near the Governor in case the Irishman gave the plot away. Minchin probably fell out with Macarthur because, like Abbott, he was unaware that Johnston/Macarthur planned to retain power after deposing Bligh.

The final timing of the plot was dictated by events. On 25 and 26 January 1808, Surgeon Harris certified that Major Johnston was too ill to answer Governor Bligh's summons. By mid-afternoon on the 26th, with Macarthur in the County Jail and Bligh refusing to respond to the demands of the six officers of the Criminal Court to replace Judge Advocate Atkins, as they knew he would, Johnston had been driven to Harris' property, Ultimo, where Minchin knew to collect him. We know from Court Martial testimony and various letters that as Minchin drove out to Ultimo and picked up Johnston in his chaise, Kemp and Lawson were at the Sydney house of Dr Robert Townson while Townson drafted a requisition for Johnston to arrest Bligh. Passing sentry Private Gray on their way, this trio went to Johnston's barrack with Townson's draft, where Townson continued to work on it.

When Johnston and Minchin arrived in Sydney, Minchin sent Sergeants Bremlow and Johnston to tell civilian junta members including Nicholas Bayly, Garnham Blaxcell, John and Gregory Blaxland, and Simeon Lord that Johnston had arrived and the plot was in motion, before the sergeants went to the Guard House to join the Governor's Guard. Bayly and Blaxcell went to the County Jail with a written order from Johnston for jailer Riley to release Macarthur. Macarthur was released and he and his two bondsmen then joined the others in the Major's barrack. Several rebel supporters paced nervously up and down outside, unwilling at first to fully commit to Bligh's overthrow, the Blaxland brothers among them.

Inside, Macarthur, hearing that Townson was writing a long-winded document, went into another room with Johnston and wrote his own short requisition and a brief letter calling on Bligh to resign. Townson was told to forget his draft, as the rebels now had a suitable requisition from Macarthur's pen. With the civilians at the barrack hesitating to put their signatures to the requisition, Macarthur signed first. Eight others followed. Johnston gave the letter calling on Bligh to resign to Captain Kemp.

Kemp, Lawson, Draffin and Moore enthusiastically hurried out the door and headed for Government House. Someone, possibly Johnston, decided that a note was necessary cautioning the Corps to treat the Governor and all at Government House with civility. This was quickly scrawled and Minchin ran with it, catching up with the four officers who had preceded him in Bridge Street.

Outside, the drums were rolling, the Corps was assembling, and the guns on the Parade Ground were being loaded and aimed at Government House by Private Gillard and his gunners. The sound of the drums was the signal to the Guard House that the coup was to be launched. Ensign Bell and the Governor's Guard quickly formed up outside the gates to Government House. The men of the Guard fixed bayonets. Mary Putland began to scream . . .

25

Admiral Bligh's Finale

New South Wales was Bligh's final command. Made a Rear Admiral immediately after the Johnston Court Martial and a Vice Admiral a year later, he never again went to sea. He would be consulted by the Admiralty and House of Commons committees on various issues, and in 1812 he helped his protégé, explorer Captain Matthew Flinders, who, in Flinders' own words, had been Bligh's 'disciple in surveying and nautical astronomy'[391] while sailing around the world with him in the *Providence*. Bligh was in 1812 'remarkably obliging and attentive to me', said Flinders,[392] aiding him both with publication of the account of his voyage of exploration in HMS *Investigator* and by introducing him to the Duke of Clarence, younger brother of the Prince Regent. But Bligh's career was in effect at an end. In April 1812, his beloved and loyal wife Betsy passed away, after years of declining health exacerbated by the stresses of the Johnston Court Martial which she had shared with her husband.

Shortly after, Admiral Bligh moved with four of his daughters from London to a manor house at Farningham, Kent. The plucky Mary, Mrs O'Connell, who had shared his ordeal in the colony, did not stay long in New South Wales. Governor Macquarie lobbied London hard to have the 73rd Regiment transferred out of the colony to remove William Bligh's daughter from his bailiwick, and in 1814 he succeeded. The O'Connells went with the 73rd to its new posting, Ceylon, today's Sri Lanka. In 1834, Maurice O'Connell was knighted; Mary became Lady O'Connell. In 1838 the couple returned to Sydney, where Sir Maurice, now a general, became commander of all British forces in the now numerous Australian colonies. Lady O'Connell put her time into charity work, including serving on the committee that supported Caroline Chisholm's work with immigrant women. After General Sir Maurice O'Connell died in 1845, Lady Mary returned to England, where she died in 1881. Several of her children and grandchildren remained in Australia.

Mary's father long predeceased her. William Bligh was diagnosed with cancer in 1817, and began regularly travelling up from Kent to see a specialist in London. On 7 December 1817, nine weeks after John Macarthur arrived back in New South Wales, sixty-three-year-old Bligh collapsed in Bond Street while in London on one of these visits, and died. Bligh had known that Macarthur had been allowed to return to Australia that same year, and perhaps this knowledge had contributed to the Admiral's rapidly declining health. It certainly wouldn't have cheered him. Bligh was buried next to his wife Elizabeth at St Mary's, Lambeth. The death of Vice Admiral William Bligh, FRS, 'a gentleman well versed in astronomy and other sciences',[393] 'the celebrated navigator' who 'bravely fought his country's battles',[394] would be widely lamented by friends and admirers in Britain and Australia. Unlike Macarthur, Bligh kept his friends.

In a tribute to Bligh, on the eightieth anniversary of 'the Great Rebellion' – as his overthrow was known well into the twentieth century – the *Sydney Illustrated News* of 26 January

1888 would say: 'He was a man by no means lacking in the elements of greatness. His worst faults appear to be those of temper and manner, and certainly not of heart.'

Just as the reputation of his bitter foe Macarthur was given a makeover in the twentieth century, Bligh's reputation was to take some crippling blows from Hollywood and the school of authors who hopped onto the large anti-Bligh bandwagon and went along for the ride. The words 'cruel' and 'tyrant' became inextricably linked with the name Captain Bligh. Many unsubstantiated claims about Bligh made by Macarthur and fellow New South Wales rebels were taken as fact. After former Chief Justice of Australia, Dr H. V. Evatt, in 1938 published his book *Rum Rebellion*, which was highly critical of John Macarthur and his junta, and also of historians who had up to that time misrepresented or omitted crucial facts relating to the rebellion so that Bligh was seen in a bad light, a storm of pro-Macarthur propaganda ensued, which continued for decades.

Over the last twenty years, there has been a revision of attitudes toward the *Bounty* mutiny. The black and white Hollywood view has been replaced by a more studied appraisal which shares the blame for that mutiny across a number of factors and people. Not that Bligh was entirely blameless. In the same way, Bligh's oft-painted role of villain of the 1808 rebellion in New South Wales needs revision. If anyone was a villain in that affair, it was John Macarthur, who conceived and stage-managed the coup and then ran the colony like a dictator. Macarthur's coup was not spur of the moment; it was premeditated by at least six weeks. A word Macarthur biographers have been fond of applying to Bligh is 'wicked'. If anyone was wicked, it was John Macarthur. He was not alone – Foveaux and Bayly were just as wicked, just as mercenary; while Johnston, Paterson, Abbott, Kemp, Minchin and Finucane should also be condemned by history for their complicity.

As Bligh protégé Captain George Tobin said sadly of Bligh after his death, 'Perhaps he was not altogether understood.'[395] It's time to dispel the myths about William Bligh and the Macarthur coup of 1808. Bligh never threatened a single life in New South Wales. He did not order floggings, or any other form of punishment, and didn't interfere with the courts. Bligh was not corrupt and did not wickedly plunder the colony or keep prostitutes, as opponents hysterically claimed. No charges of graft against him were ever proven. Nonetheless, his acceptance of the land grant from Governor King was unwise.

Far from being a tyrant, Bligh was highly popular with the vast majority of ordinary settlers in New South Wales, as demonstrated by the fact that some named their children after him and others were prepared to risk severe punishment to support him. John Macarthur had no such popular support, and for six months it was Macarthur who was the tyrant. Not a single complaint about Bligh went from New South Wales settlers to the authorities in London during his term of office – a strange thing when considering the rebel claim that they had to act to remove Bligh before there was a widespread revolt against his tyrannical and corrupt rule. Bligh's measures against corruption in New South Wales were working – that was why he had to be forcibly removed by the officer cartel.

Did Bligh contribute to his own overthrow? Yes, without doubt. His hot temper, which he himself acknowledged, even if it did quickly subside, did not serve him well. And his quarterdeck language rubbed many people up the wrong way. Although, it seems not to have bothered his supporters, few of whom mentioned it, and were never sufficiently offended by it to abandon him, as Macarthur's friends abandoned him. Bligh's inflexibility, the trait that made him such a formidable opponent to Macarthur, turned out to be a chink in his armour that Macarthur was able to exploit. Macarthur's nephew Hannibal, while not exactly a neutral observer, made the nonetheless pertinent remark that while Governor Macquarie was just as arbitrary as Bligh, at least 'he has a manner of reconciling people to his measures'.[396] Bligh was not accustomed to explaining himself or his decisions. Just as the captain of a ship expects his commands to be obeyed without question, Bligh expected his commands in the colony to be obeyed.

The British Government can also share some of the blame for the coup of 1808, for London had certainly not helped Bligh's position or that of his predecessors by appointing naval officers as governors of the colony, commanding army men, or by appointing such an inadequate judge advocate in Atkins, mistakes only rectified after Bligh's overthrow.

Was Bligh outsmarted by Macarthur? Certainly; Bligh didn't see the coup coming. But, as the Johnston Court Martial proved, no one could get away with the sort of mutiny practised by the New South Wales Corps in 1808, and Bligh simply did not imagine that Macarthur or Johnston would take so suicidal a step. It was that lack of imagination and an inability to see a situation from other peoples' perspectives that led to the disappointments and downfalls that marked Bligh's life.

So, was Bligh the wrong man for the Governor's job? Many people have thought so, but another question can quickly provide an answer to that. Had John Macarthur not been in New South Wales, would there have been a rebellion in 1808? I believe the answer to that is very definitely, no. It was Macarthur who plotted the coup, and who used himself as the bait. He very cleverly trapped Bligh into making the coup possible. No one else in the colony was as devilishly cunning as Macarthur, or had his diabolical skills. And no one was quite as mad to dare what he dared. Had Macarthur not been there, there would have been no invented crisis in the Criminal Court, and no rebellion. Bligh would have served out his intended governorship of five years. He may not have been the most polished governor, but he was a dedicated servant of his king and country, and was getting the anti-corruption job done, by winning the battle against the officer cartel, who had as good as surrendered to him. No Macarthur, no coup.

Macarthur *was* there, so what would have happened if another governor had been sent out instead of Bligh? With Macarthur in dispute with every past governor, his track record suggests that he would have engineered the removal of any governor who stood in his path, one way or another. The fact remains, Macarthur was there and Bligh was there. Their collision was inevitable, the Macarthur coup was inevitable. From the moment that William Bligh stepped ashore at Sydney Cove in 1806, the clock was ticking down to 26 January 1808, and Captain Bligh's other mutiny.

Appendix: 'The *Brothers* Case'

In late February 1808, taking the side of Captain Oliver Russell and London shipping firm Hulletts & Co in Russell's dispute with John and Gregory Blaxland, John Macarthur wrote to earnestly advise the co-owner of the ship *Brothers*, John Blaxland, not to detain the vessel in Sydney as he wished to do. Why Macarthur became involved in this dispute is open to question. Perhaps it was because he wanted to send Governor Bligh to England on the *Brothers*, which he couldn't do if the ship remained in the colony as Blaxland desired. Perhaps he wanted to look after the interests of Hulletts, his own maritime partners. Perhaps he simply wanted to best the Blaxlands.

Next, Macarthur tried to bribe John Blaxland into letting the ship go, sending him a letter from Major Johnston suggesting that any application from Blaxland for convicts, stock and land would be favourably considered. Still Blaxland would not relent.

On 2 March, Blaxland dismissed Captain Russell from the command of the *Brothers*, threatening him with criminal charges if he didn't give up the ship. Russell refused to leave the *Brothers*, and Blaxland three times approached Major Johnston for redress. Each time, Macarthur wrote to Blaxland in Johnston's name, rebuking him for not directing his correspondence to the Secretary to the Colony, and each time, Blaxland continued to ignore Macarthur.

Blaxland then instigated legal proceedings against Russell before a bench of magistrates made up of Lieutenant Minchin, Surgeon Harris, Assistant Surgeon Jamieson, and Lieutenant Symons of HMS *Porpoise.* When the magistrates declined to commit Russell to trial, Blaxland protested to Johnston, again bringing a rebuke from Macarthur. He then asked Johnston to accept his resignation as a magistrate of the colony, as he planned to take possession of the *Brothers* and proceed to England in her. Macarthur, through Johnston, replied that Blaxland's resignation might be accepted but Blaxland could not leave the colony until the *Brothers* dispute was resolved.

Blaxland then dared Macarthur to detain him as a prisoner, and produced a letter from Acting Judge Advocate Grimes saying that another suitable person could be found to replace Blaxland on the bench. This told Macarthur that Grimes was now also in the Blaxland camp. On 19 March, John and Gregory Blaxland and Simeon Lord boarded the *Brothers*. Lord was there because he was secretly in partnership with the Blaxlands in their half share of the *Brothers.* Ex-convicts were not permitted to own ships, but Lord neatly side-stepped the law by mortgaging his interest in ships he purchased to London financiers such as Hulletts, so that the mortgage holder's name appeared on the ship's papers, not his. Ostensibly, the trio had come aboard the *Brothers* to inspect the accommodation that John Blaxland would use when he sailed in the ship to England. Gregory Blaxland laid hands on Captain Russell, a scuffle broke out, Russell called the Blaxlands and Lord names, and they reciprocated. Crew members separated the combatants. After the merchant trio left his ship, Russell went straight to Macarthur and subsequently laid charges of assault against the three merchants.

On 27 March, Captain Anthony Fenn Kemp declared in a deposition that, three days before, Gregory Blaxland had complained to him 'that Mr Macarthur has used him and his brother very ill, in interfering in their shipping concerns'. Blaxland had also told Kemp that he had heard that assassins had been employed by Hawkesbury settlers to murder John Macarthur in Sydney.[397] This tale was either a mischievous invention of Blaxland's, to put the wind up Macarthur, or it was a creation of the invention-prone Kemp, to make Blaxland look bad.

The assault case came to court on 28 March. Captain Russell read several long written addresses to the court during the course of this trial, all of which bore the stamp of John Macarthur. Macarthur's fingerprints on the prosecution truly became apparent when, during cross examination, Russell admitted that Macarthur had promised him money if Blaxland refused to pay for provisions for his crew and himself, and had given Russell advice on how to handle his case. Russell and his chief officer, Robert Daniels, then testified that an assault had taken place, but five other witnesses gave evidence that Daniels hadn't even been on deck at the time and therefore could not have witnessed the alleged scuffle. Russell then announced that he wished to withdraw the charges, but it was too late. The magistrates summarily ruled that both Russell and Daniels had committed perjury, and sentenced them to seven years' transportation. John Blaxland and Lord were then found not guilty, but Gregory Blaxland was found guilty of assault, and fined £5.

Russell appealed to Major Johnston who, on 3 April, issued a proclamation annulling the sentences against Russell and Daniels, as the pair should have been committed for trial for perjury at another time. On Macarthur's advice, Johnston then fired Charles Grimes from the post of Acting Judge Advocate.

Grimes had been enjoying his prestigious new role and was livid at his dismissal. He now accused Macarthur of saying that he had taken down the evidence incorrectly and of offering to finance Russell in suing Grimes. Macarthur countered by declaring that he would sue Grimes for defamation, and that if necessary 'he would expend his last guinea'[398] to gain satisfaction. Grimes was fortunate that Macarthur had come to consider the courts a more effective weapon than the duelling pistol.

Next day, John Blaxland threw his next countering punch, by appearing before magistrates Surgeon Harris, Lieutenant Symons, Lieutenant Minchin and Lieutenant Lawson, complaining that Captain Russell had committed perjury in the previous case, and that he had subsequently committed piracy by throwing a skipper appointed by Blaxland off the *Brothers*. The magistrates referred the case to the next day's sitting. On the following morning, Macarthur totally disrupted proceedings by having Harris and Symons dismissed from the magistracy. The case was adjourned. On 7 April, Russell appeared before magistrates Lieutenant Lawson and Garnham Blaxcell, and he was committed to the next Criminal Court sitting, but only on the perjury charge. On 11 April, Blaxland announced he was sending a letter of protest to London in which he would complain against Johnston, Macarthur, and the magistrates who had not committed Russell on the piracy charge.

On the 18th, Captain Russell petitioned Major Johnston to be released on a £2000 bond on condition he report to the British Government once he arrived in England to answer any charge preferred against him. This was a typical Macarthur tactic, a nonsense clothed in legalese, for Russell had been charged with perjury in the colony and could only answer to it in the colony, not in England. But it was enough for Johnston to approve the bond. Captain Russell was free to sail away in the *Brothers*. Macarthur had won, again.

Notes

Introduction

1. Joseph Holt, *Memoirs of Joseph Holt*, Vol II.
2. Maurice Margarot, in *Report of Select Committee on Transportation*, 1812.
3. *Cambridge History of the British Empire*, Vol VII.
4. Gov Hunter in a letter to Lord Portland, 14 September 1796. HRA Series I, Vol 1.
5. Gov King to Secretary of State for the Colonies, first half of 1806. HRA, Series IV, Vol 1.
6. Macarthur to Capt John Piper, 11 October 1807. Piper Papers, A256.
7. Elizabeth Macarthur to Piper, 8 February 1808. Piper Papers, A256.
8. Francis Oakes, Johnston Court Martial testimony. Trial transcript: *Proceedings of a General Court Martial . . . for The Trial of Lieut-Col Geo Johnston*, 1811.
9. Bremlow, Johnston Court Martial. He stood to attention by the Corps' colours throughout the mess dinner.

Chapter One

10. Sydney Bureau of Meteorology: the average top temperature for 26 January in Sydney. Records of daily temperatures in Sydney go back to 1858. There is no record of the maximum temperature in Sydney on 26 January 1808.
11. Gray, Johnston CM.
12. John Macarthur had reputedly been apprenticed to a stay-maker before joining the 68th Regiment as an ensign.
13. Whittle testified at the Johnston CM that he had met Macarthur in the Sydney street days prior to the coup and Macarthur had asked him to prepare a list of enlisted men worthy of receiving the wine at a reduced rate. This exercise implies that Macarthur was trying to win the support of Whittle and of those troops who were nominated by Whittle. It was also put to Whittle at the court martial that he said the soldiers should have been given 'the whole pint' prior to marching on Government House. Whittle denied making this remark, but the implication is that the troops at the barracks were given half a pint of wine with their supper that evening.
14. Minchin, Johnston CM.
15. Gillard, Johnston CM.

16. Ibid.
17. Sir Joseph Banks in a letter to the then Governor of NSW, Captain John Hunter, 1 February 1799. NSWHR, Vol III.
18. Whittle, Johnston CM.
19. Bremlow and Sgt Robert Hall, Johnston CM.
20. Ibid.
21. Taylor, *Discovering Military Traditions.*
22. That Mary Putland carried a parasol on this occasion is more legend that provable fact. But it is true to her feisty character. It was reported in Ellis, *John Macarthur.*
23. Bligh, Johnston CM.
24. Bligh and John Dunn, Johnston CM.
25. Gore, Johnston CM. Gore also testified that the Governor's Guard appeared to him to prime and load their muskets. The testimony of Sgts Bremlow and Hall, who were involved, and of the majority of other witnesses, was that the infantrymen of the NSW Corps only fixed bayonets that day.
26. NSWHR, Vol VI.
27. Ellis, *John Macarthur.*
28. Campbell, Johnston CM.
29. Fulton, Johnston CM.
30. Minchin, Johnston CM.
31. Gore, Johnston CM.
32. Fulton, Johnston CM.
33. Kemp, Johnston CM.
34. Ellis, *John Macarthur.*
35. Figures quoted by various authoritative witnesses at the Johnston Court Martial put sixty troops at Parramatta, fifteen at the Hawkesbury, sixteen at Newcastle. Another twenty could be expected to have been on Norfolk Island, and eighty in two understrength companies in Van Diemen's Land; leaving 300 at Head Quarters in Sydney.
36. Tait, Johnston CM.
37. James Dowse Harris, Johnston CM.
38. George Suttor, *Memoirs*, and *Sketches of Events in New South Wales, 1800–20.*
39. Dr John Harris, Johnston CM.
40. JD Harris, Johnston CM.
41. Oakes, Johnston CM.
42. Palmer, Johnston CM.
43. Bligh, Johnston CM.
44. Dunn, Johnston CM.
45. Sgt Sutherland and Lt Minchin, Johnston CM.
46. Hutton, Johnston CM.
47. Ibid.
48. Bligh, Johnston CM.
49. Ibid.
50. Minchin, Johnston CM.
51. Ibid.
52. Ibid.
53. Ibid.
54. Ibid.
55. Ibid.

Chapter Two

56. Bligh, Johnston CM.
57. Dr Harris, Johnston CM.
58. Bligh, Johnston CM.
59. Johnston CM, Appendix IX.
60. Johnston, Johnston CM.
61. Johnston and Minchin, Johnston CM.
62. Ibid.
63. Bligh, Johnston CM.
64. Palmer, Johnston CM.
65. Campbell, Johnston CM.
66. Dunn, Johnston CM.
67. Minchin, Johnston CM.
68. Minchin and Dr Harris, Johnston CM.
69. Suttor. *Memoirs.*
70. Ibid.
71. Ibid.
72. Oakes, Johnston CM.
73. Griffin, Johnston CM.
74. Bligh to Castlereagh, 30 April 1808. NSWHR, Vol VI.
75. Ibid.
76. Gore, Johnston CM.
77. Ibid.
78. Abbott, Johnston CM.
79. Elizabeth Macarthur to Piper, 8 February 1808. Piper Papers, A256.
80. Elizabeth Macarthur to Piper, 4 December 1801. Piper Papers, A256.
81. Elizabeth Macarthur to Piper, 8 February 1808. Piper Papers, A256.
82. Bligh's list of *Bounty* Mutineers, SLNSW, ZS1/43.

83. Bligh to Castlereagh, 30 April 1808. NSWHR Vol VI.

Chapter Three

84. Champion, Johnston CM.
85. The sentry box and the sentries on the front path are shown in an 1808–09 painting by out of work surveyor George William Evans, while several civilians are seen waiting on the veranda.
86. Bligh, Johnston CM.
87. Palmer, Johnston CM.
88. NSWHR, Vol VI.
89. Palmer, Johnston CM. Palmer couldn't remember who the third member of the committee was, but events of the following day, when Jamieson was a member of the committee sent to study the Governor's papers along with Bayly, Blaxcell and Capt Abbott, strongly suggest he was a member of this committee on the 27th.
90. Campbell, Johnston CM.
91. Ibid.
92. Bremlow, Johnston CM.
93. Johnston Proclamation of 27 January 1808. *Proceedings*, Appendix XIX.
94. Suttor, Johnston CM.
95. Ibid.
96. Walker, Johnston CM.
97. Gore, Johnston CM.
98. Walker, Johnston CM.
99. Ibid.
100. Champion, Johnston CM.
101. Tait, Johnston CM.
102. Finnegan, Johnston CM.
103. Macquarie. NSWHR, vol VII.
104. Williamson, Johnston CM.
105. Divine and Minchin, Johnston CM. Divine couldn't remember exactly which day he was questioned. He thought it was either the Saturday or the Monday following Bligh's overthrow – to suggest that so many people had signed the requisition to arrest Bligh by that time that adding his signature hardly seemed to matter. Minchin said it was the night of Tuesday the 26th, but that is unlikely; only the interrogation of Griffin appears to have taken place then. It may have been the night of the 26th, but most of the senior officials were questioned on the 27th, and this is most likely to have been the day of Divine's meeting with the committee.
106. Divine, Johnston CM.

Chapter Four

107. Ellis, *Macarthur.*
108. Oakes, Johnston CM.
109. Bligh, Johnston CM.
110. *Proceedings*, Appendix XVIII.
111. Abbott, Johnston CM.
112. Dr Mason, Johnston CM. In confirmation of this, the *Illustrated Sydney News* of 26 January, 1888, in an article commemorating the eightieth anniversary of 'the Great Rebellion', said of Bligh: 'His interest in the settler population made him immensely popular amongst them.'
113. Malcolm Turnbull, email to the author, 7 March 2007. It is Turnbull family lore that other Hawkesbury settlers also named their sons after Bligh.
114. Dr Mason, Johnston CM.
115. Ibid.
116. Ibid.
117. Ibid.
118. Arndell to Bligh, 6 March 1808. *Proceeding*, Appendix LI.
119. Oakes, Johnston CM.

Chapter Five

120. Abbott to King, 13 February 1808. King Papers, NSWHR, Vol VI, A1976.
121. Abbott, Johnston CM.
122. Ibid.
123. Macarthur to Elizabeth Macarthur, 30 January 1808. *Some Early Records of the Macarthurs of Camden.*

Chapter Six

124. *Proceedings*, Appendix XVIII.
125. Ibid.
126. Ibid.
127. Elizabeth Macarthur to Piper, 8 February 1808. Piper Papers, A256.

128. Paterson to Johnston, May 1808. HRA, Series I, Vol VI.
129. Evatt, *Rum Rebellion*.
130. Abbott to King, 13 February 1808. King Papers.
131. Bligh, Johnston CM.
132. Ibid.
133. Ibid.
134. Bligh to Windham, 31 October 1807. HRA, Series I.
135. Bligh, Johnston CM.
136. Evatt, *Rum Rebellion*.
137. Abbott to King, 13 February 1808. King Papers.
138. John Blaxland, Johnston Court Martial Testimony.
139. Ibid.
140. Ibid.
141. Ibid.
142. Proceedings, Appendix XVIII.

Chapter Seven

143. *Proceedings*, Appendix XIV.
144. Evatt, *Rum Rebellion*, based on an analysis of three reports of John Palmer which in turn were based on returns made by Macarthur and Robert Fitz.
145. Jamieson to Bligh, 28 April 1808. NSWHR, Vol VI.
146. Ibid.
147. Ibid. The pro-Macarthur author Ellis, in *Macarthur*, claimed that the recipients of these cattle paid 28 pounds per head for them, still well below market price. He excused this distribution of government stock by claiming that the junta desperately needed the money from these sales because few people in the colony were accepting the rebel administration's bills of exchange – their written promises of payment (the fore-runners of bank notes). The cattle may well have been valued at 28 pounds per head but, as the later investigations of Commissary Palmer found, no money actually changed hands; the grain receipts fiddle covered these deals. Besides, the rebel administration had little need to issue bills of exchange, because they had reverted to the corrupt practice, which Bligh had wiped out, of forcing both colonists and the soldiery to accept wine and spirits instead of money as payment.
148. Hassall to Bligh, February 1808. Rowland Hassall Papers (A859).
149. Hayes to Castlereagh, 13 October 1809. NSWHR, Vol VII.
150. Evatt, *Rum Rebellion*, (as for note 136).
151. Johnston to Castlereagh, 11 April 1808. *Proceedings*, Appendix XIV.
152. Abbott to King, 13 February 1808. King Papers.
153. Kennedy, *Bligh*.

Chapter Eight

154. Johnston to Castlereagh, 11 April 1808. *Proceedings*, Appendix XIV.
155. Ibid.
156. Ibid.
157. Ibid.
158. Ibid.
159. Ibid.
160. Ibid.
161. Ibid.
162. Ibid.
163. Finucane, Journal. *Distracted Settlement*.
164. Macarthur to Piper, May 1808. Piper Papers.
165. HRA, series I, vol VI.
166. Ibid.
167. Ibid.
168. Ibid.
169. Paterson to Johnston, 12 March 1808. *Proceedings*, Appendix L.
170. Ibid
171. Johnston to Castlereagh, 11 April 1808. *Proceedings*, Appendix XIV.
172. Macarthur to Piper, 24 May 1808. Piper Papers.
173. Ibid.
174. Ibid.

Chapter Nine

175. NSWHR, Vol VI.
176. Ibid.
177. Ibid. 'Song on the New South Wales Rebellion', 1808.

178. Johnston's letter to the officers, 26 April 1808. HRA, Series I, Vol VI.
179. Ibid.
180. Caley to Banks, 7 July 1808. NSWHR, Vol VI.

Chapter Ten

181. Bligh, Johnston CM.
182. Evatt, *Rum Rebellion.*
183. Caley to Banks, 7 July 1808. NSWHR, Vol VI.
184. Ibid.
185. N Shakespeare, *In Tasmania.*
186. NSWHR, Vol VI.
187. Bligh to Castlereagh, 30 June 1808. HRA Series I, Vol VI.
188. Kennedy, *Bligh.*

Chapter Eleven

189. Ellis, *Macarthur.*
190. Ibid.
191. Macarthur to Piper, 24 May 1808. Piper Papers.
192. Ibid.
193. Mrs Elizabeth Bligh to Bligh, 12 February 1808. Bligh Family Correspondence, Safe 1/45.
194. Ibid.
195. Kennedy, *Bligh.*
196. Ibid.
197. Ibid.
198. Ellis, *Macarthur.*
199. *Proceedings*, App A.
200. Ibid.
201. Mrs Bligh to Bligh, 12 February 1808. BFC, Safe 1/45.
202. NSWHR, Vol VI.
203. Finucane, Journal, 28 July 1808. *Distracted Settlement.*
204. Bligh, Johnston CM.
205. Finucane, Journal, 28 July 1808. *Distracted Settlement.*
206. Ibid.
207. Ibid.
208. Hayes to Castlereagh, 13 October 1809. NSWHR, Vol VII.
209. Finucane, Journal. *Distracted Settlement.*
210. Ibid.
211. Ibid.
212. Ibid.
213. Ibid.
214. Foveaux to Castlereagh, 4 September 1808.NSWHR, Vol VI.

Chapter Twelve

215. Lt Kent testimony, Johnston CM.
216. Ibid.
217. Kennedy, *Bligh.*
218. Mrs Bligh to Bligh, 12 February 1808. BFC, Safe 1/45.
219. Tobin to Francis Bond, 15 December 1817. ML Ab 60/8.
220. Bligh, *Warrior* Court Martial transcript. TNA Adm 1/5368.
221. Tobin to Bond, 15 December 1817.
222. Sgt Mason, Johnston CM.
223. Dr Mason, Johnston CM.
224. Foveaux to Castereagh, 3 September 1808. NSWHR, Vol VI.
225. Ibid.
226. Foveaux to Colonial Office, 10 September 1808. NSWHR, Vol VI.
227. Finucane, Journal. *Distracted Settlement.*
228. Flinders to Hope, 17 September 1811.
229. Foveaux to Colonial Office, 10 September 1808. NSWHR, Vol VI.
230. Finucane, Journal. *Distracted Settlement.*

Chapter Thirteen

231. Dr Mason testimony, Johnston CM.
232. *Proceedings*, App XXXIV.
233. Ibid.
234. Finucane, Journal. *Distracted Settlement.*
235. Ibid.
236. Ibid.
237. NSWHR, Vol VII.
238. Suttor, *Memoirs.*
239. Ibid.
240. NSWHR, Vol VI.

Chapter Fourteen

241. Finucane, Journal. *Distracted Settlement.*
242. Ibid.
243. Donald, *Lincoln.*
244. Finucane, Journal. *Distracted Settlement.*
245. Ibid.
246. Ibid.

247. Elizabeth Macarthur to Foveaux, 2 February 1810. NSWHR, Vol VII.

Chapter Fifteen

248. Bligh, Johnston CM.
249. Ibid.
250. Abbott, Johnston CM.
251. Bligh, Johnston CM.
252. Ibid.
253. Finucane, Journal. *Distracted Settlement.*
254. Ibid.
255. Ibid.
256. *Proceedings*, Appendix XXVI.
257. Finucane, Journal. *Distracted Settlement.*
258. Ibid.

Chapter Sixteen

259. Bligh, Johnston CM.
260. Ibid.
261. Hayes to Castlereagh, 13 October 1809. NSWHR, Vol VII.
262. Fulton to Banks, 1809. NSWHR, Vol VII.
263. Finucane, Journal. *Distracted Settlement.*
264. Ibid.
265. *Proceedings*, App XXVII. John Blaxland and Charles Grimes were not included on this list as they had already left the colony.
266. Gore, Johnston CM.
267. NSWHR, Vol VII.
268. Godwin, *Emigrant's Guide.*
269. Kennedy, *Bligh.*
270. Hayes to Castlereagh, 13 October 1809.
271. Bligh, Johnston CM.
272. Ibid.
273. Weate & Graham, *Captain William Bligh.*
274. Kennedy, *Bligh*; Whitaker, *Distracted Settlement.*
275. Fulton to Banks, 1809, NSWHR VII.
276. Bligh, Johnston CM.

Chapter Seventeen

277. Finucane, Journal. *Distracted Settlement.*
278. *Proceedings*, App XXIII.
279. Ibid.
280. Bligh testimony.
281. Elizabeth Macquarie, 1809 Journal. ML, Lachlan Macquarie Papers.
282. Ibid.
283. Macquarie to Castlereagh, 10 May 1810. NSWHR, Vol VII.
284. Ibid.
285. Bligh to Mrs Bligh, 8 March 1810. BFC, ML, Ms Safe 1/45.
286. Minchin testimony, Johnston CM.
287. Macquarie to Castlereagh, 10 May 1808.
288. *Journal of the Royal Australian Historical Society*, Vol 16, Part 1, 1930.
289. Elizabeth Macquarie, 1809 Journal.
290. *Sydney Gazette*, 9 March 1810. NSWHR, Vol X.
291. *Proceedings*, App XX.
292. Gore, Johnston CM.
293. Ibid.
294. Ibid.
295. Ibid.
296. Gore and Kemp, Johnston CM.

Chapter Eighteen

297. Bligh to Mrs Bligh, 11 August 1810. BFC, ML, Safe 1/45.
298. Bent to his brother, 1810. NSWHR, Vol VII.
299. Ibid.
300. Bligh to Mrs Bligh, 11 August 1810.
301. Ibid.
302. Ibid.
303. Ibid.

Chapter Nineteen

304. Castlereagh to Bligh, 15 May 1809. *Proceedings*, Appendix XXIV.
305. Bligh, Opening Statement, Johnston CM.
306. *Edinburgh Advertiser*, 17 May 1811.
307. Flinders to Commissioner Shield, 1 February 1811.
308. Abbott to Piper, 24 January 1811. Piper Papers, A254.
309. NSWHR, Vol VII.
310. Hanging, drawing and quartering was still the punishment for High Treason in Britain in 1811. The last instance of this punishment being carried out was in the case of the Cato Street Conspirators, their public executions

taking place outside Newgate Prison in London on 1 May 1820.
311. Macarthur to Elizabeth Macarthur, 14 February 1810. Macarthur Papers, A2898.
312. Macarthur to Elizabeth Macarthur, 30 July 1809. Macarthur Papers, A2898.
313. *Proceedings*, Johnston CM.
314. Ibid.
315. Ibid. The actual expletives were deleted by shorthand writer Bartrum at the time, and their location within Bligh's explosive reaction to the Defence question has been guessed at by the author.
316. *Proceedings*, Johnston CM.

Chapter Twenty

317. 21 February 1807. *Proceedings*, App XXXI.
318. Bligh, Johnston CM.
319. Ibid. The *Bounty* mutiny took place in 1789, yet twice in a short space of time the trial transcript quotes Bligh as saying it occurred in 1787. Either this is a transcription error by Bartrum or, with the *Bounty* mission beginning in 1787, the trauma of the mutiny had caused a mental aberration on Bligh's part so that he habitually gave the date of the mutiny as 1787.
320. *Encyclopaedia Britannica*, Vol 2.
321. Kennedy, *Bligh*; Wilkinson, *Newgate Calendar*.
322. *Proceedings*.
323. Frazier, *Warrior* CM.
324. Bligh, *Warrior* CM.
325. *Proceedings*.
326. Ibid.
327. Ibid.
328. Ibid.
329. Ibid.
330. Ibid.
331. Ibid.
332. Ibid.
333. Campbell, Johnston CM.
334. Oakes, Johnston CM.
335. Gillard, Johnston CM.
336. Gray, Johnston CM.
337. Champion, Johnston CM.
338. Finnegan, Johnston CM.

Chapter Twenty-one

339. Johnston, Opening Statement, *Proceedings*.
340. Ibid.
341. Ibid.
342. Ibid.
343. Atkins, Johnston CM.
344. Ibid.
345. Ibid.
346. Macarthur, Johnston CM.
347. Ibid.
348. Ibid.
349. Ibid.
350. Bligh to Banks, 23 May 1811. Banks Papers, Series 40.136.
351. Macarthur, Johnston CM.
352. Bligh to Banks, 24 May 1811. Banks Papers, Series 40.137.
353. Macarthur, Johnston CM.
354. *Proceedings*.

Chapter Twenty-two

355. Kemp, Johnston CM.
356. Ibid.
357. *Proceedings*.
358. Minchin, Johnston CM.
359. Bligh to Banks, 25 May 1811. Banks Papers, Series 40.138.
360. Minchin, Johnston CM.
361. *Proceedings*.
362. Bligh to Banks, 29 May 1811. Banks Papers, Series 40.139.
363. Bligh to Banks, 30 May 1811. Banks Papers, Series 40.140.
364. *Proceedings*.
365. Bligh to Banks, 30 May 1811.
366. Elizabeth Macquarie, 1809 Journal.
367. Dr John Harris, Johnston CM.
368. Ibid.
369. Bligh to Banks, 30 May 1811.
370. *Proceedings*.
371. Abbott, Johnston CM.
372. Mann, Johnston CM.
373. Whittle, Johnston CM.
374. Ibid.
375. Ibid.
376. Baird, Johnston CM. The transcript only refers to him as 'A Member', but

Bligh identified him as Baird in his letter to Banks about that day's witnesses.
377. Sgt Mason, Johnston CM.
378. Johnston, summation, *Proceedings*.
379. Bligh, summation, *Proceedings*.

Chapter Twenty-three

380. Bligh to Banks, 31 May 1811. Banks Papers. Series 40.141.
381. Bligh, closing statement, Johnston CM.
382. *Proceedings*.
383. Ibid.
384. Ibid.
385. Baird to Macquarie, 30 March 1813. Macquarie Letterbooks, A797.
386. Bligh to Banks, 13 August 1811. Banks Papers, Series 40.145.
387. Grimes to Liverpool, 1811. NSWHR, Vol VII.

Chapter Twenty-four

388. Macarthur to Elizabeth Macarthur, 4 March 1812. Macarthur Papers, A2898.
389. Macarthur to Elizabeth Macarthur, 11 November 1810, Macarthur Papers, A2898.
390. Robert Scott to his mother, 14 May 1822. Scott Papers, A2263.

Chapter Twenty-five

391. Flinders to James Wiles, 5 March 1812. Matthew Flinders Electronic Archive, Vol 3.
392. Ibid.
393. Citation on Bligh's Royal Society Fellowship proposal, 1801, (RS GB117).
394. Bligh's epitaph, St Mary's, Lambeth.
395. Tobin to Bond, 15 December 1817.
396. Hannibal Macarthur to Macarthur, 30 November 1812. Macarthur Papers, A2901.

Appendix

397. Kemp, deposition, 27 March 1808. HRA, Series I, Vol VI.
398. Bayly to Grimes, 5 April 1808. HRA, Series I, Vol VI.

Bibliography

Books

A Charge of Mutiny: The Court Martial of Lieutenant Colonel George Johnston for deposing Governor Bligh in the Rebellion of January 26, 1808 (Introd by John Ritchie), Canberra, National Library of Australia, 1988.

Alexander, C., *The Bounty: The True Story of the Mutiny on the Bounty*. London, HarperCollins, 2003.

Allen, K. S., *The Bounty Bastard: The True Story of Captain William Bligh*. London, Robert Hale, 1976.

Australian Dictionary of Biography, Melbourne, MUP, 1967.

Baldick, R., *The Duel: A History of Duelling*. London, Chapman & Hall, 1965.

Bartrum, *Proceedings of a General Court Martial Held at Chelsea Hospital, for the Trial of Lieutenant-Col Geo Johnston, Major of the 102nd Regiment, late the New South Wales Corps, on a charge of Mutiny*. London, Sherwood, Neely & Jones, 1811.

Bickel, L., *Australia's First Lady: The Story of Elizabeth Macarthur*. Sydney, Allen & Unwin, 1991.

Bigge, J. T., *The Report of the Commissioner of Inquiry into the State of the Colony of New South Wales, 6 May, 1822*. London, 1822.

Bligh, W., *A Narrative of the Mutiny Aboard His Majesty's Ship Bounty*. London, Nicol, 1790. Republ London, Unicorn, 1901.

Broadbent, J., *Elizabeth Farm, Parramatta: A History and a Guide*. Sydney, Historic Houses Trust, 1984.

Brunton, P., (Ed), *Awake Bold Bligh! William Bligh's Letters Describing the Mutiny on HMS Bounty*. Sydney, Allen & Unwin/SLNSW, 1989.

Bryant, A., *The Age of Elegance: 1812–1822*. London, Collins, 1954.

Bryant, A., *Years of Victory: 1802–1812*. London, Collins, 1975.

Byron, Lord, *The Island: or Christian and his Comrades*. London, 1823.

Cambridge History of the British Empire, Vol VII – Australia. Cambridge, CUP, 1933.

Clark, M., *A History of Australia, Vol 1: From the Earliest Times to the Age of Macquarie*. Melbourne, MUP, 1962.

Cunningham, C., *A Narrative of Occurrences that took place during the Mutiny at the Nore, in the Months of May & June, 1797*. Chatham, 1829.

Currey, J., *David Collins: A Colonial Life*. Melbourne, MUP, 2000.

Davis, R. P., *The Tasmanian Gallows: A Study of Capital Punishment*. Hobart, Cat & Fiddle, 1974.

Dening, G., *Mr Bligh's Bad Language: Passion, Power & Theatre on the Bounty*. Sydney, CUP, 1992.

Dilorenzo, T., *The Real Lincoln: A New Look at Abraham Lincoln*. New York, Random House, 2004.

Donald, D. H., *Lincoln*. New York, Simon & Schuster, 1996.

Ellis, M. H., *John Macarthur*. Sydney, Angus & Robertson, 1955.

Ellis, M. H., *Lachlan Macquarie: His Life, Adventures & Times*. Sydney, Angus & Robertson, 1947.

Encyclopaedia Britannica, Vol 2. Chicago, 1987.

Evatt, H.V., *Rum Rebellion: A Study of the Overthrow of Governor Bligh by John Macarthur and the New South Wales Corps*. Sydney, Angus & Robertson, 1938.

Finucane, J., (Ed A-M Whitaker), *Distracted Settlement: New South Wales After Bligh, from the Journal of Lieutenant James Finucane, 1808–1818*. Melbourne, Miengunyah/MUP, 1998.

Fletcher, B., *John Macarthur: A Man of Controversy*. Sydney, Historic Houses Trust of NSW, 1984.

Godwin, *Godwin's Emigrant Guide to Van Diemen's Land*. London, Sherwood, Jones, 1823; facs edtn, Hobart, Tas Govt Printing Office, 1990.

Hassal, Rev. J. S., *In Old Australia: Records & Reminiscences from 1794*. Brisbane, Hews, 1902.

Hirst, W., (Ed), *My Dear Betsy: A Treasury of Australian Letters*. Sydney, Hale & Ironmonger, 1993.

Holt, J., *Memoirs of Joseph Holt, General of the Irish Rebels*, London, Colburn, 1838.

Hughes, R., *The Fatal Shore: A History of the Transportation of Convicts to Australia 1787–1868*. London, Collins, 1987.

Keneally, T., *The Commonwealth of Thieves*. Sydney, Random House, 2005.

Kennedy, G., *Bligh*. London, Duckworth, 1978.

King, H., *Elizabeth Macarthur & Her World*. Sydney, SUP, 1980.

Knopwood, R. (Ed A. Nicholls), *Diary of the Rev Robert Knopwood, 1803–1838: First Chaplain of Van Diemen's Land*. Launceston, Tasmanian Historical Research Society, 1977.

Macarthur Onslow, S. (Ed), *Some Early Records of the Macarthurs of Camden*. Sydney, 1914.

Mackaness, G., *The Life of Vice-Admiral William Bligh, RN, FRS*. New York, Farrar & Rhinehart, 1931.

Mackaness, G., *Sir Joseph Banks: His Relations with Australia*. Sydney, Angus & Robertson, 1936.

Mann, D. D., *Present Picture of New South Wales*. London, Booth, 1811; facs edtn, Sydney, Fergusson/RAHS, 1979.

Norman, L., *Pioneer Shipping in Tasmania*. Hobart, Walch, 1938.

Shakespeare, N., *In Tasmania*. Sydney, Random House/Knopf, 2004.

Smith, G. (Ed), *Military Small Arms*. London, Salamander, 1994.

Stancombe, G. H., *Highway in Van Diemen's Land*. Launceston, National Trust of Australia, 1974.

Statham, P., *A Colonial Regiment: New Sources Relating to the New South Wales Corps, 1789–1810*. Canberra, ANU, 1992.

Taylor, A., *Discovering Military Traditions*. Herts, Shire, 1969.
Weate, P. and C. Graham, *Captain William Bligh*. Sydney, Hamlyn, 1972.
Whitaker, A-M, *Joseph Foveaux: Power & Patronage in Early New South Wales*. Sydney, UNSW Press, 2000.
Wilkinson, G. W. (Ed), *Newgate Calendar*. London, Kelly, 1820.
Wyatt, Major D. M., *A Lion in the Colony*. Hobart, Sixth Military District Museum, 1990.

Document Collections & Newspapers

Banks Papers, State Library of NSW, Mitchell Library, Sydney.
Bent Journals & Papers, National Library of Australia, Canberra.
Bligh Family Correspondence, State Library of NSW, Mitchell Library, Sydney.
Edinburgh Advertiser, 1811.
Elizabeth Macquarie, 1809 Journal, State Library of NSW, Mitchell Library, Sydney.
Historical Records of Australia, Series I, Vols VI–X, & Series IV, Vol I, National Library of Australia, Canberra.
Illustrated Sydney News, 1888 & 1891.
Journal of the Royal Australian Historical Society, 1930, Sydney.
King Papers, State Library of NSW, Mitchell Library, Sydney.
Lachlan Macquarie Papers, State Library of NSW, Mitchell Library, Sydney.
Launceston *Examiner*, 2005.
London Times, 1811.
Macarthur Papers, State Library of NSW, Mitchell Library, Sydney.
Matthew Flinders Electronic Archive, Vol 3, State Library of NSW.
New South Wales Historical Records Vols I, VI & VII, State Library of NSW, Mitchell Library, Sydney.
Piper Papers, State Library of NSW, Mitchell Library, Sydney.
Report of the Select Committee on Transportation, 10th July 1812, British Parliamentary Papers (543), London.
Rowland Hassall Papers, State Library of NSW, Mitchell Library, Sydney.
Royal Society Archive (GB117), London.
Scott Papers, State Library of NSW, Mitchell Library, Sydney.
Suttor, G., *Memoirs*, NSWHR, Vol VI (A3072), State Library of NSW, Mitchell Library, Sydney.
Suttor, G., *Sketches of Events in New South Wales, 1800–20*, NSWHR, Vol VI (C783), State Library of NSW, Mitchell Library, Sydney.
Sydney Gazette, 1806–1823 (NSWHR), State Library of NSW, Mitchell Library, Sydney.
Tobin Correspondence, ML Ab 60/8, The National Archives, London.
Warrior Court Martial Transcript, Adm 1/5368, The National Archives, London.

Glossary of Characters

The Bligh Camp

ARNDELL, Thomas 'Foolish Tom': magistrate

BANKS, Sir Joseph: President of the Royal Society, previously chief botanist on Captain James Cook's Australian voyage in the *Endeavour*; Bligh's patron in England

BLIGH, Governor William

BLIGH, Elizabeth 'Betsy': Bligh's wife, in England

BROOKS, Richard: sea captain, master of the *Rose*

CALEY, George: free settler at the Hawkesbury

CAMPBELL, Robert: Naval (Customs) Officer of NSW, magistrate, ship owner, and merchant. Dismissed and tried by rebels

CAMPBELL, Sophia, (née Palmer) Robert Campbell's wife, 'Little Jack' Palmer's sister

CASTLEREAGH, Lord Robert Stewart: Secretary of State for War and the Colonies, a senior minister in the British government (later Foreign Secretary)

CLARENCE, Duke of: brother of Prince Regent

COOKE, Edward: Under Secretary of State for War and the Colonies, a junior minister in the British Government

COX, William Jr.: Hawkesbury settler, son of former NSW Corps captain; unlike his father, he supported Bligh, and both William and his mother signed the January 1808 pro-Bligh Hawkesbury settler address

CROSSLEY, George: Parramatta settler, shopkeeper and sometime legal adviser, former Old Bailey attorney, ex-convict; sent to coal mines by rebels

DAVOREN, Lawrence: ex-convict, author of 'The Song of the New South Wales Rebellion'; sent to coal mines by rebels

DUNN, John: personal servant to Governor Bligh

FLINDERS, Lt. Matthew: Bligh's navigational protégé

FULTON, Rev. Henry: Acting Principal Chaplain of Sydney, and magistrate. Dismissed by rebels

GORE, William: Provost Marshal of NSW and Superintendent of Police, Sydney; sent to coal mines by rebels

GRIFFIN, Edmund: Secretary to Governor Bligh

HARRIS, James Dowse: Sydney shipwright, ex-convict

HASSALL, Rev. James: Parramatta clergyman

HAYES, Sir Henry Brown (Sir Harry Hayes): eccentric Irish free settler, former Sheriff of Cork, owner of Vaucluse Estate, ex-convict; sent to coal mines by rebels

HOOK, Charles: free settler, business partner of Robert Campbell; imprisoned by rebels

JUBB, George: Governor Bligh's steward

MARSDEN, Rev. Samuel: Principal Chaplain of Sydney, friend of Bligh family, absent in England during Bligh's overthrow

MASON, Dr Martin: surgeon and free settler at Green Hills (Windsor); harassed by rebels

OAKES, Francis: Chief Constable of Parramatta; dismissed by rebels

PALMER, John 'Little Jack': Commissary-General of NSW, magistrate, and merchant. Dismissed and imprisoned by rebels

PALMER, Mrs Susan (née Stillwell): 'Little Jack' Palmer's American wife

PORTEOUS, Captain John (RN): commander of HMS *Porpoise*

PRINCE REGENT, the future King George IV: effectively king from 1811 after his father George III declared insane in 1810

PUTLAND, Mary: Bligh's widowed daughter, acting as her father's First Lady in Australia

PUTLAND, Lieutenant John: Bligh's son-in-law and ADC, who died in Sydney two weeks prior to the coup

SUTTOR, George: botanist and free settler at Baulkham Hills, NSW; imprisoned by rebels

TAIT, Thomas: clerk in Commissary-General's office, Sydney, ex-convict

TURNBULL, John: Scottish free settler at the Hawkesbury; named his son after Bligh

WALKER, Charles: sea captain, previously in employ of John Macarthur; gave evidence against Macarthur and other rebels

WILLIAMSON, James: Deputy Commissary at Sydney, given an appointment by rebels, later dismissed, probably secretly helped Commissary Palmer, gave evidence against Johnston

The Rebels & Their Supporters

ABBOTT, Captain (later Major) Edward: commander of troops at Parramatta, and a magistrate

BADGERY, James: had a flour mill and bakery in Sydney, and several small farms on the Hawkesbury and Nepean Rivers; granted 840 acres by the rebels; Badgery's Creek is named after him

BAYLY, Nicholas: Parramatta farmer, former lieutenant in NSW Corps. With Abbott and Piper, one of Macarthur's closest friends since their time in NSW Corps together. With Blaxcell, went bail for Macarthur. Later plotted against Macarthur

BELL, Ensign Archibald: NSW Corps officer, Commander of the Main or Governor's Guard in 1808

BLAXCELL, Garnham: free settler, Sydney merchant, formerly Provost Marshal under Governor King. With Bayly, one of Macarthur's bondsmen

BLAXLAND, Gregory: free settler, ship owner, Sydney merchant

BLAXLAND, John: free settler, ship owner and Sydney merchant, elder brother and business partner of Gregory Blaxland. Later crossed Blue Mountains with Wentworth and Lawson

BRABYN, Lieutenant John: NSW Corps officer. Promoted to captain in late 1808

COLLINS, Colonel David: Lieutenant Governor of southern Van Diemen's Land, Commandant at Hobart Town

COX, William Snr.: Hawkesbury settler, former captain and paymaster with NSW Corps; not in colony at time of coup, he had returned from England by early 1810, when he supported the rebels

DAVIDSON, Walter: young free settler, nephew of the Prince of Wales' surgeon, close to Macarthur

DRAFFIN, Lieutenant Cadwallader: NSW Corps officer, considered mad

ELLISON, Lieutenant William (RN): naval officer serving in NSW

FINUCANE, Lieutenant John: NSW Corps officer, Secretary to Lt Col Foveaux

FITZ, Robert: Assistant Commissary at Green Hills (Windsor), formerly an Army officer and paymaster with a regiment in Ireland. Made a magistrate by the rebels

FOVEAUX, Lieutenant-Colonel Joseph: NSW Corps officer, took over rebel leadership in NSW in July 1808

GRIMES, Charles: Surveyor-General of NSW

HARRIS, John: NSW Corps Surgeon and farmer
HOBBY, Thomas: free settler at Hawkesbury, former NSW Corps lieutenant
HUNTER, Admiral John: former Governor of NSW
JAMIESON (also spelled Jamison), Thomas: NSW Corps Assistant Surgeon
JOHNSTON, Major (later Lt-Col) George: NSW Corps commandant at Sydney leading up to, during, and following the coup
JULIAN, Esther (formerly Abrahams): mistress and later wife of Major George Johnston
KABLE, Henry: successful Sydney merchant, ex-convict
KEMP, Captain Anthony Fenn: NSW Corps officer
KENT, Captain William (RN): naval officer, formerly wealthy landowner in NSW, plotted to have Bligh removed so he could be appointed Governor of NSW in his place
KENT, Lieuitenant William (RN): naval officer stationed in NSW, nephew of Captain Wm Kent
KING, Philip Gidley: former Governor of NSW, plotted to have Bligh removed so he could regain his old post at twice the pay
LAWSON, Lieutenant William: NSW Corps officer, later found Blue Mountains crossing with Blaxland and Wentworth
LAYCOCK, Lieutenant Thomas: NSW Corps officer, son of a former Quartermaster of the Corps, also Thomas, who had become a settler
LIVERPOOL, Lord: successor to Lord Castlereagh as Secretary of State for War and the Colonies; not exactly a supporter of the rebels, but wanting to sweep the coup under the carpet
LORD, Simeon: wealthy Sydney merchant, ex-convict
MACARTHUR, Edward: eldest son of John Macarthur
MACARTHUR, Elizabeth: wife of John Macarthur
MACARTHUR, Elizabeth: daughter of John Macarthur
MACARTHUR, Hannibal: nephew of John Macarthur
MACARTHUR, John: free settler at Parramatta, former Captain with NSW Corps
MANN, David Dickinson: free settler at Sydney, formerly Secretary to Governor King
MILEHAM, James: NSW Corps Assistant Surgeon
MINCHIN, Lieutenant William: Adjutant and Artillery Officer of NSW Corps, and magistrate
MINCHIN, Ann: wife of Lt Minchin
MOORE, Thomas: former NSW Corps sergeant, father of Lt William Moore
MOORE, Lieutenant William: NSW Corps Officer
NICHOLLS, Isaac: Sydney innkeeper, de facto son-in-law of Major George Johnston
NICHOLLS, Rosanna: wife of Isaac Nicholls, daughter of Esther Julian
OXLEY, Lieutenant John (RN): naval officer stationed in NSW
PATERSON, Lieutenant-Colonel William: Commander of NSW Corps, Lieutenant Governor of NSW, commandant of settlements in northern Van Diemen's Land, took nominal control of rebel leadership in NSW in 1809
PATERSON, Elizabeth: wife of Lt-Col Paterson
PIPER, Captain John: NSW Corps officer, Commandant of Norfolk Island settlement
REDMAN, John: Chief Constable of Sydney
RILEY, Alexander: Secretary to Lt-Col Paterson
RILEY, Barnaby: Keeper of the County Jail, Sydney, appointed Chief Constable of Parramatta by rebels
RUSSELL, Oliver: sea captain, master of the *Brothers*; sought Macarthur's aid against Blaxlands and Lord

SHIRWIN, Ann: mistress of Lt-Col Foveaux, the wife of a NSW Corps sergeant

SYMONS, Lieutenant James (RN): naval officer serving in NSW

TOWNSON, Dr Robert: free settler, formerly Captain in NSW Corps

UNDERWOOD, James: successful Sydney shipbuilder, ex-convict

WENTWORTH, D'Arcy: dismissed NSW Corps Assistant Surgeon, reinstated by rebels

WENTWORTH, Charles: son of D'Arcy; crossed Blue Mountains with Blaxland and Lawson, bought Vaucluse Estate from Sir Harry Hayes

Changed Sides

ATKINS, Richard: Judge Advocate under Bligh. Against Macarthur, dismissed by rebels but later accepted reappointment by them, and gave evidence for Johnston

DIVINE, Nicholas: Superintendent of Convicts, Sydney, initially sided with rebels, but later switched sides and gave evidence against Johnston

JAMIESON, John: NSW Superintendent of Stock, initially supported Bligh, but later accepted a post from rebels

NSW Corps Enlisted Men

BREMLOW, Sergeant William: Sydney Commandant's Orderly Sergeant in January, 1808; gave evidence against rebels

CHAMPION, Sergeant-Major Isaac: in charge of Governor Bligh's close confinement in 1808, later reduced to the ranks by Major Johnston; gave evidence against rebels

COX, Sergeant-Major James; gave evidence for rebels

MARLBOROUGH, Corporal Michael: member of Governor's Guard, one of three men to locate Govenor Bligh on evening of 26 January 1808. Claimed he dragged Bligh from under a bed

DAVIS, Private Robert: gave evidence against rebels

FINNEGAN, Private Thomas; gave evidence against rebels

GILLARD, Private John: artilleryman, ex-convict; gave evidence against rebels

GRAY, Private John: on sentry duty on 26 January 1808; gave evidence against rebels

HALL, Sergeant Robert: senior NCO of Governor's Guard on 26 January 1808; gave evidence against rebels

HUTTON, Private William; gave evidence against rebels

MASON, Private Richard; gave evidence for rebels

SUTHERLAND, Sergeant John: member of Governor's Guard on 26 January 1808; gave evidence for rebels

WHITTLE, Sergeant-Major Thomas; gave evidence for rebels

WILFORD, Private William: member of Governor's Guard on 26 January 1808; one of three men to locate Governor Bligh that evening

Key Figures at Johnston Court Martial, Chelsea, 1811

ADOLPHUS, John: co-counsel for Lt-Col Johnston

BAIRD, Lieutenant-General Sir David: commander of British forces at the Battle of Corruna, Portugal, where he was severely wounded; Member of the court

KEPPEL, Lieutenant-General William: Commanding Officer 67th Regiment; court President

LARPENT, Francis Seymour: counsel for the Crown; later Judge Advocate General to the Army of the Duke of Wellington

MANNERS-SUTTON, Rt Hon Charles: Judge Advocate General to His Majesty's Forces; later Speaker of the House of Commons, later Viscount Canterbury

POLLOCK, Frederick: counsel for Governor Bligh; later Sir Frederick Pollock, later Chief Baron Pollock

WILLIAMS, C. F.: co-counsel for Lt-Col Johnston

Index